The Practice of Qualitative Data Analysis

Research Examples Using MAXQDA, Volume 2

The Practice of Qualitative Data Analysis

Research Examples Using MAXQDA, Volume 2

Edited by

Stefan Rädiker

Michael C. Gizzi

MAXQDA PRESS

ISBN: 978-3-948768-17-1 (paperback)
ISBN: 978-3-948768-18-8 (eBook PDF, identical page numbers as paperback edition)
https://doi.org/10.36192/978-3-948768188

MAXQDA Press is a division of VERBI Software. Consult. Sozialforschung. GmbH
Invalidenstr. 74, 10557 Berlin, Germany, info@maxqda-press.com, www.maxqda-press.com

Printed by Books on Demand, Norderstedt, Germany

Contents

Introduction 13
Stefan Rädiker & Michael C. Gizzi

Word-Based, AI-Assisted, and Rapid Analysis

1 Using MAXQDA's Word-Based Features and AI Assist: Processing Large Numbers of Documents in Strategic Foresight 17
Matthew H. Loxton

2 Using MAXQDA for Word-Based Content Analysis: Nature and Climate Change Perceptions in Qualitative Interviews 33
Leandro Mahalem de Lima

3 Using MAXQDA for Dictionary-Based Content Analysis: An Example Exploring the Business Strategy of Netflix Over Time 49
Richard L. Vail & Michael C. Gizzi

4 Using MAXQDA's Code Comments for Rapid Analysis: Writing Summaries for Analyzing and Reporting in Evaluation 71
Stefan Rädiker

Survey and Mixed Methods Analysis

5 Using MAXQDA to Analyze Open-Ended Survey Responses:
An Example From an Evaluation Project 87
Christina Silver

6 Using MAXQDA for Mixed Methods Research:
An Example Integrating Interview, Survey, and Social Network Data 107
Sinem Toraman Turk

Thematic, Visual, and Interpretative Analysis

7 Using MAXQDA for a Large Qualitative Dataset:
Identifying Relevant Data and Analyzing It With Thematic Analysis 127
Christian Schmieder & Allison Rogers

8 Using MAXQDA for Combining Visual and Textual Analysis:
An Example From a Participatory Photovoice Research Project 149
Elena Samonova

9 Using MAXQDA for Interpretative Analysis:
Analyzing Four Interviews (Almost) Without Coding 165
Andreas Müller

Table of MAXQDA Key Features Covered

Consult the following table to locate chapters in which your MAXQDA feature of interest is described in a research example. The table is ordered by the MAXQDA main menu. Features accessible through the context menu but not the main menu are included under the relevant main menu category and are highlighted in italics. Entries beginning with "Vol. 1" refer to the first volume of *The Practice of Qualitative Data Analysis,* which is available as an eBook on the MAXQDA Press website (www.maxqda-press.com) or as a paperback edition at your favorite bookstore.

MAXQDA feature	**Book chapters (chapter's starting page)**
Home	
Teamwork Export/Import	Vol. 1: Schmieder et al. (p. 169)
Import	
Import Documents from Excel Spreadsheet	Schmieder & Rogers (p. 127) Vol. 1: Schmieder et al. (p. 169)
Survey Data: Import Data from Excel Spreadsheet	Silver (p. 87) Toraman Turk (p. 107)
Import Focus Group Transcripts	Vol. 1: Loxton (p. 89)
Codes	
Coding	Samonova (p. 149)
Color coding (highlight coding)	Müller (p. 165) Vol. 1: Jacques (p.17)
Creative Coding	Loxton (p. 17) Samonova (p. 149) Vol. 1: Jacques (p.17)
Smart Coding Tool	Vail & Gizzi (p. 49) Rädiker (p. 71) Vol. 1: Jacques (p. 17) Vol. 1: Gizzi & Harm (p. 71) Vol. 1: Gugushvili & Salukvadze (p. 107)

Feature	Reference
Comments on coded segments	Rädiker (p. 71)
	Schmieder & Rogers (p. 127)
	Vol. 1: Schmieder et al. (p. 169)
Transform into Categorical Document Variable	De Lima (p. 33)
Activate Documents Containing This Code	Schmieder & Rogers (p. 127)
Memos	
Project memo	Schmieder & Rogers (p. 127)
Document group memos	Vol. 1: Schmieder et al. (p. 169)
Document memos	Müller (p. 165)
	Vol. 1: Jacques (p. 17)
	Vol. 1: Leimbigler (p. 121)
	Vol. 1: Casasempere-Satorres & Vercher-Ferrándiz (p. 149)
Code memos	Silver (p. 87)
	Schmieder & Rogers (p. 127)
	Vol. 1: Gugushvili & Salukvadze (p. 107)
	Vol. 1: Casasempere-Satorres & Vercher-Ferrándiz (p. 149)
	Vol. 1: Schmieder et al. (p. 169)
In-document memos	Müller (p. 165)
	Vol. 1: Jacques (p. 17)
	Vol. 1: Maksutova (p. 135)
Link codes to memos	Müller (p. 165)
Free memos	Vol. 1: Jacques (p. 17)
Variables	
Document Variables	Vol. 1: Müller (p. 55)
	Vol. 1: Gizzi & Harm (p. 71)
Document Variable Statistics	Silver (p. 87)
Import Document Variables	Vol. 1: Gugushvili & Salukvadze (p. 107)
Speaker Variables	Vol. 1: Loxton (p. 89)

Analysis	
AI Assist (summaries)	Loxton (p. 17)
AI Assist (suggest subcodes)	Loxton (p. 17)
QTT: Questions – Themes – Theories	Loxton (p. 17) Silver (p. 87)
Text Search & Autocode	Schmieder & Rogers (p. 127) Vol. 1: Gizzi & Harm (p. 71) Vol. 1: Loxton (p. 89) Vol. 1: Casasempere-Satorres & Vercher-Ferrándiz (p. 149)
Word Explorer	Vail & Gizzi (p. 49)
Complex Coding Query	Schmieder & Rogers (p. 127)
Compare Cases & Groups: Qualitative	Samonova (p. 149)
Compare Cases & Groups: Quantitative	Vol. 1: Müller (p. 55)
Summary Grid Summary Tables	Loxton (p. 17) Vail & Gizzi (p. 49) Vol. 1: Santos et al. (p. 35) Vol. 1: Gizzi & Harm (p. 71) Vol. 1: Loxton (p. 89) Vol. 1: Maksutova (p. 135)
Categorize Survey Data	Silver (p. 87)
Code Configurations	Vol. 1: Gugushvili & Salukvadze (p. 107)
Code Frequencies	Vol. 1: Gizzi & Harm (p. 71) Vol. 1: Leimbigler (p. 121)

Mixed Methods	
Activate Documents by Variables	De Lima (p. 33) Silver (p. 87)
Interactive Quote Matrix (renamed to "Segment Matrix" in MAXQDA 24)	Vail & Gizzi (p. 49) Silver (p. 87)
Crosstabs	Toraman Turk (p. 107)
Side-by-Side-Display of Results	Toraman Turk (p. 107)

Visual Tools	
MAXMaps	De Lima (p. 33) Rädiker (p. 71) Silver (p. 87) Samonova (p. 149) Müller (p. 165) Vol. 1: Santos et al. (p. 35) Vol. 1: Gugushvili & Salukvadze (p. 107)
Code Matrix Browser	Vail & Gizzi (p. 49) Toraman Turk (p. 107) Vol. 1: Santos et al. (p. 35) Vol. 1: Müller (p. 55) Vol. 1: Gizzi & Harm (p. 71)
Code Relations Browser	Toraman Turk (p. 107) Vol. 1: Jacques (p. 17) Vol. 1: Santos et al. (p. 35) Vol. 1: Müller (p. 55) Vol. 1: Gizzi & Harm (p. 71) Vol. 1: Leimbigler (p. 121)
Code Map	De Lima (p. 33)
Document Comparison Chart	Vol. 1: Müller (p. 55) Vol. 1: Loxton (p. 89) Vol. 1: Gugushvili & Salukvadze (p. 107)
Document Portrait	Vol. 1: Santos et al. (p. 35) Vol. 1: Loxton (p. 89)
Word Cloud	Loxton (p. 17) De Lima (p. 33) Silver (p. 87) Vol. 1: Gizzi & Harm (p. 71)
Code Cloud	De Lima (p. 33)
Reports	
Overview of Coded Segments	Schmieder & Rogers (p. 127)

MAXDictio	
Word Frequencies	De Lima (p. 33) Vail & Gizzi (p. 49)
Word Combinations	Loxton (p. 17) Silver (p. 87) Vol. 1: Casasempere-Satorres & Vercher-Ferrándiz (p. 149)
Keyword-in-context	Vol. 1: Loxton (p. 89)
Word Tree	Loxton (p. 17)
Word Matrix Browser	Vail & Gizzi (p. 49)
Dictionary-based Content Analysis	Vail & Gizzi (p. 49)
Category Matrix Browser	Vail & Gizzi (p. 49)
Autocode with Dictionary	Vail & Gizzi (p. 49)
Stats	
Stats: Frequencies	Toraman Turk (p. 107)
Stats: Descriptive Analysis	Toraman Turk (p. 107)

Introduction

Stefan Rädiker & Michael C. Gizzi

In 2021, we published the first volume of *The Practice of Qualitative Data Analysis: Research Examples Using MAXQDA*. That book contains ten case studies with real-world examples illustrating how MAXQDA is used in practice. The authors present how they used MAXQDA in actual research projects, addressing numerous questions, like how the coding system was developed, how they implemented a methodological approach, what tools were used, and how they informed the results. The book has proven to be a popular resource for MAXQDA users around the globe and is one of the leading publications by MAXQDA Press.

We are excited to present to you the second volume of all new research examples, which cover topics we did not have room to include in the first volume, as well as features that have emerged since we published the first book. MAXQDA 2022 was introduced in November 2021, and received many updates, adding many new features and tools, such as enhanced searching capability with Word Explorer; a Word Matrix Browser to explore the use of words or phrases across documents; the development of a worksheet tool to store your analysis results, named "QTT: Questions – Themes – Theories;" and the introduction of AI Assist, which uses artificial intelligence to aid the user in creating summaries of text, coded segments, and even suggest codes and subcodes. As we go to press, MAXQDA 24 has been recently released, with even more enhancements. While this volume provides examples using MAXQDA 2022, users of the new software will be completely at home in learning from the research examples presented here, as the basic principles of using MAXQDA are still the same.

This book follows the same structure and concept of the original, but includes different methodologies, data types, and usage examples, while retaining our commitment to example-based learning. As we wrote in volume 1, "this book does something unique. It offers the reader insights into actual research projects, providing examples that can serve to inspire the researcher. […] Case studies of how others have completed a project, with a clear description of what they did, can serve to inspire the reader in ways that a textbook often cannot do" (p. 10). Volume 2 provides you with an entirely different set of examples to draw on. Many of these presents what some might say are specialized or advanced uses of MAXQDA, but we think all of the chapters in both volumes offer something to all users, whether novice or experienced researcher.

The organization of each chapter should feel familiar to readers of the first volume. Each chapter or case study provides an abstract, an introduction to the research example written to be understood by the lay reader, a discussion of the methodological approach and data

Rädiker, Stefan & Gizzi, Michael C. (2024). Introduction. In: S. Rädiker & Michael C. Gizzi (Eds.), The practice of qualitative data analysis. Research examples using MAXQDA, volume 2 (pp. 13–15). Berlin: MAXQDA Press.
https://doi.org/10.36192/978-3-948768188_0

collection, and then an in-depth exploration of how MAXQDA was used by the authors to accomplish their goals. Each chapter then ends with the lessons learned by the contributors, how they might do something different, and how you as a reader can benefit from it. Care has been taken that the process of MAXQDA usage is clearly explained with references to the tools used and the steps taken to complete each task, while minimizing the use of "tutorial" or "user manual" style language. We think this makes the book even more valuable to the researcher, whether they are a student or established scholar.

Structure of the book

When we sought out contributors, we were looking for interesting case studies using rigorous methodological approaches, and innovative uses of MAXQDA, from a variety of disciplines. We are quite pleased with the results, and volume 2, consisting of nine contributions, is organized into three parts:

The first section of the book focuses on word-based, automatic, and rapid analysis techniques. *Matthew Loxton* provides a chapter that explores how he used word-based tools and AI Assist to identify key themes from a large data set to develop an evidence-based coding system. *Leandro Mahalem de Lima* provides a case study of how he used word-based tools like Word Frequencies within a word-based content analysis to analyze cultural models of nature and climate change perceptions in an exploratory set of 18 semi-structured interviews in Brazil. *Richard Vail and Michael Gizzi* demonstrate how they used numerous MAXQDA tools to conduct a dictionary-based content analysis to perform a longitudinal study of five years of Netflix' business strategy through autocoding for a first cycle of coding. Finally, *Stefan Rädiker*'s chapter illustrates how an evaluation project can be done rapidly using summaries of coded segments in code comments and creative uses of MAXMaps.

The second section includes two chapters that explore ways to effectively analyze open-ended survey question responses, and innovative ways of doing mixed methods research. In the first chapter, *Christina Silver* offers a comprehensive overview of how she analyzed free-text responses to open-ended survey questions in a project evaluation, utilizing a variety of MAXQDA tools, and providing a process others can follow. A similar exploration of mixed methods research with MAXQDA is authored by *Sinem Toraman Turk* in a chapter that shows how she used MAXQDA functions in a mixed methods research project, focusing on organization and management of data, data analysis, integration and visualization and reporting.

The book ends with three chapters that provide case studies illustrating thematic analysis, visual analysis, and interpretative analysis. *Christian Schmieder and Allison Rogers* describe how they used MAXQDA features to both manage and refine a very large dataset to identify relevant data that could be analyzed using analytic steps common in thematic analysis. *Elena Samonova*'s chapter focuses on a photovoice participatory research project involving both visual and textual data and explores how MAXQDA can be used to conduct a combined analysis. Finally, *Andreas Müller*'s chapter explains how he used MAXQDA in an interpretative analysis that draws on techniques from grounded theory and sequential analysis in a strongly theory-guided analysis that relies heavily on memos and color coding to conduct an interpretative analysis almost without coding.

How to best read this book?

Each chapter in *The Practice of Qualitative Data Analysis* offers unique and valuable insights that we hope you the reader can benefit from in your own research journey. You do not need to approach this book linearly—while the organization of chapters into sections provides some common points in terms of the type of MAXQDA features used, but each chapter is unique in itself. To the contrary, it might make more sense for you to first examine the table of MAXQDA key features (p. 7) if you are interested in learning more about how the authors used specific tools. This table includes references to key features discussed in both the current and the previous volume. Or you could skim through the book, looking at the more than 120 screenshots to spark innovation. Together, the 19 research examples offered in the two volumes of the book provide one of the most comprehensive sets of examples available anywhere of the ways MAXQDA can be used in qualitative and mixed methods research. We hope you get as much out of it as we did in bringing it together.

Acknowledgments

This book goes to press as the MAXQDA research community is about to gather together in person at the MAXQDA International Conference (MQIC) in Berlin, for the first time since the pandemic. We developed the first volume of *The Practice of Qualitative Data Analysis* in 2020, publishing the book in the spring of 2021. The success of the book, and the collaborative process of working together inspired us to add a second volume of research examples.

This book would not have come to fruition were it not for the talented individuals in the MAXQDA trainer network who submitted proposals for chapters. We are grateful for the response we had to our call for chapters and wish we could have accepted all the proposals we received. We pushed hard for short-deadlines, and the authors all were cooperative.

Michael Gizzi wants to especially thank his co-editor and friend Stefan Rädiker for his expertise on all things MAXQDA, and the detailed work he did in formulating comments to authors, all with the goal of making this the best book it could be. I constantly learn from Stefan.

Stefan Rädiker would also like to thank Michael Gizzi for all his invaluable inputs in this book's creation. His focus on ensuring each chapter's accessibility and each paragraph's value to the reader has been crucial. This collaboration has been a rewarding journey, also enhancing my proficiency in the English language.

Using MAXQDA's Word-Based Features and AI Assist: Processing Large Numbers of Documents in Strategic Foresight

Matthew H. Loxton

Abstract

This chapter describes the use of MAXDictio and AI Assist by a strategic foresight team of analysts. We used these tools in identifying the key themes from a large body of data to develop an evidence-based code system. MAXDictio enabled us to extract prevalence data on word combinations, and we used the Interactive Word Tree to explore context and meaning once common words or phrases had been identified. We used AI Assist features extensively to automatically summarize coded segments in the Summary Grid and in code memos and to suggest subcodes for further breaking down coded segments. Creative Coding gave us a vehicle to brainstorm and a means to pull the results of the sessions into an initial coding system. The team also used MAXQDA "Questions – Themes – Theories" (QTT) to develop a primary hypothesis and research questions for further detailed analysis within a tight timeframe. QTT helped to focus the research analysis process, and to generate a working document that later formed the basis of our communication with the project sponsor.

Key MAXQDA features covered

- ✓ Word Combinations
- ✓ Word Cloud
- ✓ Word Tree
- ✓ AI Assist
- ✓ Summary Grid
- ✓ Creative Coding
- ✓ Questions – Themes – Theories (QTT)

1 Introduction

Strategic foresight is a domain of action research that focuses on plotting a course to the most preferred future, by describing the instrumental forces of change and stasis involved, and potential points of influence. One of the bigger challenges in conducting strategic foresight research is to balance the client's needs for a quick and plausible initial answer about an underexplored topic, and yet still be able to trace assertions back to their primary

Loxton, Matthew H. (2024). Using MAXQDA's word-based features and AI Assist: Processing large numbers of documents in strategic foresight. In: S. Rädiker & Michael C. Gizzi (Eds.), The practice of qualitative data analysis. Research examples using MAXQDA, volume 2 (pp. 17–31). Berlin: MAXQDA Press.
https://doi.org/10.36192/978-3-948768188_1

sources. Many researchers in foresight studies use a hypothesis-driven approach[1], which in practice, means developing a code system that reflects the core risks, issues, and opportunities in the domain represented by forces of change, and which answer the concerns of the sponsor—in essence a take on "what is this all about" that is grounded in evidence rather than assumptions or received wisdom.

Acquiring a sufficiently large sample of documents to frame the environment and research question is crucial to ensure that the initial code system is based on the "voice of the documents," reflects what stakeholders see as salient risks, issues, and opportunities, and that can be defended and explained by means of evidence. However, the larger the document corpus grows, the greater the orientation workload to form the initial hypothesis and relevant research questions, and historically this has meant either sacrificing precision and accuracy, or validity during the formation of the initial taxonomy and hypothesis.

The experience in our team from quality and process improvement reviews of past projects suggested that two common failure modes in prior projects were:

- Spending so much time gathering data, that by the time the research started, the basic research question had been overcome by events and was no longer of interest or use to the client, but also,
- a tendency to jump too quickly to the analysis phase, without a more careful examination of what the data pointed to as the most significant questions to be answered by the research.

To balance these failure modes in the example project of this chapter, we used a form of the World Health Organization (WHO) "Hypothesis-Driven Approach" (HDA) (WHO, 2022). We gathered as large a corpus of documents as we could within the tight timeframe of emergent situations but used MAXQDA to shorten the time spent in orienting to the problem and defining its basic outline by developing a code system that focused on the key issues revealed by the rapid data collection phase.

MAXQDA has proven to be a game-changer in the field of strategic foresight by shifting the work from disconnected but overlapping paper-based processes and spreadsheet work, to an integrated process that has inbuilt traceability and reporting. In the MAXQDA Press guide on performing strategic foresight projects using MAXQDA (Loxton, 2021), I described the methodology of applying MAXQDA to the Houston Model, and in this chapter, I look at greater detail at one of the early steps in foresight in which the foundational taxonomy is built and a code system developed that will be used for ongoing horizon scanning and anal-

1 The hypothesis-driven approach is recommended by the World Health Organization as a means to respond to rapidly emerging topics and threats. See https://www.who.int/publications/i/item/WPR-2023-DHP-001

ysis. The same foundational framing phase is also pivotal when foresight is used to answer specific stakeholder questions about the future.

In this chapter, I cover one of the initial and foundational steps in conducting a strategic foresight domain assessment: the discovery process using internal organizational documents and communications, industry guides, press releases, whitepapers, and transcriptions of stakeholder interviews. The steps are demonstrated using an example project that focuses on the future of work and the future workplace. Stemming partially from the effect of COVID-19 and the need to increase the number of people working from home, one client sponsor asked a broader question of what the future of work and the future workplace were likely to be. There was limited time to get from framing an initial hypothesis and developing formal research questions, to delivering answers capable of informing decisions that would help to orient the organization, support collecting data in a purposeful ongoing manner, and initiate more long-term and in-depth research.

MAXQDA was used to develop two essential deliverables:

1. A suitable initial code system to use in subsequent ongoing monitoring and scanning.
2. A report describing the key forces of change and events related to the future of work and the workplace.

2 Data collection

Data collection involved four researchers, each harvesting documents based on their individual focus from interview transcripts and notes, client materials, and industry documents. The approach was to brainstorm search terms that could be used by the team to find documents that matched the need, and periodic updates were made to the search terms as we began to collect documents.

Each researcher in our team had one or more focus areas, and this is pertinent because the data corpus later reflected this specialization. The team split its focus into areas such as:

- Science & Technology
- Wounds & Health
- Regional Impacts of Environment & Climate Change
- Social & Demographics
- Statute & Policy/Politics

We anticipated that many search terms would remain standard across all our individual topic areas, but there was some customization to suit each topic, since a term used in science and technology might not suit a similar concept in statute. To speed up this process, we made use of a combination of Microsoft Visio, and MAXMaps to document the brainstorming sessions.

We used a combination of collection methods, including:

- Harvesting from known sources, such as PubMed, World Bank, social science collections, and libraries.
- Snowball sampling by using bibliographies in key documents already collected.
- Google search with specified terms.

Some of the documents were downloaded with the MAXQDA Web Collector, an extension for Google Chrome browsers that allowed us to enter a document title and document memo during collection, while the others were downloaded directly. At the end of the time allotted for data collection, we had accumulated 225 documents, with a mean size of 13.7 PDF pages per document, ranging from zero (an image) to 306 pages, for a sum total of 3,111 pages.

3 Setting up the MAXQDA project

We imported the 225 documents into MAXQDA via drag and drop into the Document System area and via ***Import > Web Pages > Web Pages from Web Collector***. The documents were organized in document groups per topic area, as follows (number of documents in parentheses):

- Science & Technology (72)
- Healthcare (7)
- Statute & Policy (73)
- Climate Change (73)

This structure aligned with our team organization, and how we divided work in the team. There was a small amount of crossover between researchers, and on occasion a document was found during the analysis that fitted more in someone else's category. We made use of document sets to contain the documents that were activated through particular search terms. In this way particular topics could be explored and visualized.

4 Autocoding word combinations

At the heart of our methodological approach is the argument that with some notable exceptions related to taboos (Argyris, 2010), word and phrase prevalence in a body of documents reflect the policies, plans, processes, and activities of an organization, community of practice, or industry, and are an unbiased predictor of the things that they regard as salient and important.

We used MAXDictio to identify the most frequent non-trivial phrases in the documents. Fig. 1 illustrates the settings used in ***MAXDictio > Word Combinations*** to capture phrases while ignoring hyperlinks, email addresses, hashtags, and numbers. We applied a general list of stop words to limit the number of "junk words" retrieved in the count and used lemmatization to capture different forms of each root word.

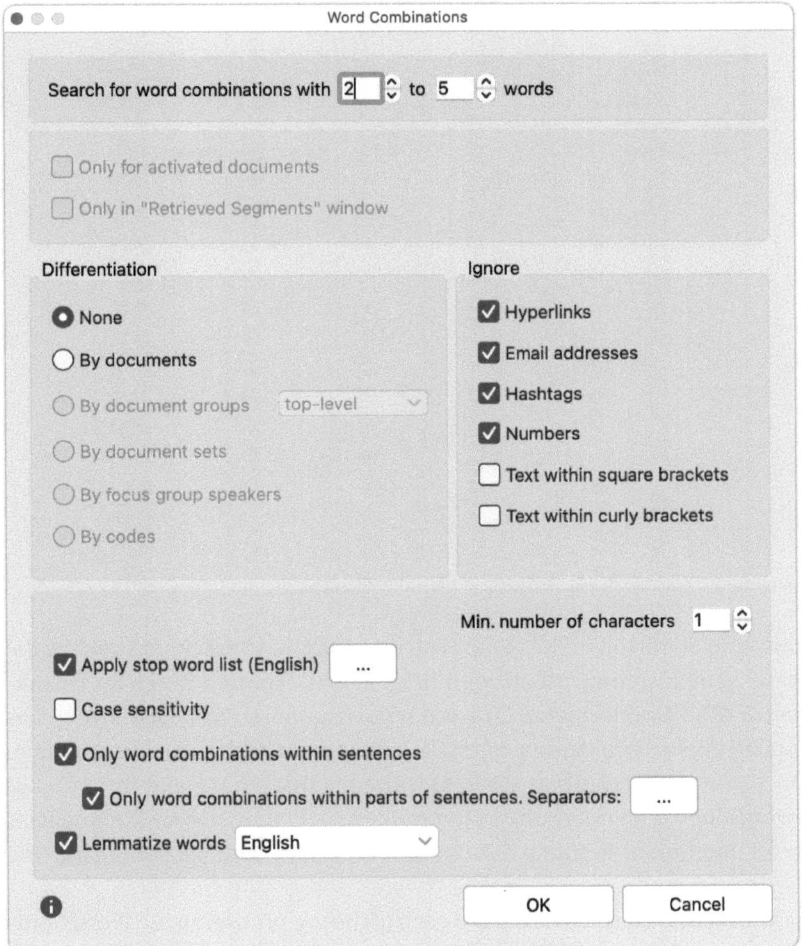

Fig. 1: MAXDictio Word Combinations to identify phrase frequency in corpus

The results shown in Fig. 2 reflect the top fifteen phrases in order of total frequency. The display can be made more manageable by using the ***Display Top Ranks*** dropdown list to limit the display to the selected number of items sorted by count. Selection of phrases was based on frequency but influenced by the percentage of documents in which it occurred. This was to prevent a single document that used a phrase a great many times from being over-represented compared to a slightly less frequent phrase that occurred over several documents. In the sense of document voice, this attempts to ensure that a single loud voice does not drown out a choir of voices. Of note is that we retained "the pandemic" and "the office" as valid terms but chose to reject "the covid."

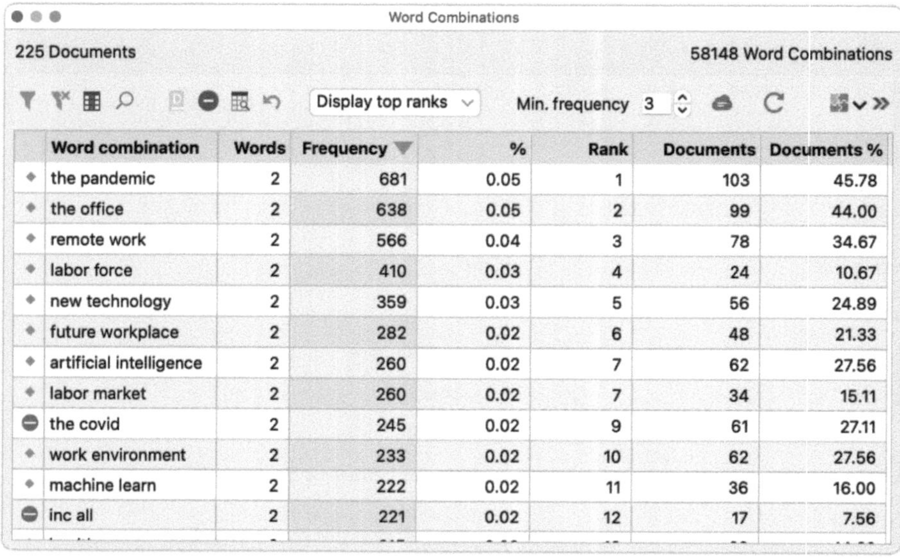

	Word combination	Words	Frequency	%	Rank	Documents	Documents %
	the pandemic	2	681	0.05	1	103	45.78
	the office	2	638	0.05	2	99	44.00
	remote work	2	566	0.04	3	78	34.67
	labor force	2	410	0.03	4	24	10.67
	new technology	2	359	0.03	5	56	24.89
	future workplace	2	282	0.02	6	48	21.33
	artificial intelligence	2	260	0.02	7	62	27.56
	labor market	2	260	0.02	7	34	15.11
	the covid	2	245	0.02	9	61	27.11
	work environment	2	233	0.02	10	62	27.56
	machine learn	2	222	0.02	11	36	16.00
	inc all	2	221	0.02	12	17	7.56

Fig. 2: List of most frequent word combinations. Red stop icons indicate excluded combinations.

Clicking on the cloud icon at the top in the results list, we created a word cloud showing the most frequent phrases. The resulting visualization (Fig. 3) was exported into a QTT worksheet using the ***Send to QTT Worksheet*** icon. QTT is a reporting tool in MAXQDA which lets the user create worksheets to store various analysis outputs and add notes or insights to them. In this instance, the word cloud was saved as a graphic that would later form part of reports. While the word cloud does not provide any unique insight that a table of frequencies does not, it is a useful instrument to frame discussions, especially with people outside the research team.

At this point in the process, the team discussed each of the top phrases in the Word Combinations results list, excluded those that were deemed irrelevant, and then moved down the list until a point was reached at which phrases were no longer common across the corpus or considered by the team to be pertinent to the sponsor's question. Each of those phrases were double-clicked to reveal context to help inform decisions, but also to identify text segments to be autocoded, because they related to the underlying concept. This was often a highly labor-intensive task, since in some cases, a phrase occurred a great many times that needed to be inspected for relevance. For example, Fig. 4 shows the context for the term "the pandemic." After excluding any non-relevant text segments (by clicking on the red "stop symbol" icon in the toolbar), the remainder were autocoded at the paragraph level with the relevant phrase—in this case "the pandemic." This was a suitable time to add the collective thoughts on the code meaning and scope to the code memo which was later refined and expanded.

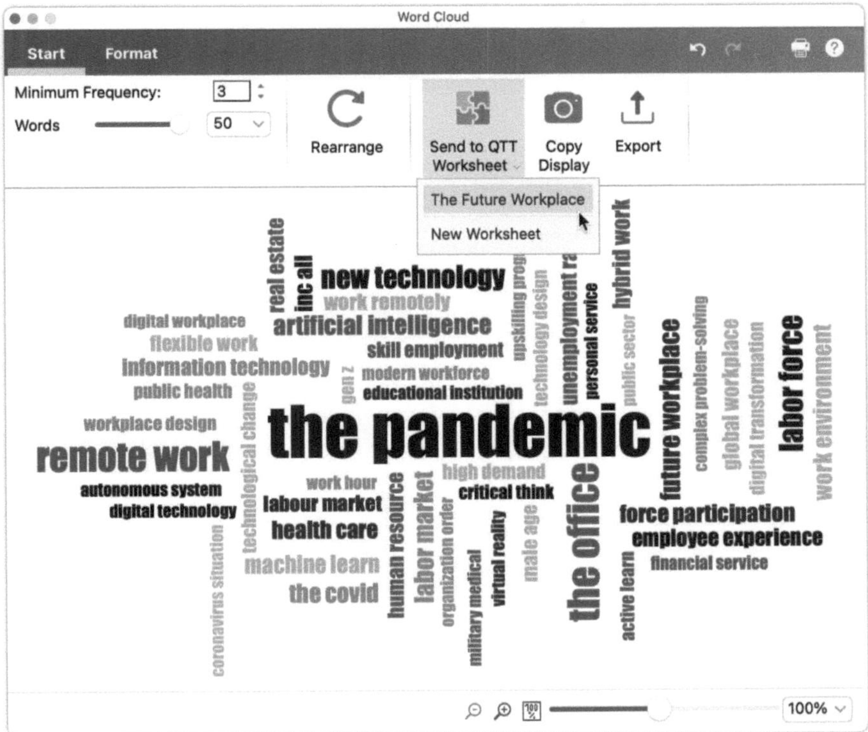

Fig. 3: Word cloud illustrating the phrase frequency

Overall, fifty-nine phrases were autocoded following this process before the list ran dry, resulting in fifty-nine codes on the top level of the code system (Fig. 5). Autocoding in this fashion is highly efficient and allows a large number of segments to be coded without manual effort that would take time. Even at this early point, the sponsor was already able to get an initial impression on what the terrain looked like based on evidence, rather than assumptions and suppositions.

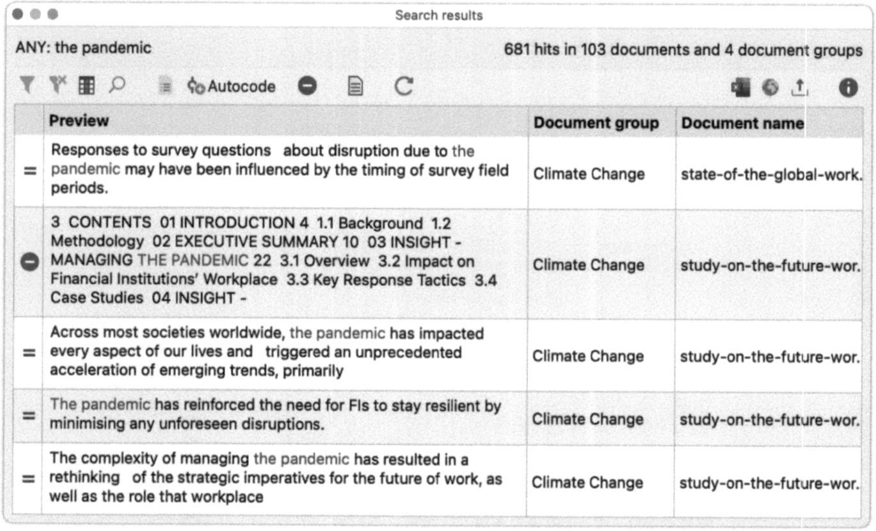

Fig. 4: Context of phrases

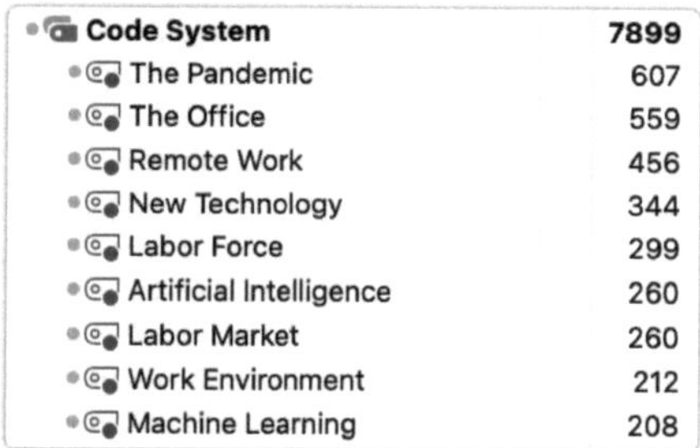

Fig. 5: Code System after autocoding word combinations

5 Auto-summarization using AI Assist

Once the code system had been created, the next step was to develop a better understanding of the topic realm of each code by summarizing the coded segments using AI Assist. MAXQDA's built in AI Assist utilizes a large language model to automatically create summaries and to perform other language related analysis tasks. We launched AI Assist by right-clicking on the code in question and selecting ***AI Assist*** from the context menu (Fig. 6).

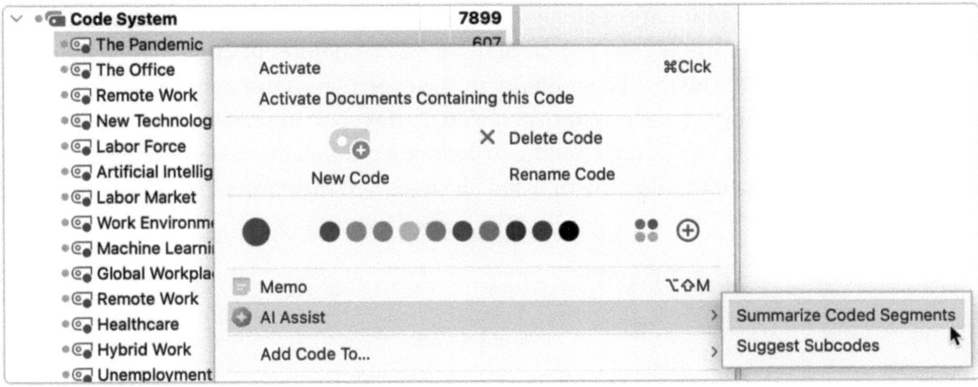

Fig. 6: Initiating AI Assist on coded segments

In the AI Assist dialogue (Fig. 7), we selected the desired language and summary length. We typically repeated the process twice and used both the "Standard" summary length and the bulleted summary. In practice, we found that the standard summary could later be used in overviews and descriptions, while the bulleted list tended to be more granular and highly suitable to be dropped into PowerPoint slides.

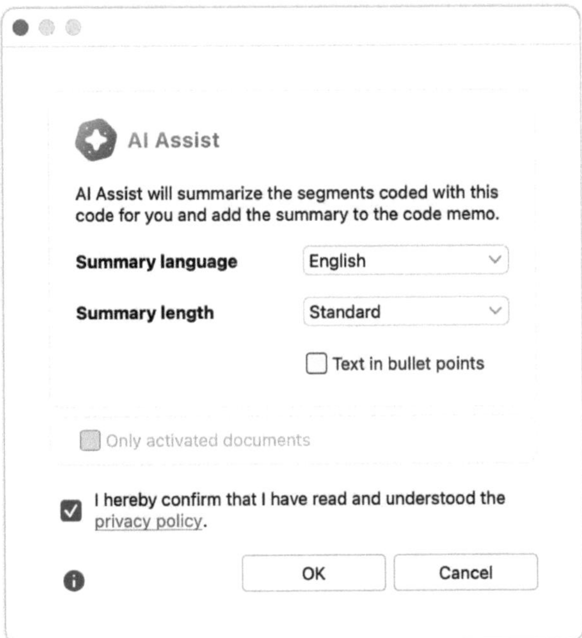

Fig. 7: AI Assist dialog pane for summarizing coded segments

The process captured a summary of all segments coded with the selected code, and AI Assist inserted the results into a new code memo (if none existed before) or appended to an existing code memo (Fig. 8). Having the summary in the code memo was important to support the next steps in refining the code system and also made reporting easier since these would appear in the codebook. We found it helpful to generate a codebook as a reference guide via ***Reports > Codebook***, since this document listed all codes and the content of their memos.

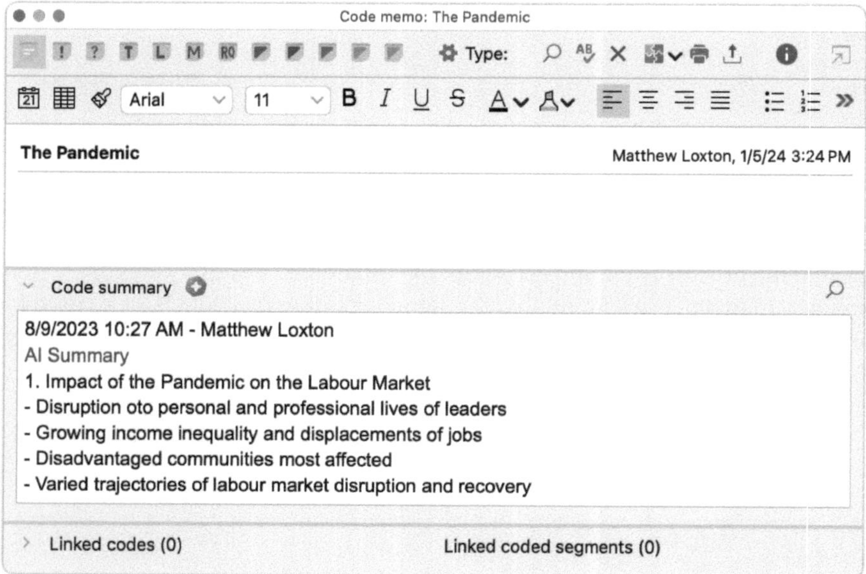

Fig. 8: Code memo with AI Assist summary of coded segments

6 Using Creative Coding for refining the code system

We used ***Codes > Creative Coding*** as a whiteboard to arrange codes and a brainstorming and discussion tool to progress from a plain list of codes to a structured hierarchy that could be used to understand the dimensions and facets of the topic, and to serve as the basis for further monitoring, scanning, and analysis going forward. In foresight research, the stakeholder values a snapshot of what the future might look like from the perspective of a point in time, but far more values a foundation upon which to build ongoing scanning that can drive continuous adjustment towards a desired future. For that purpose, a more developed code system is an essential foundation.

To use Creative Coding in this way, we dragged all fifty-nine codes into the workspace and selected ***Start Organizing Codes***. We then collaboratively moved codes into clusters in the traditional card sorting process (Best, 2022), and created new codes or merged codes where this was appropriate (Fig. 9). For example, "External Forces of Change" was a new code created to be the parent to subcode elements such as "The Pandemic," "Social Media," and "Labor Market." In the same way, "Worker Characteristics" was created to provide a new collective code for those that related to attributes a successful worker might need in the future.

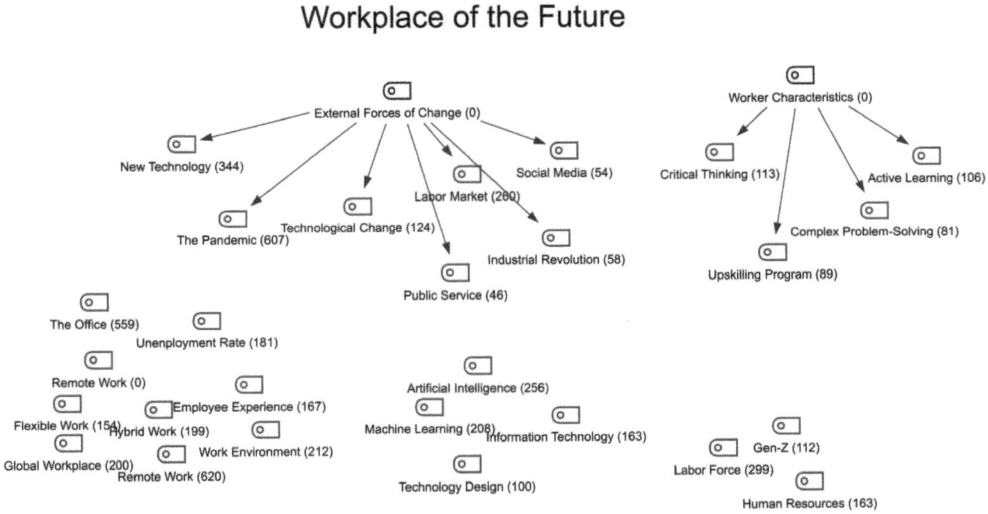

Fig. 9: Card sorting in Creative Coding workspace

At this time, while the discussion and thought process was fresh, it was important to capture the code memos for new codes, especially those acting as higher-level parent codes for the clusters created during card sorting (Fig. 10). The memos described the purpose, definition, and scope of each code. This allowed us to limit code meanings from "creeping" and expanding too far beyond the intent.

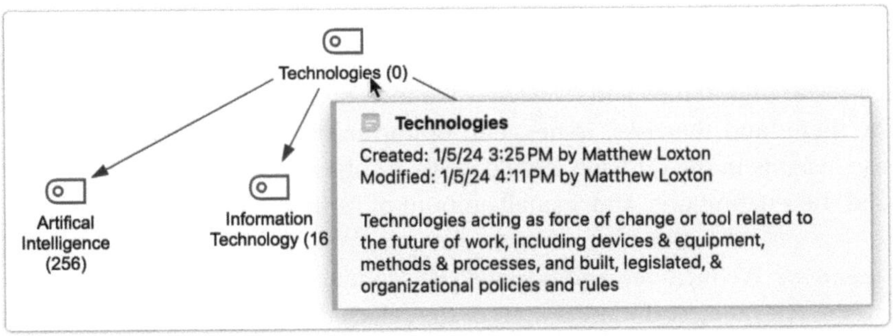

Fig. 10: Capturing code memos during card sorting

We chose a significant color for the top-level codes we regarded as key to answering the stakeholder question, so that they could easily be identified later during the more in-depth analysis stages. We also moved the code families in the code system to indicate those at the top represented the forces of change and events that we believed were the most impactful and relevant to the sponsor's questions.

Before ending the Creative Coding session and updating the code system composition and structure with the changes, we used the icon ***Save as a Map in MAXMaps*** to save the graphic code structure as a map that could be worked on later in ***Visual Tools > MAXMaps***, the environment for creating concept maps in MAXQDA. The maps were further edited in a separate MAXMaps session to add conceptual links, icons and shapes, and images and explanatory text. The resulting map was exported to a QTT worksheet for inclusion in a report.

With the code system developed, a conceptual map created, and the AI-generated summaries in hand, traditional thematic analysis could proceed. In this phase, we reviewed the higher-order coded segments, and added code comments and memos, and updated the summaries where the AI content was insufficient, missed a key aspect, or where wording needed to be better aligned with the stakeholder interests and internal language. These were also saved to a QTT worksheet.

7 Synthesizing the analysis process using Questions – Themes – Theories (QTT)

At this point, the initial code system was complete and one of the key deliverables achieved. What remained to be completed, was an analytical narrative that bound the code system, summaries, and analysis together to provide the sponsor with an answer to their question about the future of the workplace.

The QTT environment (Fig. 11) proved to be a highly effective way to channel efforts towards a research product, and we used it to guide activities for the remainder of the project. Concretely, we used the sections of each QTT worksheet for different purposes, including:

- *Related Codes & Themes.* In this section, we added the codes that were color-coded to indicate high-order importance and relevance. We then discussed the forces of change identified by them, and the risks, issues, and opportunities represented, and documented these insights in the QTT tab. This process resulted in some changes made to the codes and their definitions, and a small amount of further adjustment to the code hierarchy.
- *Important Segments.* We included and reviewed key coded segments and captured our insights as to the relevance and implications of the selected segments. These segments were also used in the final report to underpin our insights, or to provide the sponsor with

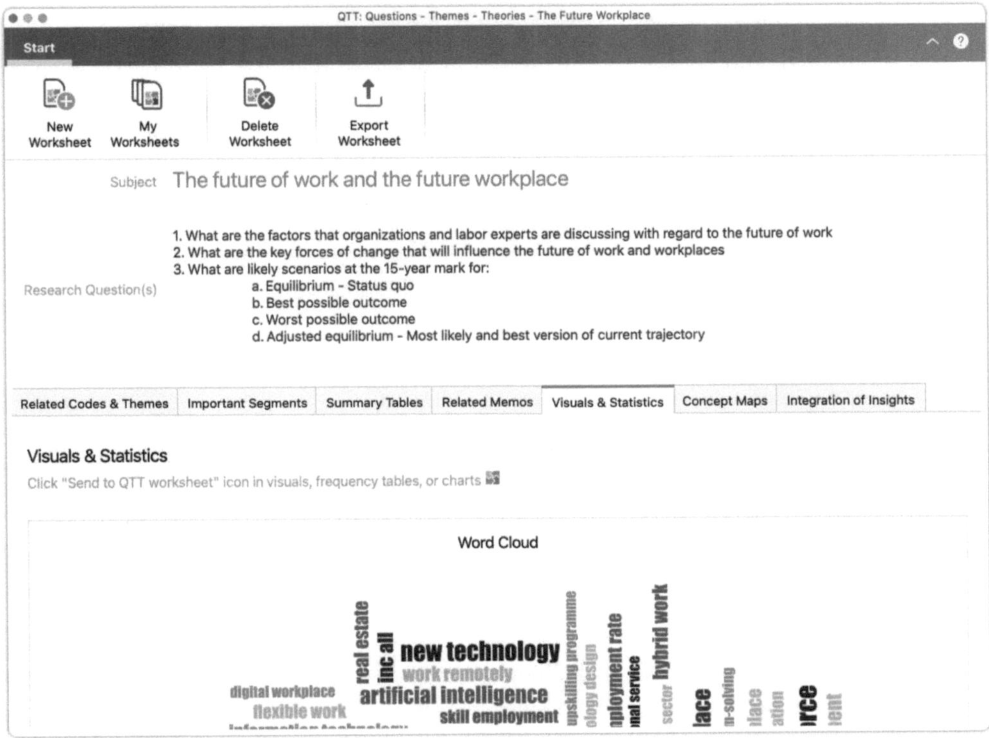

Fig. 11: QTT worksheet Visuals & Statistics view

examples of the direct quotes from source documents that were relevant to their question. With that crystallization of thought, we added any additional relevant coded segments that were pertinent and amended the insights.

- *Summary Tables.* Although this was not described in detail in this chapter, we reviewed the summary tables containing all summaries created by AI Assist, and captured our insights, especially regarding key points in the AI Assist summaries that underlined the major forces of change that had emerged.
- *Related Memos.* We added and reviewed memos. These were used to write the insights, and we added additional memos for insight elements that needed further support.
- *Visuals & Statistics.* We described the visuals and document statistics and added insights into the context and implications of these related to forces of change relevant to the future of work.
- *Concept Maps.* We used the concept maps, such as the MAXMaps image sent to QTT to help describe the relationships and hierarchies that existed in the various elements of forces of change and risks, issues, and potential opportunities that they reflected.

- *Integration of Insights.* At the conclusion of the QTT process, we used all the previous tabs to organize and support an integrated perspective that listed and described the forces of change, the implications we saw, and the potential risks, issues, and opportunities that the material had uncovered. We further used AI Assist to summarize the integrated insights into a bulleted list (by copying the insights into a new document).

The final step in the process with MAXQDA was to publish the QTT worksheet by clicking on ***Export Worksheet*** to generate a Word document, which could be further edited to satisfy organizational formats and themes.

8 Lessons learned

MAXQDA's MAXDictio and AI Assist features made it possible to respond to urgent questions about emergent situations within a timeframe that matched the required immediacy, but without unduly sacrificing reliability or validity. The ability to ingest a large document corpus and use word-based analysis to provide traceable insights was particularly useful to stakeholders. The creation of a code system from the corpus in this way also provided the foundation for further monitoring and evaluation and horizon scanning projects. Here are some specific lessons learned:

- Using AI Assist effectively was a challenge. We sometimes found validation of the AI-generated material difficult because it was not always clear where the AI was getting a specific fact from. We would like to emphasize that AI output should always be checked.
- Given many previous examples using AI chatbots, such as Bard, ChatGPT, etc., we were surprised to find no evidence of hallucination with AI Assist. Where we were expecting to see the AI generated false content, in our validation we found no instances in which AI Assist hallucinated.
- Compared to some previous projects using manual methods, MAXQDA enabled us to greatly expand the number of source documents typically used to inform the initial hypothesis and research questions, and it also reduced the time taken to conduct the initial generation of suitable questions and topics.
- Using a hypothesis-driven methodology and process provided an excellent way to conduct the initial exploration of a problem. It was fast and satisfied sponsor needs for informed initial appraisal of problems and laid a solid groundwork for subsequent traditional research.
- The success of our method combined with MAXQDA created somewhat of a monster, and we are receiving requests for analysis of ever bigger and more urgent problems.

Bibliography

Argyris, C. (2010). Organizational traps: Leadership, culture, organizational design. OUP Oxford.

Best, P. B. (2022). Participatory theme elicitation: Open card sorting for user led qualitative data analysis. *International Journal of Social Research Methodology, 25*(2), 213-231. https://doi.org/10.1080/13645579.2021.1876616

Loxton, M. H. (2021). *Using MAXQDA for strategic foresight.* MAXQDA Press. https://doi.org/10.36192/978-3-948768126

WHO (2022). *Hypothesis-driven approach for problem-solving in the context of global public health.* World Health Organization.

About the author

Matthew Loxton is a Principal Analyst at Serco, focused on healthcare improvement and strategic foresight, serves on the board of directors of the Blue Faery Liver Cancer Association, and holds a master's degree in Knowledge Management from the University of Canberra. Matthew is also a MAXQDA professional trainer.

ORCID: https://orcid.org/0000-0003-3650-596X

ResearchGate: https://www.researchgate.net/profile/Matthew-Loxton

LinkedIn: https://www.linkedin.com/in/mloxton

Mastodon: https://med-mastodon.com/@mloxton

Using MAXQDA for Word-Based Content Analysis: Nature and Climate Change Perceptions in Qualitative Interviews

Leandro Mahalem de Lima

Abstract

This chapter provides an example of how I used MAXQDA to analyze cultural models of nature and climate change perceptions in an exploratory set of 18 semi-structured interviews, conducted among indigenous peoples in Lower Tapajos region (Santarem, Brazil). Firstly, I demonstrate how I used word frequency analysis to synthesize and map the major components that frame the content about which interviewees talked about. Next, I describe how I analyzed, quantified, and mapped instances when participants raised the theme of climate change, evidencing patterns, and variable factors that cut across multiple cases. My goal is to show how word-based content analysis, assisted by MAXQDA's key features, can bring new ways to describe and visualize different ways of thinking, by creating simple and meaningful lists, tables, and concept maps.

Key MAXQDA features covered

- ✓ Word Frequencies
- ✓ Word Cloud
- ✓ Code Cloud
- ✓ Code Map
- ✓ MAXMaps: Free map
- ✓ MAXMaps: Code Co-Occurrence Model
- ✓ Activate by Variable
- ✓ Transform into Categorical Document Variable

1 Introduction

This research example is based on ethnographic research and data I collected in the Brazilian Amazon. It is part of a larger cross-cultural project on which a group of anthropologists working in six continents investigated cultural models of nature held by primary food producers who are experiencing the impacts of environmental degradation and climate change. Our main goal was to describe underlying conceptual models, causal relations and cultural practices that impact environmental resources and climate change policy implementation. We have applied a common set of qualitative and quantitative strategies, within

Leandro Mahalem de Lima (2024). Using MAXQDA for word-based content analysis: Nature and climate change perceptions in qualitative interviews. In: S. Rädiker & Michael C. Gizzi (Eds.), The practice of qualitative data analysis. Research examples using MAXQDA, volume 2 (pp. 33–48). Berlin: MAXQDA Press.
https://doi.org/10.36192/978-3-948768188_2

the field of cognitive anthropology, to analyze linguistic data at word, sentence, and discourse levels.[1]

2 Data collection and methodological approach

The 18 audio recorded semi-structured interviews explored in this research example were conducted among residents of two small-scale riverine villages in Santarem (Brazil): Caruci, in the border of a lake, and Garimpo, in the margins of a forest small stream. They are inhabited by the Arapium and the Tapajo, Portuguese-speaking indigenous peoples, representing here several villages with similar characteristics in the region. Four participants were interviewed in Alter do Chão, a village inhabited by the Borari, and an increasingly popular tourist site, where they were moving to for job prospects.

Cultural models are defined as systematically organized mental representations that are shared by members of a culture, while the analytical concept of nature may include everything that exists in the world people live in. In that sense, a cultural model of nature refers to the ways a community understands how the existing world works—establishing relationships among its major components (Bennardo, 2019). In a comparative study about the native mind and the cultural construction of nature, Scott Atran and Douglas L. Medin (2008) identified six major components across cultures: humans, plants, animals, weather/climate, physical environment, and supernatural. These components drove the development of categories for the content analysis presented in this chapter.

Primary food producing was the core criterion for the selection of sites and the main subject of the semi-structured interviews. The interviews focused on daily food-producing activities because talking about them is supposed to activate the interviewee's cultural model of nature as they explain the activities and their beliefs about them. Therefore, frequent words used when discussing these topics can be explored to reconstruct the major components that underlie the interviewees discourses.

In the following, I will demonstrate how I applied word analysis in the 18 interview transcripts to describe the underlying major components, co-occurrences and causal elations that frame cultural models of nature and climate change perceptions, following seven steps:

1. Setting up and structuring the MAXQDA project.
2. Retrieving and comparing frequent words.
3. Turning frequent words into codes and creating code clouds.
4. Visualizing relationships of codes with conceptual maps.

1 The research was funded by the National Science Foundation (NSF). Preliminary results are available in Cultural Models of Nature: Primary Food Producers and Climate Change (Bennardo, 2019). In this chapter, I present a revised and expanded version of two posts I published on MAXQDA Research Blog (2019, February 25 and 2019, June 11).

5. Lemmatizing keywords to retrieve and code a theme.
6. Reading segments of a code and creating subcodes.
7. Visualizing co-occurrences of codes in MAXMaps.

3 Data analysis using MAXQDA

3.1 Setting up and structuring the MAXQDA project

I set up and structured my interview analysis project in MAXQDA following three basic steps. First, I imported the transcriptions of the 18 interviews into the Document System into a single document group, which I named "Interviews" (Fig. 1). Second, I imported document variables for each interview from a Microsoft Excel spreadsheet (***Variables > Import Document Variables***), including basic information such as gender, age group, residence place, ethnic affiliation, schooling. Third, I used the feature ***Mixed Methods > Activate Documents by Variables*** with variables "Gender" and "Age group (2015)" to create document sets representing different subgroupings, such as "Female," "Male," and "Female (60+) Seniors."

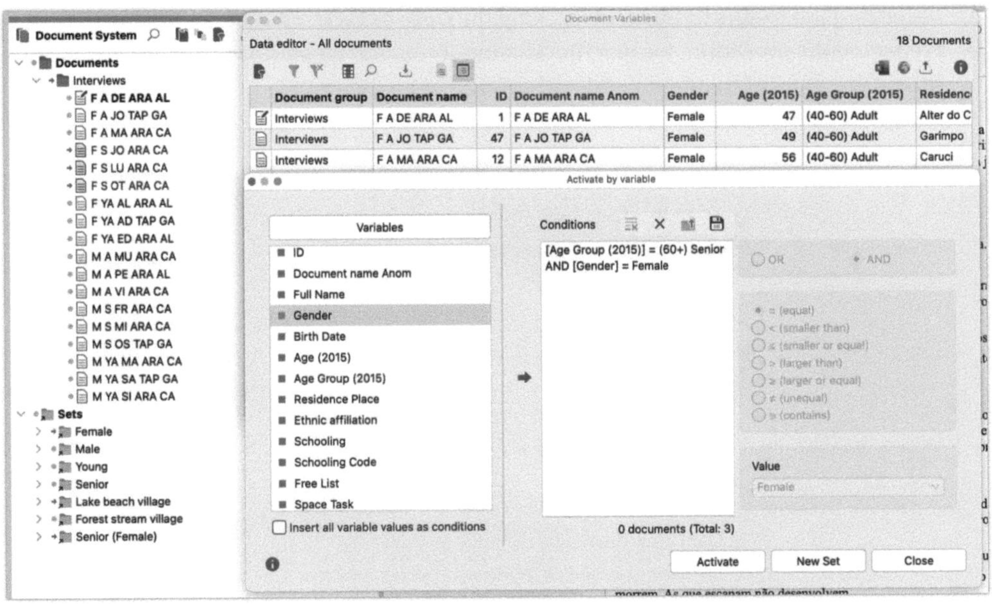

Fig. 1: Document System with some created sets. Data Editor for Data Variables showing the variable values. Activate Documents by Variables window used for creating the sets.

Mainly, these document sets were used for analysis because they allowed performing group comparisons. To ensure participant anonymity in the document names, I used acronyms for gender (Male, Female), age group (Young Adult, Adult, Senior), personal name (various), ethnic group (Arapium, Tapajos), and village (Cacuri, Garimpo, Alter do Chao).

3.2 Retrieving and comparing frequent words

Frequent words in interviews provide a way to access the conceptual building blocks that frame the world interviewees talked about. I utilized MAXQDA's word frequency and word cloud feature to explore the interviewees' usage of words:

1. I opened ***Word Cloud*** in the ***Visual Tools*** menu tab, selected all documents, and created a cloud showing the most frequent words. By clicking on the ***Word Frequencies*** option in the menu bar of the word cloud, I opened a table listing all used words and their frequencies in all interviews, as illustrated in Fig. 2 (please note that it is also possible to get this table via ***MAXDictio > Word Frequencies***).
2. I excluded uninteresting words by selecting them and using the ***Add to Stop List*** icon in the toolbar, while keeping only nouns.
3. I exported the results to Excel, by clicking the ***Open as Excel table*** icon.
4. I repeated the procedure for specific document sets and created a comparative table that shows the 15 most frequent words overall and per subgroup.

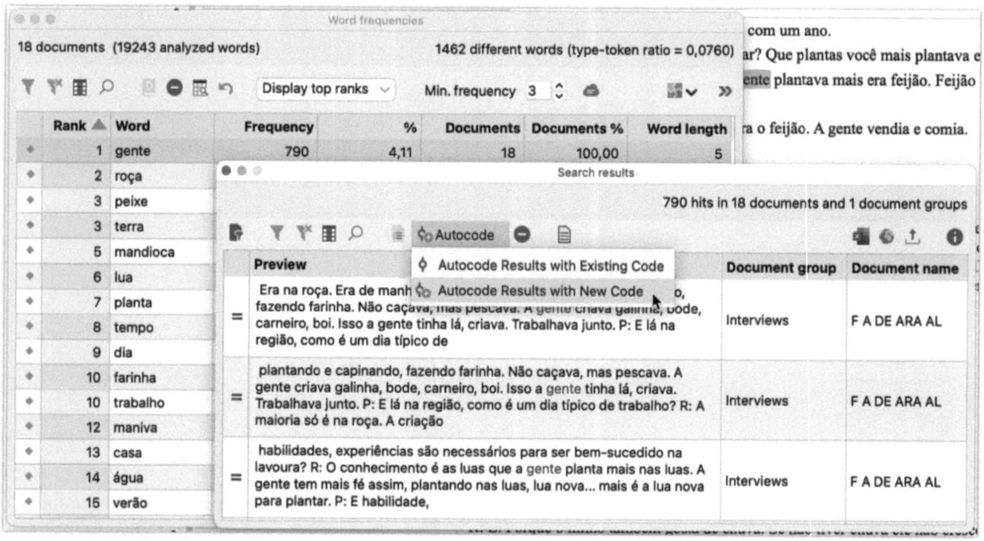

Fig. 2: Word cloud frequencies (first 15 entries) for all documents and search results after double-clicking the search hit "gente"

Tab. 1 presents the comparative table. The first column contains the most frequent words overall. The other eight represent smaller sub-groupings formed by combining gender, age, and place of residence. Understanding these sub-groups was crucial in our analysis as it helped reveal words that are significant within different social segments.

Tab. 1: Comparative table made with lists exported from MAXQDA containing frequent words overall and for different subgroupings (De Lima, 2019, p. 75, Table 3.1 "Key words in interviews for all respondents and sub-groupings" reproduced with permission of the licensor through PLSclear.)

			Male								**Female**							
	Overall (n = 18)		**Young (n = 3)**		**Senior (n = 3)**		**Lake beach village (n = 2)**		**Forest stream village (n = 2)**		**Young (n = 3)**		**Senior (n = 3)**		**Lake beach village (n = 2)**		**Forest stream village (n = 2)**	
	Word	**n**	**Word**	**n**	**Word**	**n**	**Word**	**n**	**Word**	**n**	**Word**	**n**	**Word**	**n**	**Word**	**n**	**Word**	**n**
1.	people	790	people	170	people	91	people	75	people	112	people	200	people	79	people	70	people	124
2.	garden	265	fish	94	fish	54	moon	75	game	45	garden	65	garden	49	plant	29	m.root	60
3.	fish	219	moon	82	garden	40	fish	67	garden	36	m.root	63	soil	33	garden	27	garden	54
4.	soil	219	game	54	time	39	force	43	time	28	soil	44	plant	27	year	25	m.plant	34
5.	m.root	195	hours	52	soil	25	day	39	path	25	flour	40	time	20	m.root	25	soil	27
6.	moon	188	force	49	day	20	hours	35	m.root	20	m.plant	38	house	19	soil	23	mother	26
7.	plant	153	day	43	flour	20	water	24	moon	18	labor	35	m.root	17	house	19	plant	25
8.	time	148	time	35	water	19	lake	23	forest	18	house	32	beach	16	corn	19	flour	24
9.	day	121	garden	33	moon	19	m.root	23	soil	18	mother	29	year	13	flour	18	moon	21
10.	flour	119	m.root	28	m.root	18	time	22	hours	17	summer	29	lake	13	time	18	labor	19
11.	labor	119	forest	28	house	16	soil	21	m.plant	15	stream	28	god	12	water	13	forest	18
12.	m.plant	109	fishing	26	month	16	fishery	20	day	14	moon	27	flour	12	animal	13	house	17
13.	home	107	path	26	plant	16	money	19	labor	14	year	26	mother	11	god	13	stream	15
14.	water	99	labor	25	curupira	15	morning	18	law	12	plant	26	w.melon	10	rain	12	a.forest	13
15.	summer	98	soil	22	lake	14	plant	18	border	11	garden	24	fish	10	moon	12	family	12

m.root = manioc root; m.plant = manioc plant; w.melon = water melon; a.forest = anthrop forest
please note that these words are single words in the original language Portuguese

By compiling and comparing the 15 most frequent nouns overall and by subgroups, I derived 35 salient words. It is interesting to notice that "people" (*gente*) is the most frequent category in all lists, followed by "garden" (*roça)* and "manioc" (*mandioca)* among the females, while "fish" (*peixe*) and "moon" (*lua*) are more salient among males. This contrast reinforces the hypothesis that males' self-construction is framed by animal predation, whereas females' self-construction is more connected to the cultivation of plants. Moreover, it illustrates how useful word analysis can be, to uncover the underlying conceptual building blocks that frame the interviewees' discourses.

3.3 Turning frequent words into codes and creating code clouds

To build conceptual models out of the lists, I converted each of the 35 words in Tab. 1 into a code. To do so, I did the following:

1. I went back into the results table of word frequencies and double-clicked on specific words to open the search results table, which also displays previews of instances in which the selected word appears.
2. To autocode each salient word with a new code, I clicked the ***Autocode*** icon in the toolbar. In the options dialog, I translated each word from Portuguese to an English code name and chose to code the sentence around each search result.
3. Next, I began to organize my codes in the Code System window by using words from a higher abstraction level as parent codes (for example, "beaches" are a kind of "soil"; "maniocs" are "plants," "game" is a sort of "animal"). This organization allowed me to think about the relations between the identified words.
4. Finally, I changed the colors of each main code using the right-click menu. All 11 parent codes (and their subcodes) were assigned specific colors (Fig. 3). "Forest-weed" appears in darker green to contrast with "plants," a word the interviewees used only for species and domains that are domesticated humans.

For a first visualization of my coding work (Fig. 3), I used ***Code Cloud*** feature by right-clicking on the Interviews document group in the Document System and choosing the same-called option (also available via ***Codes > Code Cloud***). The more often a code has been applied to the interviews, the larger it appears in the cloud.

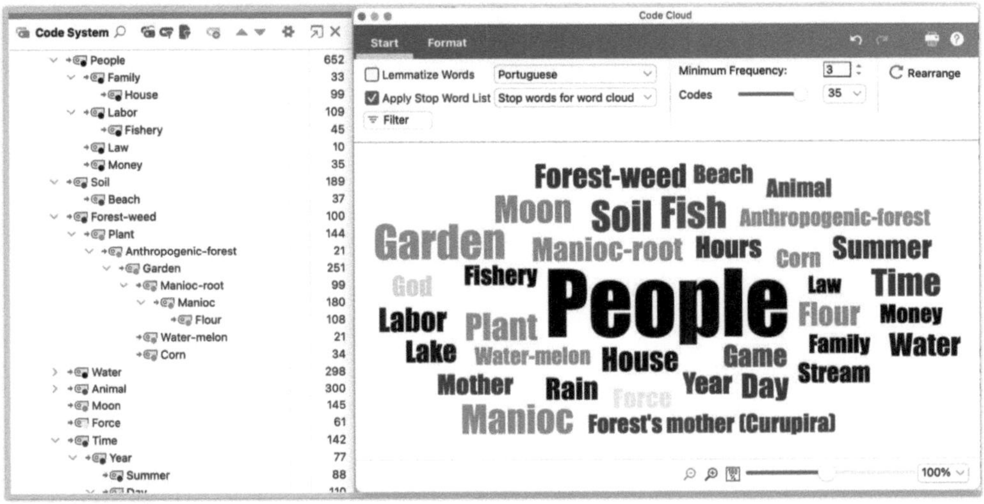

Fig. 3: Left: Code system representing 35 words as codes derived from word frequency analysis. It includes 11 parent codes and 24 related subcodes, which are color-coded for differentiation of areas. Right: Code cloud visualizing the frequency of each code.

3.4 Visualizing relationships of codes with conceptual maps

To continue the exploration, I created a series of concept maps using the analytical features available in ***Visual Tools > MAXMaps***.

Code subsystems and their relations (free model)

To visualize all subsystems, formed by 11 parent codes and 24 related subcodes, and their relations as shown in Fig. 3, I created a new blank MAXMap and then followed these steps:

1. One after the other, I dragged and dropped all parent codes into the map.
2. To insert subcodes, I right-clicked on the code and selected ***Import Subcodes*** from the context menu, with the thickness of lines representing frequencies. After that, I changed all symbols of the code icons to circles.
3. I freely placed the code groups as if representing the general relations and oppositions in the spaces where the interviewees live in and talked about. In the vertical axis: "God" above all; "people" in the middle (above the ground), "[enchanted] Mother" at the bottom. In the horizontal axis: "Soil" and "Water," "Forest" and "Lake," generating complementary landscapes on which "People," "Plants," and "Animals" live in.

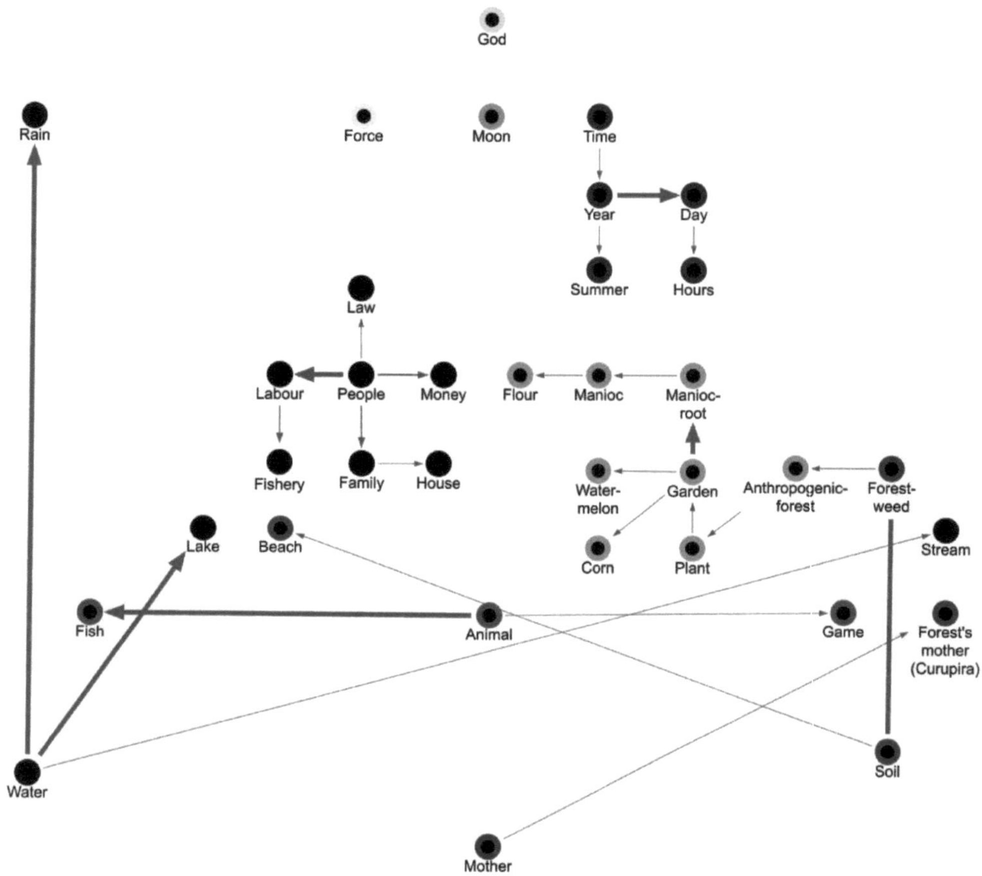

Fig. 4: Free concept map created in MAXMaps. Subsystems represented by colors and relationships between them represented by oriented lines. The thickness of lines indicates code frequencies of the subcodes.

Code co-occurrence model (model template)

To obtain an overview of common occurrences of the identified salient words within sentences, I created a Co-occurrence Model in MAXMaps. After starting the feature via ***Visual Tools > MAXMaps > New Code Model > Co-occurrence Model (Code Intersection)***, I dragged and dropped all my parent codes into the map, adjusted the options in the appearing menu (Fig. 5), and the structure shown in Fig. 6 was automatically created.

To change the properties of the code icons displayed in the map (font, symbol, borders), I multi-selected a group of related codes and right-clicked on one of the code icons to access the ***Format*** menu tab.

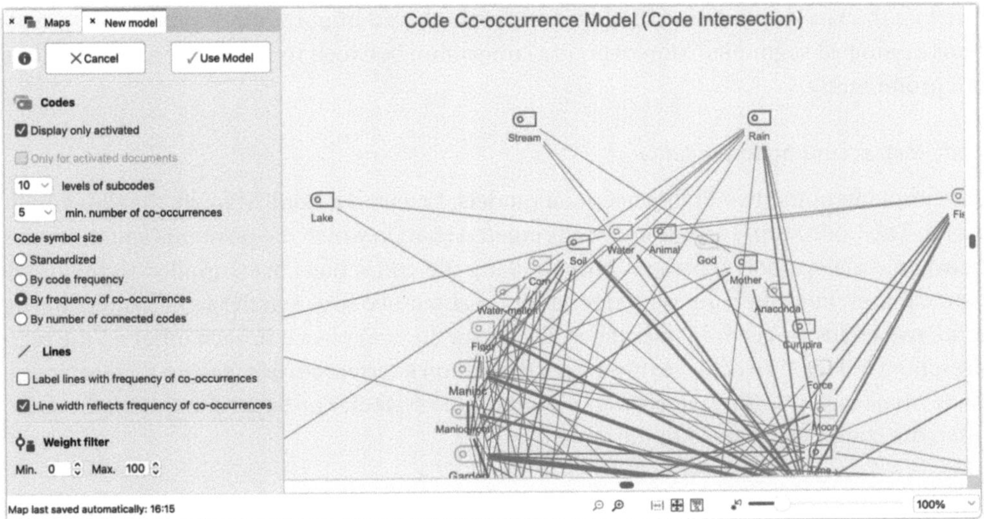

Fig. 5: Settings for creating a Code Co-occurrence Model with MAXMaps

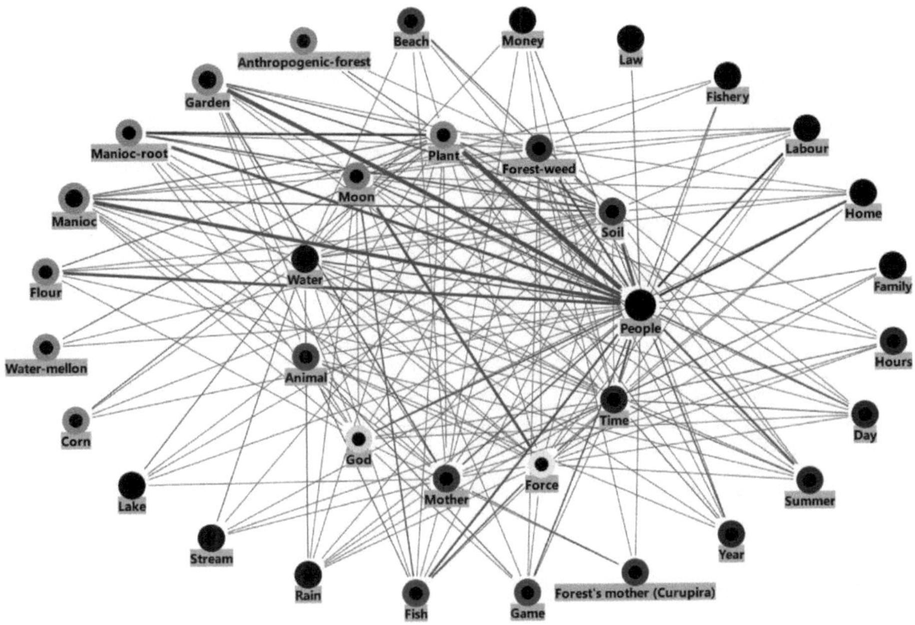

Fig. 6: Code Co-occurrence Model (Code Intersection) showing parent codes in the inner circle and subcodes in the outer. Colors represent subsystems. The red lines represent co-occurrences between codes of the same subsystem, whereas the gray ones indicate inter subsystem connections. The thickness of lines indicates frequencies of co-occurrences.

The line thickness variations clearly visualize the shared importance of people-plant relations among all segments. Moreover, the connection between moon and force also stands out prominently.

Code Map according to similarity

To complement the two first conceptual models, I created a Code Map via the ***Visual Tools*** menu. The Code Map is an automatically created chart in which the positions and distances between code symbols represent how similarly the codes have been applied to the interviews, that is, how often the respondents spoke about two topics in the same sentence. The more two codes co-occur in a sentence, the closer they are placed to each other on the map presented in Fig. 7. To achieve this, I used the option ***Intersections of codes in a segment*** in the Code Maps dialog. Colors were taken from the code system. The larger the circles, the more often the code was assigned to the data.

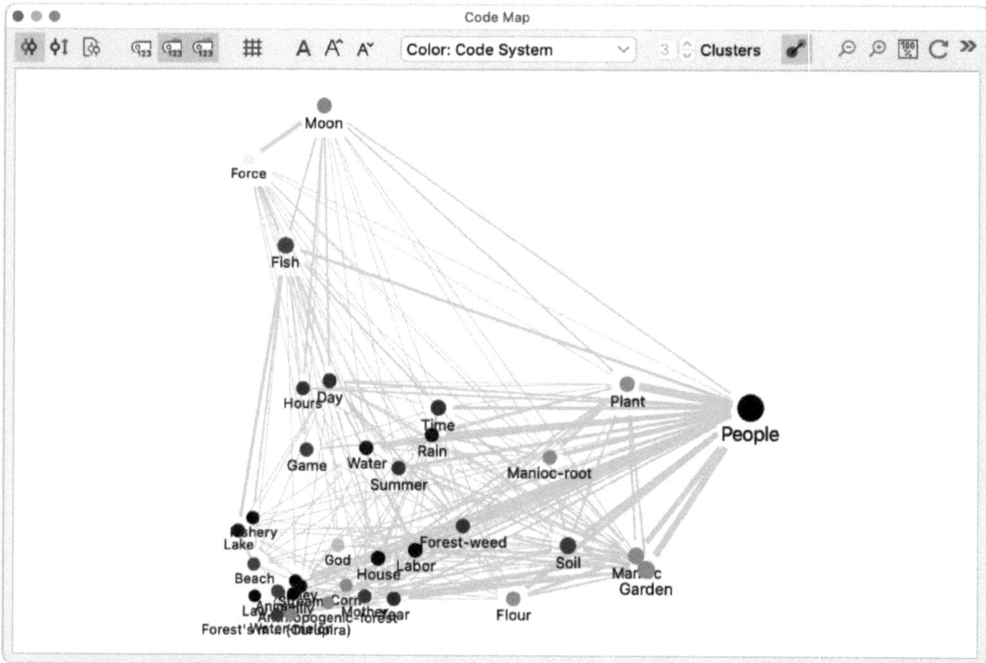

Fig. 7: Code Map indicating intersections of codes in a segment. Colors represent code subsystems.

The image clearly shows two subsystems: one formed by fish, moon, and force (upper left); and other closer to people, constituted by plants and soil system (middle below).

3.5 Lemmatizing keywords to retrieve and code a theme

I next turned my attention to analyze and map instances when individual respondents raised the theme of climate warming, looking for commonalities across multiple cases, taking advantage of MAXQDA's lemmatization tools. In linguistics, a lemma is the dictionary form of a set of words (for example, see), whereas its various forms or variants (for example, seeing, saw) are named lexemes. In content analysis, lemmatization (that is, combining different forms of a word) is very useful to look up ways specific concepts are enunciated. With MAXDictio, one can lemmatize Word Frequencies (or Word Combinations) in various languages, including Portuguese.

While searching for climate warming problems, I used lemmatizing to access and code all variations of words used to express ideas as "warm" (*quente*), "warm up" (*esquentar*), "warmth" (*quentura*) and "heat" (*calor*). In the lemmatized word frequency list, I identified 4 lemmas (plus 5 lexemes) that fulfilled such criteria: *quentar* (*quente*), *esquentar* (*esquentava, esquente, esquenta, esquentou*), *quentura, calor*. A problem with automatized lemmatization for Portuguese is that some of the lemmas presented in the word frequency list are incorrect for Brazilian Portuguese. As an example, the verb "quentar" was derived from the adjective "quente" (meaning "warm"), but the correct form with a prefix is "esquentar," which also has four variations.

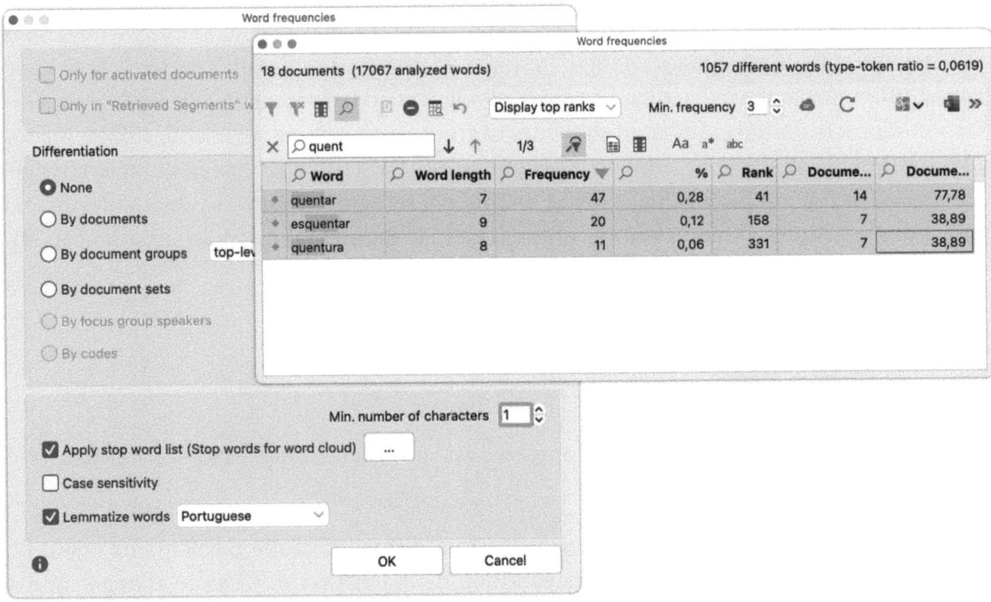

Fig. 8: MAXDictio's Word Frequencies dialog with options to lemmatize words and resulting Word Frequencies list with 3 of the 4 lemmas filtered

There are two easy ways to combine these lemmas presented in the word frequency list:

1. Drag and drop one word into another to merge them in the results table, and then double-click the resulting line to autocode all sentences in which any of the lemma variations appear; or
2. autocode lemmas one-by-one and merge them in the Code System window.

The second option might be better if you are interested in describing all your coding phases in detail. Either way, the resulting code list for "Warm/Heat" is formed by 69 automatically coded sentences. Note in Fig. 9, that once the lemmas were merged, the number of coded segments decreased from 74 to 69 because some lemmas co-occur in some segments.

Code	
Warm/Heat	69
Warm up (esquentar)	17
Warm up (quentar)	44
Warmth (quentura)	11
Heat (calor)	2

Fig. 9: Code System with four coded lemmas under "Warm/Heat"

3.6 Reading segments of a code and creating subcodes

I analyzed the content of the 69 segments coded with "Warm/Heat" to identify which ones address the subject of climate change. In the code system, I manually created a new code called "Climate change" to which I applied all relevant coded segments. By reading and interpreting each sentence, I created subcodes to group interview passages with similar meanings. Using this strategy, I compiled 20 segments that discuss the topic of climate change. According to Fig. 10, the passages could be broadly categorized into two main groups: (1) indicating a warmer climate, with 17 entries; and (2) suggesting periodic variations in climate, with 3 entries.

Code	
Climate change	20
Climate is warmer	17
Climate varies periodically	3

Fig. 10: Code System with the code "Climate change" and two subcodes that express the gist of interviewees propositions

Using the ***Visual Tools > Code Matrix Browser***, I found that all of the participants could be placed into one these two groups. I transformed the parent code "Climate change" into a categorical document variable by righting-clicking on the code and selecting ***Transform into Categorical Document Variable***. This created a new document variable named "Climate change" which values represented the subcode ("Climate is warmer" or "Climate varies periodically") per interview, as demonstrated in Fig. 11. Please note that in one interview there were no relevant climate change passages that could be coded. As a result, the document variable value for this document is blank.

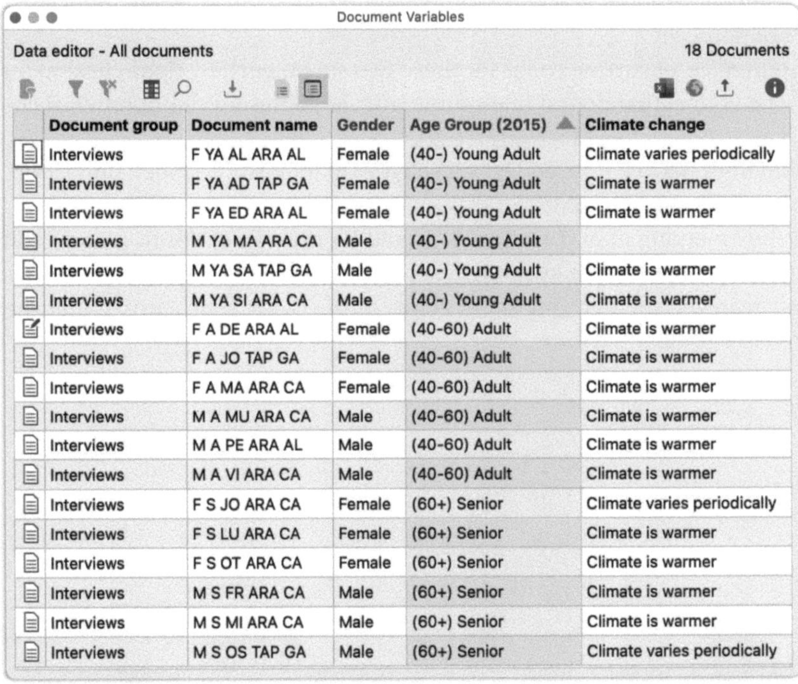

Document group	Document name	Gender	Age Group (2015)	Climate change
Interviews	F YA AL ARA AL	Female	(40-) Young Adult	Climate varies periodically
Interviews	F YA AD TAP GA	Female	(40-) Young Adult	Climate is warmer
Interviews	F YA ED ARA AL	Female	(40-) Young Adult	Climate is warmer
Interviews	M YA MA ARA CA	Male	(40-) Young Adult	
Interviews	M YA SA TAP GA	Male	(40-) Young Adult	Climate is warmer
Interviews	M YA SI ARA CA	Male	(40-) Young Adult	Climate is warmer
Interviews	F A DE ARA AL	Female	(40-60) Adult	Climate is warmer
Interviews	F A JO TAP GA	Female	(40-60) Adult	Climate is warmer
Interviews	F A MA ARA CA	Female	(40-60) Adult	Climate is warmer
Interviews	M A MU ARA CA	Male	(40-60) Adult	Climate is warmer
Interviews	M A PE ARA AL	Male	(40-60) Adult	Climate is warmer
Interviews	M A VI ARA CA	Male	(40-60) Adult	Climate is warmer
Interviews	F S JO ARA CA	Female	(60+) Senior	Climate varies periodically
Interviews	F S LU ARA CA	Female	(60+) Senior	Climate is warmer
Interviews	F S OT ARA CA	Female	(60+) Senior	Climate is warmer
Interviews	M S FR ARA CA	Male	(60+) Senior	Climate is warmer
Interviews	M S MI ARA CA	Male	(60+) Senior	Climate is warmer
Interviews	M S OS TAP GA	Male	(60+) Senior	Climate varies periodically

Fig. 11: Data Editor for Document Variables showing a categorical document variable for climate change views transformed from a parent code

3.7 Visualizing co-occurrences of codes in MAXMaps

Mapping code co-occurrences within the content of the 20 sentences coded with "Climate change" is a good way to start investigating underlying contrasts and causal relations. To do this, I turned back to the set of 35 frequent words previously selected, to unpack specific domains and elaborate relationships between them. To capture the distinct aspects of participants' propositions on climate change, I found it necessary to include four additional frequently mentioned words that were prominent within this set of coded sentences: sun, climate, warm, and deforestation.

Finally, I went to ***Visual Tools > MAXMaps*** to visualize the co-occurrence of codes. While the Code Co-occurrence Model can provide similar results, I chose to manually carry out each operation, one at a time. To accomplish this, I used the following process:

1. First, I dragged the code "Climate Change" into the blank image.
2. By right-clicking on it, I imported the two contrasting subcodes "Climate is warmer" and "Climate varies periodically."
3. After that, I imported co-occurring codes for these two statements, by right-clicking on each of them. The connecting dotted lines automatically represent the number of co-occurrences.
4. I also added solid lines between the codes of a subsystem to illustrate their connection, using the code colors as the line colors.
5. While revising the emerging map, I realized it would be more effective to remove the main code "Climate change," while keeping the contrasting subcodes only.
6. Finally, I freely organized the distribution of codes in the blank space, arriving at the model presented in Fig. 12.

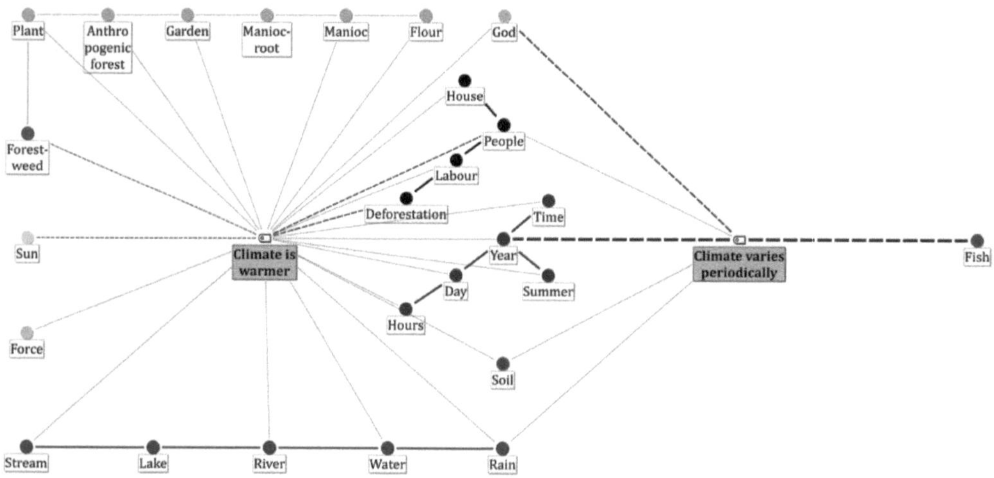

Fig. 12: Conceptual map showing codes and co-occurrences in climate change propositions

For example, the model shows that "Fish" is only mentioned in the sentences of interviewees from the 'Climate varies periodically' group, whereas all other codes co-occurring with this proposition ("God," "People," "Year," "Soil," and "Rain") are mentioned by both groups.

4 Lessons learned

From a word frequency analysis in 18 semi-structured interviews, provided by representatives of indigenous villages in Amazonia, I generated a set of 35 codes (grouped into 11 parent codes). In the subsequent analysis I learned these lessons:

- *Usefulness of Visual Tools.* MAXMaps and Code Map provided an easy way to build innovative conceptual maps out of a code system that represents constituents of the world interviewees talked about. I was also able to group, analyze, quantify, and visualize all sentences that addressed the issue of climate change very easily.
- *MAXQDA offers different ways to perform an analytical task.* Some procedures I adopted can be accomplished using advanced options or different tools of MAXQDA. For example, to compare the most frequent words overall and by subgroupings, in ***MAXDictio > Word Frequency*** there is an option to differentiate the results by document sets. Furthermore, there are new options implemented in MAXQDA that would have been interesting to use: the co-occurrences of codes presented in the ***Code Relations Browser*** can be exported as an adjacency matrix for easy import into specialized software for network analysis, such as Pajek (De Nooy et al. 2018). This export option provides the perfect means to construct innovative social and semantic networks through text analysis.

Bibliography

Atran, S., & Medin, D. L. (2008). *The native mind and the cultural construction of nature.* MIT Press. https://doi.org/10.7551/mitpress/7683.001.0001

Bennardo, G. (Ed.). (2019). *Cultural models of nature: Primary food producers and climate change.* Routledge. https://doi.org/10.4324/9781351127905

De Lima, L. M. (2019). "Plants are cooking under the soil": Food production, models of nature, and climate-change perceptions among indigenous peasant communities (Amazonia, Brazil). In G. Bennardo (Ed.), *Cultural models of nature: Primary food producers and climate change.* (pp. 66–94). Routledge. https://doi.org/10.4324/9781351127905

De Lima, L. M. (2019, February 25). Analyzing and mapping word frequencies in interviews using MAXQDA 2018. *MAXQDA Research Blog.* https://www.maxqda.com/blogpost/mapping-word-frequencies/

De Lima, L. M. (2019, June 11). Mapping climate change perceptions with MAXQDA 2018. *MAXQDA Research Blog.* https://www.maxqda.com/blogpost/climate-change-content-analysis

De Nooy, W., Mrvar, A., & Batagelj, V. (2018). *Exploratory social network analysis with PAJEK: Revised and expanded edition for updated software.* Cambridge University Press.

Kuckartz, U. (2014). Qualitative text analysis: A guide to methods, practice and using software. Sage.

About the author

Leandro Mahalem de Lima has a Ph.D. in Social Anthropology from the University of Sao Paulo, Brazil. He is a MAXQDA Professional Trainer since 2019. From 2015 on, he has used MAXQDA in a wide variety of research and teaching contexts.

Using MAXQDA for Dictionary-Based Content Analysis: An Example Exploring the Business Strategy of Netflix Over Time

Richard L. Vail & Michael C. Gizzi

Abstract

This chapter demonstrates how we used MAXQDA's dictionary-based content analysis features to aid in the initial coding of 40 quarterly letters to shareholders and transcripts from earnings call interviews to longitudinally examine the business strategy of Netflix. We developed a method to build a dictionary with search terms identified through searches using Word Frequencies, Word Explorer, and Word Matrix Browser. We tested the dictionary with the Category Matrix Browser, Dictionary-based Content Analysis, and the Word Matrix Brower. We then used Autocode with Dictionary to conduct an initial cycle of coding of themes. A second cycle of coding was completed using the Smart Coding Tool, resulting in a fully coded project that could be analyzed over time. We then used the Summary Grid to create Summary Tables.

Key MAXQDA features covered

- ✓ Word Frequencies
- ✓ Word Explorer
- ✓ Word Matrix Browser
- ✓ Category Matrix Browser
- ✓ Dictionary-based Content Analysis
- ✓ Autocode with Dictionary
- ✓ Smart Coding Tool
- ✓ Code Matrix Browser
- ✓ Interactive Quote Matix
- ✓ Summary Grid
- ✓ Summary Tables

1 Introduction

The research described here evolved from an earlier study that began with an exploratory question of whether MAXQDA could be used to examine changes in business strategy over time for a major corporation using publicly available documents from the corporate investor website. We were interested in examining the evolution of the entertainment company Netflix, using publicly available quarterly shareholder letter and earnings call transcripts. The goal in this chapter is to show how we used MAXDictio and other MAXQDA tools to explore and analyze our dataset with greater detail and thoroughness.

Vail, Richard L. & Gizzi, Michael C. (2024). Using MAXQDA for dictionary-based content analysis: An example exploring the business strategy of Netflix over time. In: S. Rädiker & Michael C. Gizzi (Eds.), The practice of qualitative data analysis. Research examples using MAXQDA, volume 2 (pp. 49–70). Berlin: MAXQDA Press.
https://doi.org/10.36192/978-3-948768188_3

Each quarter, Netflix publishes an open letter to shareholders and investors to explain the company's recent past, describe current activities, and present expectations of future results. The information comes from a specific, but consistent perspective. The letters provide a qualitative narrative, but also include tables of quantitative data on company finances. They provide the basis for both a statistical and qualitative content analysis. The same day the shareholder letter is released, an "earnings call" takes place, in a panel discussion between an investor representative who interviews senior executives to discuss the letter.

Business strategy is the practice of pursuing corporate goals through various activities and how those activities change over time. For example, in April 2018 Netflix expressed the desire to grow their subscriber base "across the world by providing amazing stories"—the content available on the Netflix streaming service. The activities need to obtain content can be termed their content strategy. Over time, Netflix's content strategy has evolved due to a variety of external events and technological changes. When we began the study, in 2018, there were two major types of content, programming licensed from intellectual property (IP) owners and a growing number of original content items produced by Netflix itself and various production partners. By 2021, the balance between these two approaches to content had changed, with a significant shift towards original content production, and building the infrastructure to support it. In addition, Netflix was in the process of introducing a new type of original content: mobile games. Finding and understanding the details of how and why these changes occur calls for longitudinal research. The time period explored—2018 through 2022—included significant growth, the entrance of new major competitors in the streaming industry, and disruption from the global pandemic.

Ultimately, our research project sought to examine how not only Netflix's strategy for content evolved, but also several other key areas of business strategy, including partnerships, competition, new subscriber forecasting, global activities, and eventually the impact of the pandemic.

2 Data collection and methodological approach

The Netflix case study provided us with the perfect dataset for a longitudinal research project examining changes in business strategy. A longitudinal approach involves collecting information about the same subject over an extended period. Longitudinal data can be analyzed using quantitative and qualitative methods. The same information is collected over specified time periods, providing a tempo to the research. Qualitative longitudinal research usually entails narrative approaches to detect changes over time and explore the processes associated with those changes (Baur, 2008; Vogl, 2023).

The quarterly letters follow a standard format. The earnings call participants are very stable. The senior executives have been largely the same, and the investor representatives usually change annually. In answering questions, executives explain their current view of past actions and events, their current activities, and their expectations. From quarter to quarter these views can change. Observing this reflexivity is one of the advantages of this form of research. Of course, these views are framed through the lens of the environment of current events, such as actions of competitors, the start of the COVID-19 pandemic, or the Russian invasion of Ukraine, all of which have had significant impacts on Netflix over time.

Our initial work began in the summer of 2019, at a time when there were a lot of changes going on at Netflix, due to increased competition, and rapid expansion of original programming. The coronavirus pandemic that began in March 2020 created new dynamics, including both disruptions to the production and availability of original and licensed programming, as well as the beginning of a never-before seen growth, with more than 40 million new subscribers. As the pandemic progressed it became clear that Netflix was a perfect candidate for longitudinal study of strategic choices.

We decided to frame the study around the impact of the pandemic on the company's growth and development. With that in mind, we included 2 years of data prior to the pandemic (2018–2019), and the three years (2020–2022) in which COVID was a global health emergency. It was also very clear to us that the data we had to use was voluminous, with more than 420 pages of printed pages in a total of 40 letters and transcripts over 5 years. Together these documents included more than 4,000 paragraphs of text and approximately 200,000 words.

A typical qualitative content analysis (Kuckartz and Rädiker, 2023) or thematic analysis (Boyatzis, 1998; Guest et al., 2013) would have been challenging, but we saw it as an opportunity to take advantage of MAXQDA's extensive word-based analysis tools to combine it with a quantitative content analysis (Krippendorff, 2018). This approach let us do the first processing of the documents with a dictionary-based analysis identifying the major themes or topics we wanted to examine, and then shift to a qualitative content analysis for the second cycle of coding, refining the codes with relevant subcodes.

3 Building the MAXQDA project

To conduct the study, we converted the letters and transcripts in Adobe PDF format from the corporate investor website into Microsoft Word format for easier use in MAXQDA. We stripped the letters of headings and footers, and eliminated several pages of accompanying charts and tables that we did not need for our work, while some of the standardized financial data was added as document variables for later mixed methods work. While we could have used the PDF files in MAXQDA, simplified Word documents contained all necessary information and allowed better recognition of paragraphs in searches and autocoding (in PDFs, paragraphs always end on a page for MAXQDA).

The MAXQDA project was structured with our intended analytical approach in mind. We imported the letters and transcripts into five document groups for each year (Fig. 1). The documents were named for the year and quarter. We then created four document sets for each year and added the letters and transcripts into the sets. It was important to list them chronologically, from the first through the fourth quarter. Together, this doubled structure provided a powerful basis for analysis when we differentiated by document group or set.

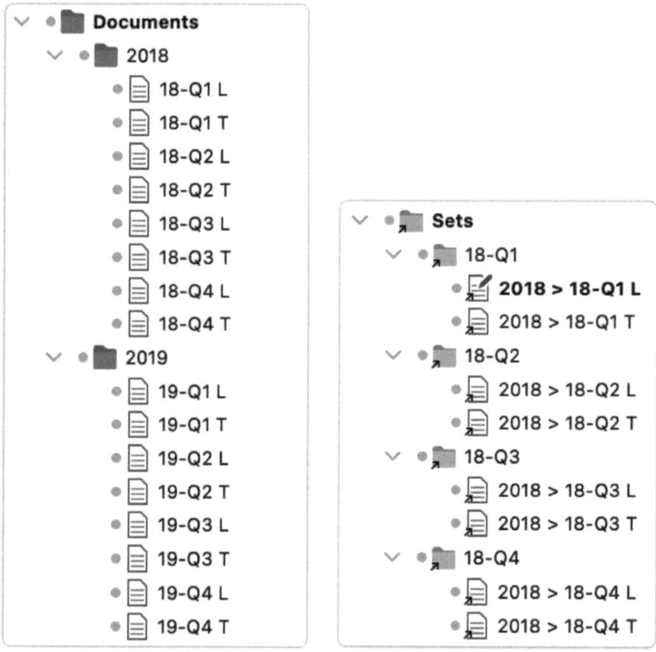

Fig. 1: An excerpt of the document groups and sets in the project

The document names distinguished letters from transcripts, but we also added a document variable labeled "type" to easily limit the analysis to just letters or transcripts using ***Mixed Methods > Activate Documents by Variables***.

4 Coding the data using a dictionary-based approach

To examine changes in strategy and behavior over time, we designed a coding approach that identified key themes occurring in the data. We did not need to start from scratch in identifying themes in the quarterly reports, as we had both a strong familiarity with the data, and a foundation in core concepts in business strategy.[1] We identified six areas that we wanted to look at, which became the primary categories we used for our initial coding of the documents.

To conduct a dictionary-based content analysis for the initial coding, we created a dictionary with categories and relevant search terms to identify text to autocode, following a five-step process:

1. Based on our pre-knowledge of the documents, test out possible search terms using Word Frequencies, Word Explorer, and Word Matrix Browser.
2. Build a dictionary in MAXDictio including search terms for each category.
3. Test the dictionary using the Category Matrix Browser, Word Matrix Browser, and Dictionary-Based Content Analysis tools.
4. Autocode the documents with the dictionary.
5. Review the results by looking at the documents and adjusting borders of the resulting coded segments to include additional paragraphs of text as necessary or merging multiple consecutive coded segments.

From here, we reviewed the coded data, and then conducted a qualitative content analysis to interpret the autocoded text, adding subcodes in a second cycle of coding, while annotating them with code comments.

4.1 Testing possible search terms using Word Explorer and Word Matrix Browser

Developing a dictionary was the first step in coding. ***MAXDictio > Dictionary*** lets the user create categories and related search terms to identify relevant text. We began with the six categories we wanted to explore: (1) partnerships, (2) original content, (3) competition, (4) global activities, (5) subscriber forecasting; and (6) impact of the pandemic.

We took each category and began testing out possible search terms. Our goal was to identify words and phrases that we thought would capture the essence of each category. This was an exploratory part of the process, in that we needed to find terms that would identify relevant passages, but not be so broad as to capture too many irrelevant passages.

We had the advantage of being familiar with this data and had a strong foundation in the types of topics we wanted to focus on. We were able to brainstorm some of the search ideas, but to assist in identifying more possible search terms we initially used ***MAXDictio > Word Frequencies*** to scan, search, and filter words we would potentially include in searches. We differentiated the results by document groups (year) and used the ***Apply Stop Word List*** option to eliminate common English words (Fig. 2).

1 One of the authors (Vail) has taught business strategy using Netflix as a case study for several years.

When we found a word that we thought was possibly relevant, we double-clicked on it to examine the search results and from there, and decided if the word was worth further examination with other tools. As an alternative, we could have also dragged those words directly into a MAXDictio Dictionary as a search term.

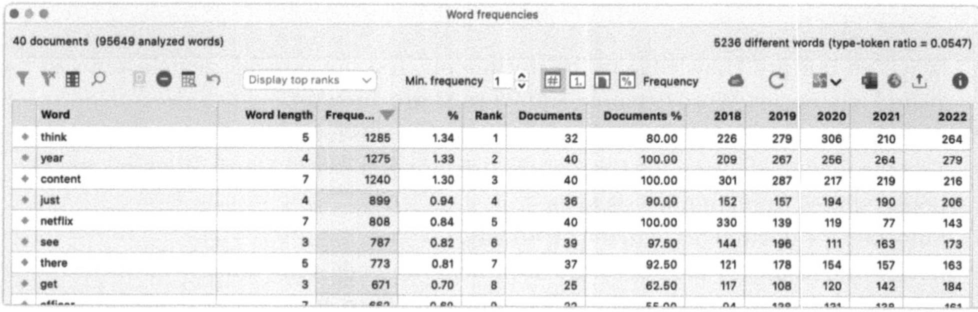

Word	Word length	Freque...	%	Rank	Documents	Documents %	2018	2019	2020	2021	2022
think	5	1285	1.34	1	32	80.00	226	279	306	210	264
year	4	1275	1.33	2	40	100.00	209	267	256	264	279
content	7	1240	1.30	3	40	100.00	301	287	217	219	216
just	4	899	0.94	4	36	90.00	152	157	194	190	206
netflix	7	808	0.84	5	40	100.00	330	139	119	77	143
see	3	787	0.82	6	39	97.50	144	196	111	163	173
there	5	773	0.81	7	37	92.50	121	178	154	157	163
get	3	671	0.70	8	25	62.50	117	108	120	142	184

Fig. 2: Word Frequency was used to initially scan the dataset for possible search terms

When we identified a search term that seemed promising, we used ***Analysis > Word Explorer*** to get a more complete picture of the word or phrase. We chose to use Word Explorer instead of ***Analysis > Text Search & Autocode*** because Word Explorer provides the ability to see word combinations, context words, and frequency of the search term in documents. It permitted us to select words or phrases and specify case sensitivity and starting letters. The lemmatization option reduced the search to its base form (the lemma) and included any variations of the word. For our purposes, we primarily used it to see how many times the search terms appeared, and then clicked on the number of hits in documents to view search results.

As an example, for the category "Original Content," we were interested in the original films and television series Netflix produces and develops, along with the more recent development of mobile games. Original content contrasts with films and series that Netflix licenses from other production companies ("licensed" content). We began the testing of search terms with the word "content," which we searched in Word Explorer with the option ***Find Whole Words*** (Fig. 3).

The Word Explorer search generated 1,239 hits in all 40 documents. The "Most frequent word combinations" section showed 297 hits for 'chief content officer' (which is the title of one of the senior Netflix executives taking part in each earnings call). We also clicked on the "1239 hits" under "In documents," to view the search results, as demonstrated in Fig. 4. This further convinced us that there were a lot of false positive results. We needed more focused search terms.

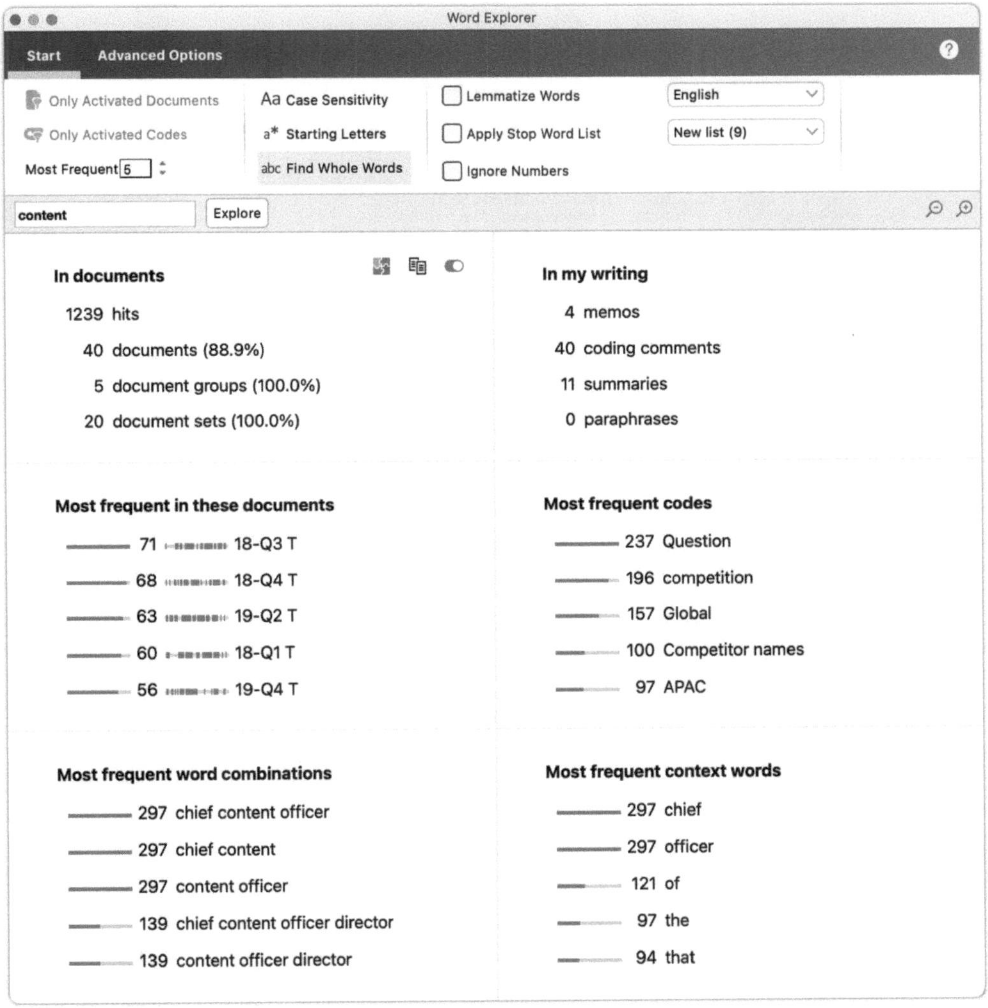

Fig. 3: A Word Explorer search for the word "content" using option to find whole words

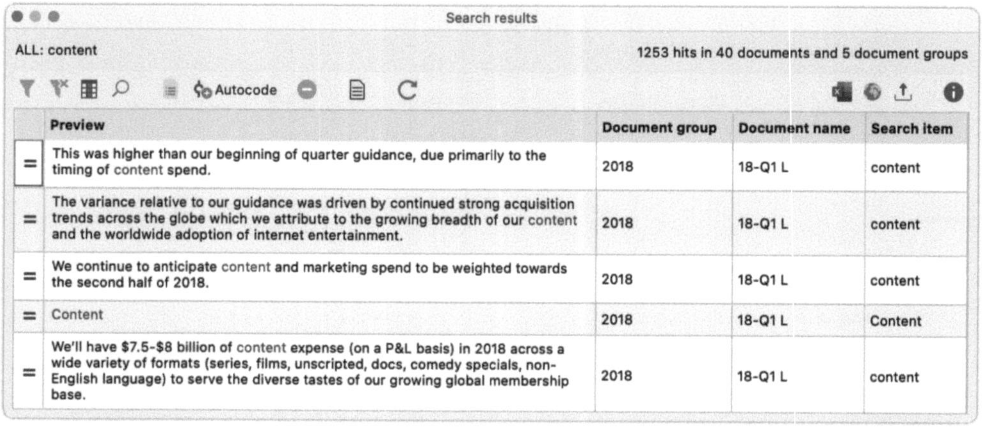

Preview	Document group	Document name	Search item
This was higher than our beginning of quarter guidance, due primarily to the timing of content spend.	2018	18-Q1 L	content
The variance relative to our guidance was driven by continued strong acquisition trends across the globe which we attribute to the growing breadth of our content and the worldwide adoption of internet entertainment.	2018	18-Q1 L	content
We continue to anticipate content and marketing spend to be weighted towards the second half of 2018.	2018	18-Q1 L	content
Content	2018	18-Q1 L	Content
We'll have $7.5-$8 billion of content expense (on a P&L basis) in 2018 across a wide variety of formats (series, films, unscripted, docs, comedy specials, non-English language) to serve the diverse tastes of our growing global membership base.	2018	18-Q1 L	content

Fig. 4: Search results from Word Explorer, accessed by clicking on the Word Explorer results

It was clear that by itself "content" was too broad, so we repeated the search, but this time looked for "original content." This produced a much smaller set of results (42 hits in 24 documents), and a brief review of the hits demonstrated they were all on point, and we added the term "original content" to a free memo for further evaluation in creating a dictionary.

We repeated this process with several possible word choices, building a set of terms to include in a dictionary, while minimizing possible "false positive" results. To provide one more example, one of the types of original content that Netflix has focused on is the development of mobile games, initially intended as a marketing hook for existing series like Stranger Things, and more recently to develop Netflix's own mobile gaming platform. A Word Explorer search showed that the use of the word "game" or "games" would result in numerous references to several Netflix productions, such as Squid Games and Sacred Games. So, we switched to the terms "gaming" and "mobile games" and were much happier with the results, with considerably fewer false positives.

Ultimately, identifying relevant search terms is a process of trial and error, but Word Explorer provided a good platform for identifying and evaluating relevant search terms. We continued our testing by shifting to the ***MAXDictio > Word Matrix Browser***, which enabled us to take the terms we identified and look at the search results over time, in a browser window similar to the Code Matrix Browser (Fig. 5). We used the search terms items, and then chose the option to set the columns to document groups, which grouped the search results by years. Since some of our categories were time dependent (such as the impacts of the pandemic and lockdowns on production and related subscriber growth), a matrix of word and phrase usage over time was valuable.

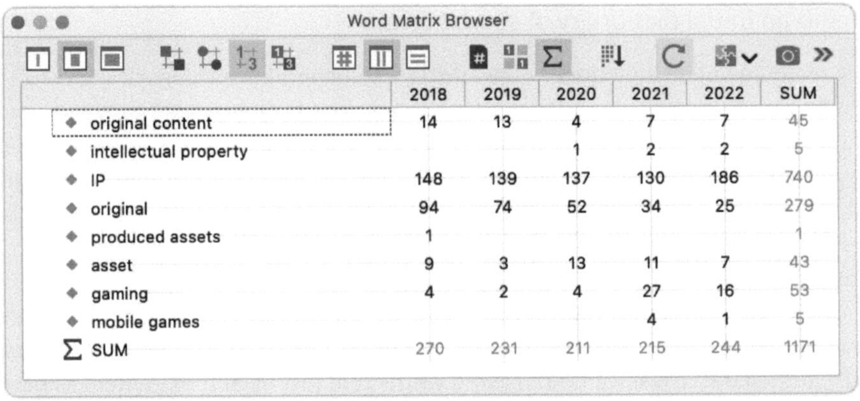

Fig. 5: Word Matrix Browser created a matrix of words and phrases identified in the project documents differentiated by year

Once again, we wanted to review the search results, but we were also interested to see how the word usage differed over time. We could double-click on any cell and then view the search results (Fig. 6). For example, in 2021 there were 27 hits for "gaming," and the search results showed us the segments of text identified.

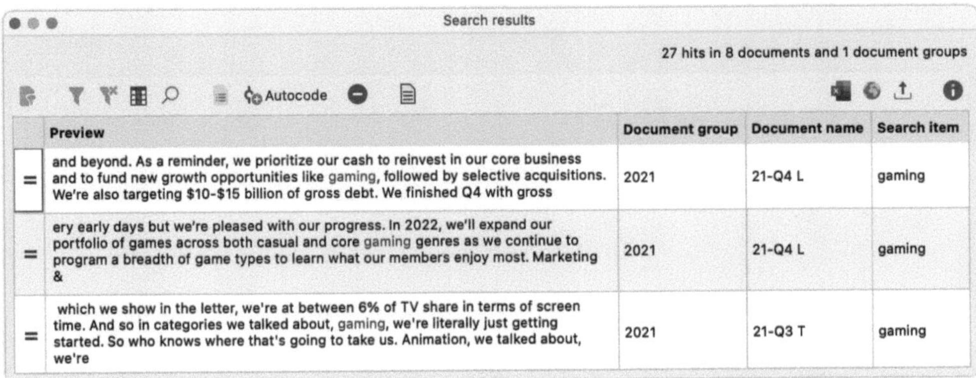

Fig. 6: The first three of 27 search results from Word Matrix Browser for gaming in 2021

4.2 Developing an initial dictionary of search terms

We were now ready to create a dictionary. ***MAXDictio > Dictionary*** uses categories and subcategories as the topics that are defined by search items. The Dictionary window lets you create separate dictionaries for different themes. Fig. 7 shows the dictionary we created for one category, "original content." We created three categories: "original content," "mobile games," and "licensed content." For each category, we then added search items, which would trigger a search hit for the relevant category. It is also important to include both abbreviations used by the panel and the full words, which are also used both in the letters and transcripts, such as "IP" and "intellectual property." For each term we specified whole word, case sensitivity, or use starting letters for our search. For example, we used the ***Whole Word*** option for "IP" and "slate" as we wanted to avoid words that just used those letters as part of irrelevant words, such as "tran*slate*" or "membersh*ip*."

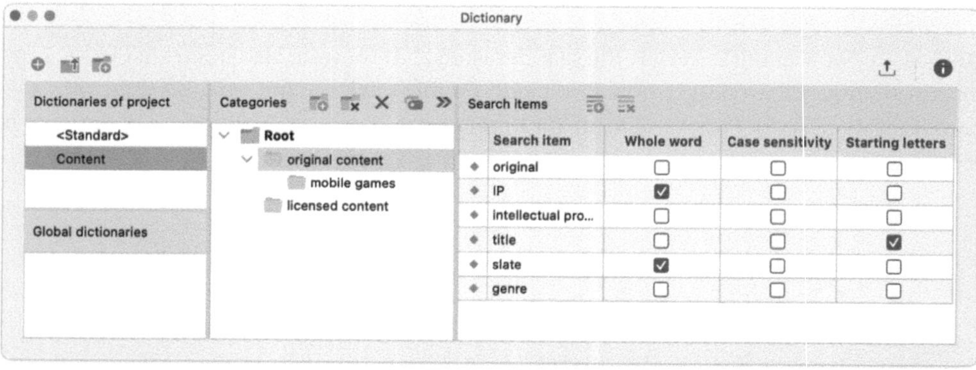

Fig. 7: The dictionary "Content" included three categories, "original content," "licensed content," and "mobile games"

4.3 Testing the Dictionary

Once the search terms were created, we used three tools to test the dictionary: Word Matrix Browser, Category Matrix Browser, and Dictionary-based Content Analysis. The first focused on the search items we created in the dictionary, while the last two displayed results for the categories. All three tools let us differentiate the results displayed by document, document group, or set. We usually used document group, collapsing the eight letters and transcripts together in one year's column, or document set, looking at each quarter of the year separately.

We used ***MAXDictio > Word Matrix Browser*** to view the individual search terms for each category with the option ***Search items of dictionary***. The tool defaults to the most recent dictionary used in the project, so it was important to open the dictionary and click on the "Original Content" dictionary before opening Word Matrix Browser (Fig. 8). Like with our usage of Word Matrix Browser described above when identifying search terms, the results in the matrix are interactive, and could be clicked on to display the search results, like we saw in Fig. 5.

Ultimately, Word Matrix Browser provided a check on the choices we made, by helping us see the detail of our search terms. With each iteration, we became more familiar with the information expressed in the paragraphs reviewed. While this might seem repetitive, we wanted to examine the results to make sure that the search terms we used to create categories were relevant and had minimal false positives before we began autocoding.

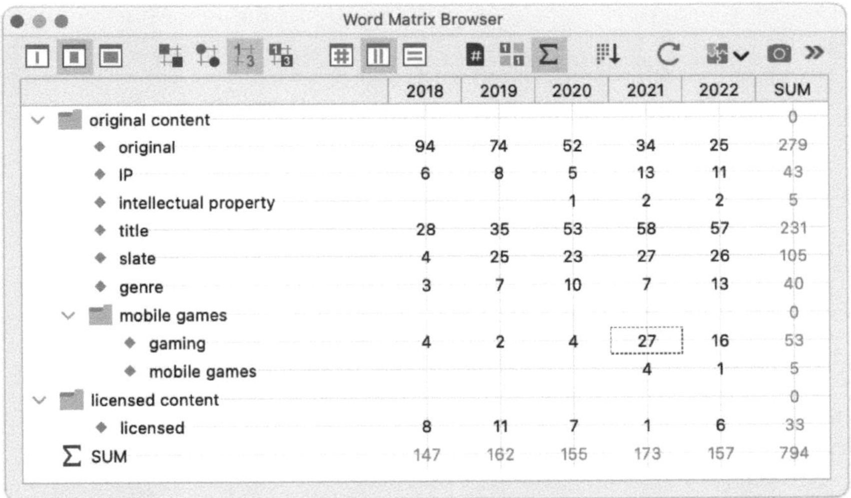

Word Matrix Browser

	2018	2019	2020	2021	2022	SUM
original content						0
original	94	74	52	34	25	279
IP	6	8	5	13	11	43
intellectual property			1	2	2	5
title	28	35	53	58	57	231
slate	4	25	23	27	26	105
genre	3	7	10	7	13	40
mobile games						0
gaming	4	2	4	27	16	53
mobile games				4	1	5
licensed content						0
licensed	8	11	7	1	6	33
Σ SUM	147	162	155	173	157	794

Fig. 8: Word Matrix Browser displaying the search terms from the dictionary sorted by document groups

Once satisfied with the search terms, we were able to view the aggregate results, focusing on the dictionary categories themselves. Here we had two options, which do similar things, but display the results and options differently. ***MAXDictio > Category Matrix Browser*** generated the search hits for each category in a matrix with the categories as rows, and documents (or document groups or sets) in columns. Its results are interactive, as we could click on any cell to view search hits.

This can be contrasted with ***MAXDictio > Dictionary-based Content Analysis,*** which displays a table of hits, with the documents/groups/sets as rows, and the categories as columns. It allowed us to change the output to show row percentages, to look for patterns in the words used (Fig. 9).

Category Matrix Browser results are interactive, as you can click on any cell to view search hits, but Dictionary-based Content Analysis required us to click on the ***Search results*** icon to view the underlying data.

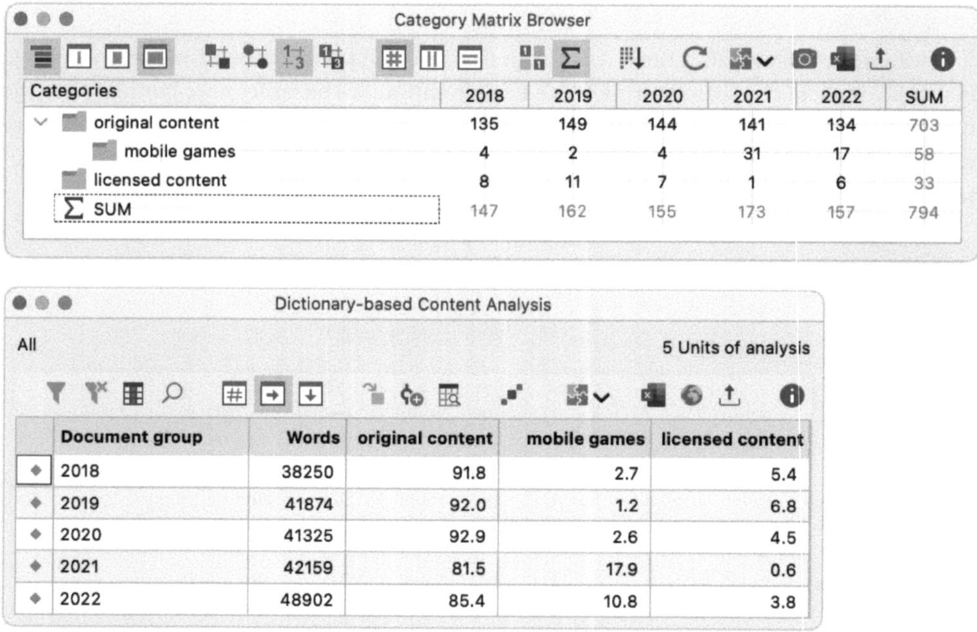

Fig. 9: Category Matrix Browser and Dictionary-based Content Analysis output, showing the hits identified by the dictionary

4.4 Autocoding categories

We were now ready to autocode categories. To do this, we used ***MAXDictio > Autocode with Dictionary*** to code each document for "original content." We began by selecting the proper dictionary and selected ***Ignore inactive categories***, which limited the autocoding to just the categories we had turned on in the dictionary. We then selected the paragraph option to autocode the entire paragraph in which the category appeared. Once we clicked "autocode," the newly coded segments appeared in the Code System under a new top-level code named "MAXDictio" with the two categories and one subcategory from the dictionary (Fig. 10).

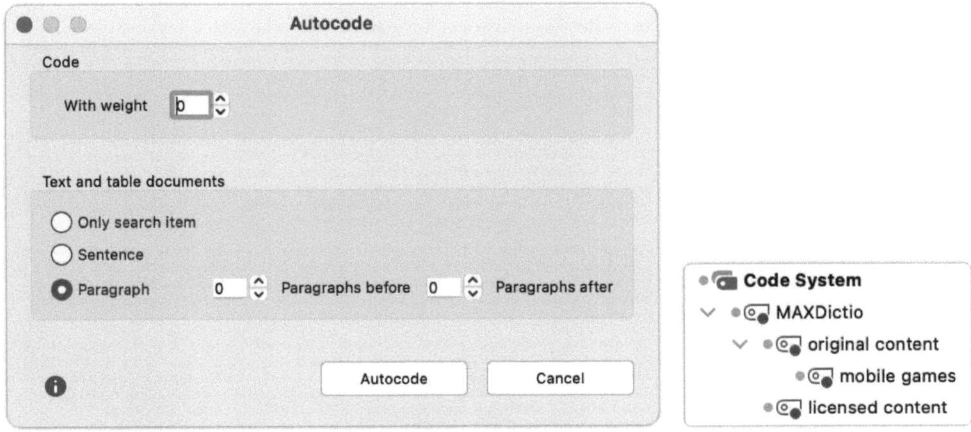

Fig. 10: The code system after using Autocode with Dictionary

4.5 Reviewing the results of the autocode and finalizing the coding system

We were now able to review the results of the auto coding. First, we were particularly interested in identifying if the autocoded segments needed to span additional paragraphs, which was a possibility in the transcripts. Or if there were paragraphs that were part of the same conversation but not autocoded, because the search terms did not identify a hit in a paragraph of the text. In this instance, we would evaluate the uncoded text and decide if it was part of the same discussion and should be coded. This is a matter of interpretation.

In contrast, there were also instances where the same code was applied to consecutive paragraphs, as separate coded segments. Fig. 11 shows an example of four paragraphs from one of the letters which were all separately coded. In this instance, we either highlighted the entire four paragraphs and then applied the same code to include the entire passage as one coded segment, or we choose to leave them alone if the segments were unique enough to merit individual codes.

The last step in the autocoding process was to move the codes we created in MAXDictio and move them out of the MAXDictio parent code, to result in a code structure that had the six categories as top-level codes. We did not do this until we were satisfied with the autocode results, because the Autocode with Dictionary tool can be run additional times, if we needed to add additional terms to the dictionary, and the coded segments would be placed in the same MAXDictio code hierarchy.

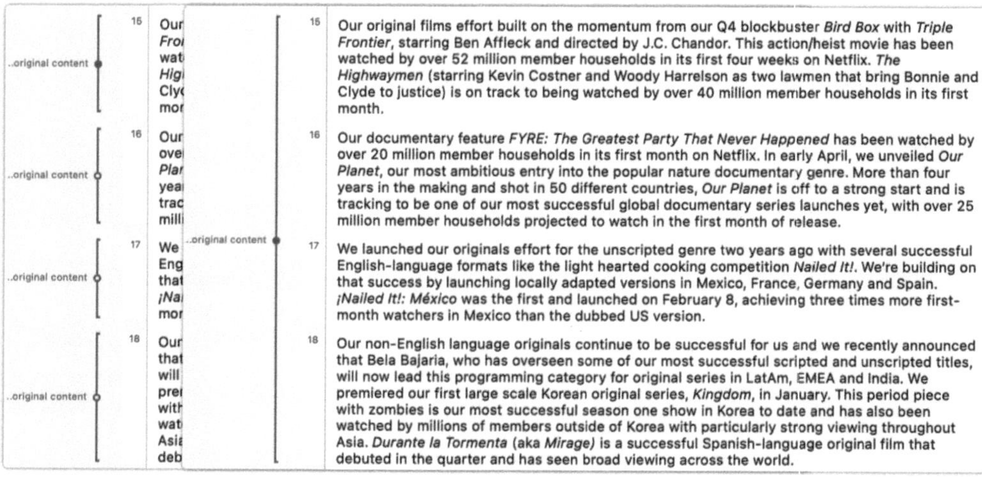

Fig. 11: Before and after. Four consecutive paragraphs coded with for separate codes, and then the same text as one coded segment.

5 Second cycle coding with Smart Coding Tool

Once the first cycle of autocoding with a dictionary was completed, we shifted to a qualitative content analysis for the second cycle of coding. Our goal was to examine each of coded segments for each category, add code comments, and then refine the code system with subcodes. We did most of this in ***Analysis > Smart Coding Tool*** and then reviewed the results when reading each document.

Before starting the process, we activated documents from an individual year, so we could examine the coding within a shorter time period. In Smart Coding Tool, we reviewed the coded segments, and then added comments, to provide a brief summary of the segment. Writing code comments was an important part of both the coding process and ultimately the analysis. A concise comment served to annotate a coded segment, capturing the key essence of why a coded segment was created. Code comments generally follow a coded segment throughout the analysis of coded data. For example, they appear in Retrieved Segments window, Overview of Coded Segments table, and in the Summary Grid when creating a document summary (see section 6 below).

Next, we reviewed the coded segments and began to identify subcodes that refine the category we were looking at. As we reviewed each segment, we could code them with a new subcode, by right-clicking on the highlighted text in Smart Coding Tool and selecting ***Create and Assign New Code.*** Or if a subcode already existed, we dragged the highlighted segment to the code and applied it (Fig. 12).

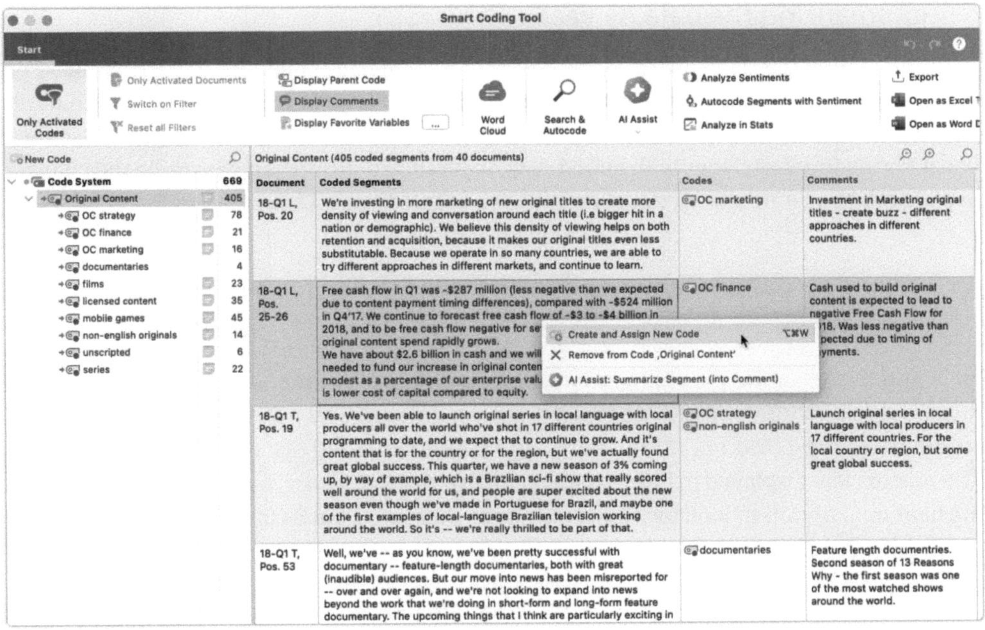

Fig. 12: Adding a new subcode in the Smart Coding Tool while conducting the second cycle of coding

The process of commenting and creating subcodes resulted in building a complete set of subcodes for the category. These codes were both descriptive and analytical. For example, we created three codes, “OC strategy,” “OC finance,” and “OC marketing” which were meant to capture specific examples of original content strategy, financial discussions of original content, and the marketing of original content. Similar codes were created in other categories, like “Partnership strategy” and “Competition strategy.” We had decided that while “strategy,” “marketing,” and “finance” were not going to be top-level categories, they would be included as subcodes in all (or most) of the categories, because the topics were at the heart of the study.

Other subcodes included more descriptive topics like documentaries, films, (television) series, non-English original content, and unscripted content. Finally, the mobile games and licensed content codes created by the dictionary-based analysis were included as subcodes. While it is distinct from original content, licensed content represented a very small part of the discussions in the dataset, and we kept it as a subcode.

6 Summarizing the data by year

With the coding done, we turned our attention to analyzing the data, initially focused on identifying patterns and changes in strategy over time. Some of this was done preliminarily when we were testing search terms for the Dictionary in the Category Matrix Browser and Word Matrix Browser. Now, with coded data, we could go deeper, and examine the changes in coded data over time with visual tools like the Code Matrix Browser.

6.1 Looking for patterns and trends with Code Matrix Browser and Interactive Quote Matrix

We wanted to examine the changes in coded segments over time, so we took advantage of the document groups and sets we created. We used ***Visual Tools > Code Matrix Browser*** to first consider the pre-covid era (2018 and 2019) by differentiating our data by document sets. The macro view displayed in Fig. 13 shows consistency in the discussions of topics. We used the heat map option to look for coded segments that stood out in the data.

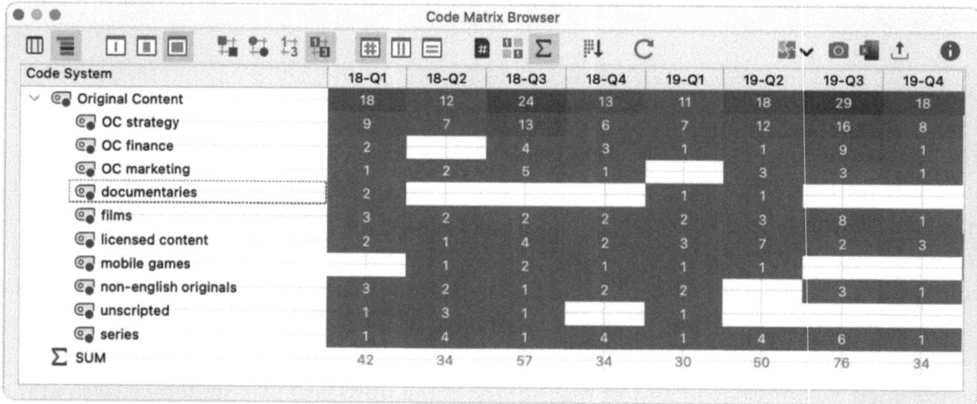

Fig. 13: Code Matrix Browser displaying results differentiated by quarter

To get to the underlying data, we could directly launch the Interactive Quote Matrix (Fig. 14) using the first icon in the Code Matrix Browser menu. This let us see the underlying coded segments, which we could draw on to seek insights. We could copy interesting, coded segments or send them to a QTT worksheet. But to truly make sense of the data and changes over time, we needed to create more detailed summaries, for which we turned to MAXQDA's Summary Grid and Summary Tables.

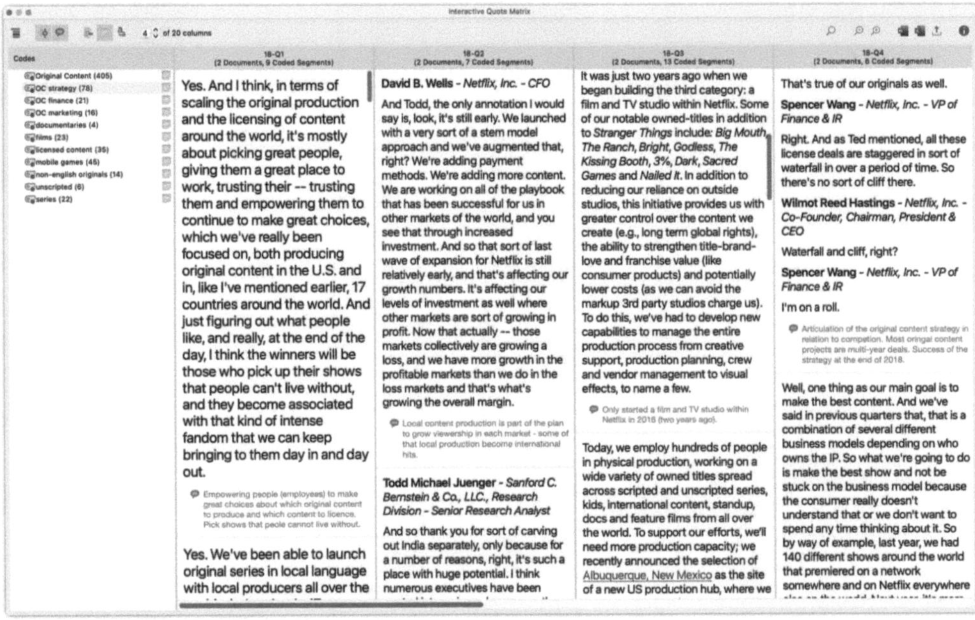

Fig. 14: Interactive Quote Matrix launched from the Code Matrix Browser

6.2 Creating Summary Tables

MAXQDA has two tools to create summaries of coded data. The process begins with ***Analysis > Summary Grid***, a matrix that lets the user read the coded segments for individual documents, and then write a summary of the segments. These summaries then become the basis for creating a Summary Table.

Our dataset included 2 documents for each quarter, 8 for the year, which we wanted to summarize. To do this we needed to create a dummy document representing the entire year. We used ***Import > Create Document > New Text Document*** to add 5 blank documents to the project, named for each year, and stored them in the relevant document group (Fig. 15).

To create the summaries for each year, we used the Summary Grid, looking at one year's data at a time. We activated the document group for the selected year, and then proceeded to review the coded segments for the relevant eight documents. The Summary Grid identifies cells that have coded segments with either blue squares, circles, or a number representing the total coded segments for a topic in the document. Once a summary is written, the background of the cell turns green. We repeated the process until every coded cell was "green" (Fig. 16).

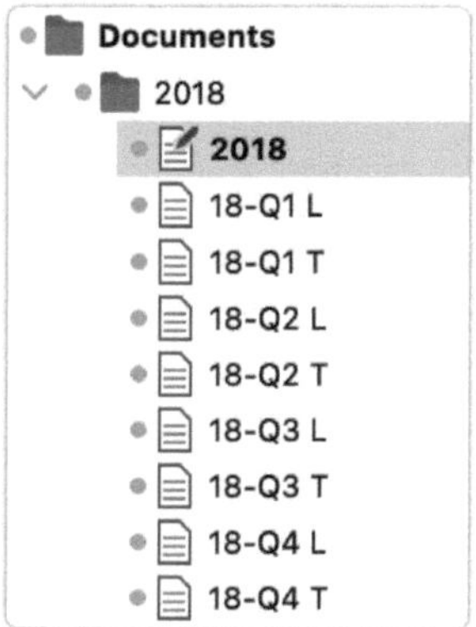

Fig. 15: The document structure with the dummy text document "2018" added to it

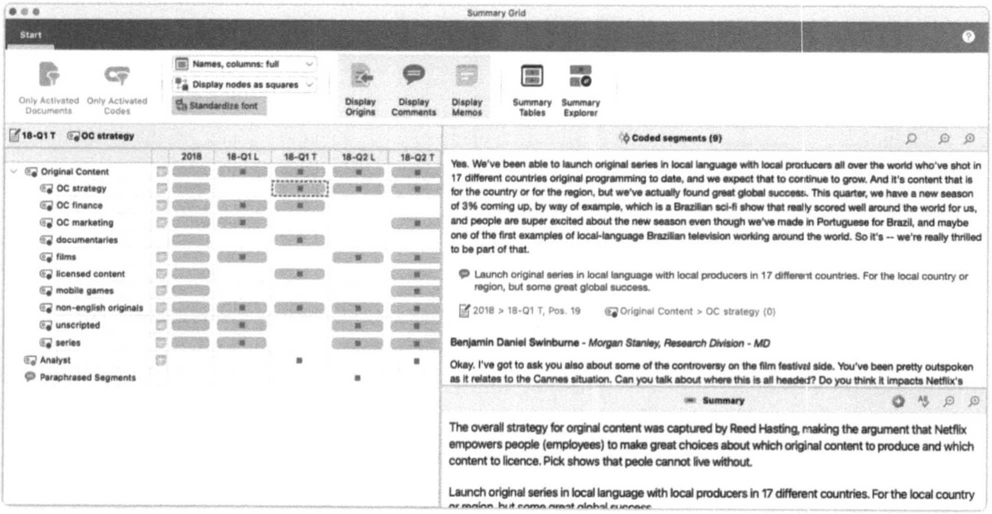

Fig. 16: Summary Grid used to write summaries of coded comments

To write the summaries we drew on the code comments we had written when coding the data, and sometimes, also took advantage of MAXQDA's support of AI Assist to create an automatic summary of the coded segments. To create the annual summary for the code, we copied the summaries we wrote, and pasted them into the empty cell for the dummy document for the year. We then used the copied text as the draft to write a combined annual summary.

After completing the summaries in the Summary Grid, we opened ***Analysis > Summary Table*** to create a tabular document summary. We first activated the dummy documents to narrow the tables to only include the data from the annual summaries. Then, in the Summary Table options, we selected the codes we wanted to include. Once the Summary Table was generated, we adjusted the margins of the cells, and renamed the table. The first summary table we created focused on subcodes, looking at summaries during a year (Fig. 17). This provided an in-depth exploration of different elements of strategy during a single year.

Next, we looked at single code summaries, over each year, focused on the evolution of strategy about mobile gaming across the entire 5-year study period (Fig. 18). The summaries illustrated how Netflix initially thought of mobile games as a competitor for customer entertainment time, and then began dabbling in the using games tied to original content as a marketing hook, but still not a primary focus of the company. In 2021, Netflix had shifted to building its own mobile platform and saw as an opportunity to expand its content as a category specifically for mobile devices. Those efforts continued in 2022 but were rarely discussed since they followed a pattern similar to the introduction of other types of original content.

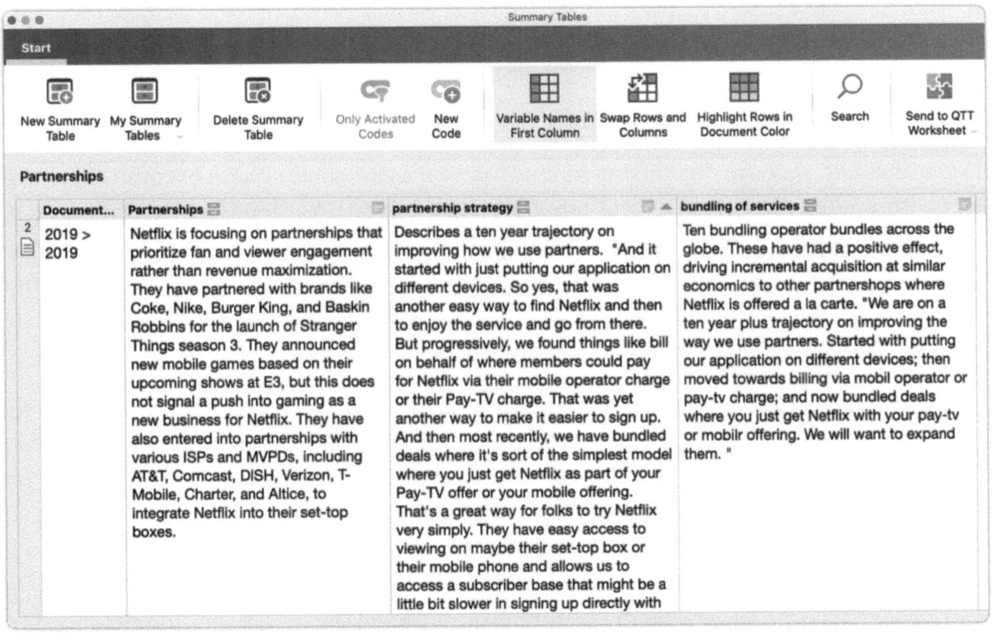

Fig. 17: Excerpt of the Summary Table displaying summaries of several codes in the same year

Mobile games strategy

		2018	2019	2020	2021
1	Documents and variables	2018 > 2018	2019 > 2019	2020 > 2020	2021 > 2021
2	mobile games	Note In 2018 gaming was seen by Netflix as a competitor for entertainment time. One of the "many ways to have great entertainment on a screen" - a significant part of the "about 1 billion hours a day" "total TV entertainment market." However, near the end of the 18-Q2 Earnings Call "gaming" was suggested by the Analyst, in a list of expansion options. The list was quickly dismissed by Hastings - opportunities in movies and TV shows were	In 2019 Netflix still saw gaming as a competitor for entertainment time. However the in the 19-Q1 transcripted they mentioned "a big new original series that we're currently shooting in Hungary called The Witcher. That is enormous European IP, very popular game and book IP that we think is going to make a really fun global series." That the game was an important part of the intellectual property involved will appear in later discussions. In 19-Q2 Letter Netflix noted	In 2020 Netflix sees video gaming still seen as a competitor for entertainment time which range "from linear TV to video gaming to user generated content on YouTube and TikTok." Prompted by a question in the 20-Q2 interview about francise potential of intellectual property in video games Hasting admits the potential and interest, but current "big plans to spend future billions in our movies, in series, in animation." Sarandos adds the idea that a francise can come from "successful	In the 21-Q1 lett were still present competitor for er time. But in the i prompted by a q relatively late in t interview, Hastin that "we're kind now because we Bandersnatch ar some very basic things." Neuman "we've kind of d gaming - interac programing, licei merchandising. "we're in the bus

Fig. 18: A longitudinal Summary Table of a single code across the study period. This table tracks the discussion of mobile gaming as part of Netflix's strategy.

7 Lessons learned

In this chapter, we have demonstrated how we used a two-stage system of coding in a project with a large dataset of several hundred pages of text. We developed a dictionary of search terms that were fully vetted and then used to autocode the first cycle of themes in the documents. We used Smart Coding Tool to review the coded data and refine the themes with several subcodes. In engaging in this process, we have learned several things that we think serve to provide lessons for other researchers.

- Dictionary-based content analysis is not an automatic process. Developing a working dictionary requires effort. We cannot reiterate enough the process of trial and error that is entailed in identifying search terms. It might seem redundant and repetitive, but on every iteration, we learn things about the meaning of the words captured.
- We chose to use a variety of tools to test search terms, instead of just using one of the options. We felt that we learned more about the data and gained greater confidence in our search terms by viewing the search results through the lenses of different tools. The Word Matrix Browser and Category Matrix Browser provided us with a glimpse of the patterns in the data, by showing how the usage of terms changed over time. Dictionary-based Content Analysis provided yet another perspective, comparing the search results using row percentages.

- Dictionary-based autocoding is not essential for all projects, but when dealing with a large amount of information it can save a lot of time, but it still requires a significant investment in time building the dictionary. If the dictionary work is shoddy, the results will not be nearly as useful.
- The second cycle of coding with the Smart Coding Tool can also seem a bit overwhelming, but like a lot of tools, once you become familiar with it, it becomes very useful for refining a coding system and capturing your comments.
- Writing code comments during the second cycle of coding was extremely valuable during out analysis stage and when creating summaries. The comments provided us with a reminder of why we coded something using a particular code and an initial summary of the coded segment itself.
- Organization matters. To examine data longitudinally, it is important to use the structural options of document groups and sets. For us, the document groups provided an opportunity to see the quarterly data over an entire year, and the sets let us look at changes from quarter to quarter. This was also valuable in the coding process, as we were able to examine yearly snapshots of data as opposed to having to consider the entire five-year dataset at once.

Bibliography

Baur, N. (2008). Taking perspectivity seriously: A suggestion of a conceptual framework for linking theory and methods in longitudinal and comparative research. *Historical Social Research, 33*(4), 191-213. https://doi.org/10.12759/hsr.33.2008.4.191-213

Boyatzis, R. E. (1998). *Transforming qualitative information: Thematic analysis and code development.* Sage.

Guest, G; MacQueen, K; & Namey, E. (2013). *Applied thematic analysis.* Sage.

Krippendorff, K. (2018). *Content analysis: An introduction to its methodology* (4th ed.). Sage.

Kuckartz, U., & Rädiker, S. (2023). *Qualitative content analysis: Methods, practice and software* (2nd ed.). Sage.

Vogl, S. (2023). Mixed methods longitudinal research. *Forum: Qualitative Social Research / Qualitative Sozialforschung, 24*(1), 1–26. https://doi.org/10.17169/fqs-24.1.4012

About the authors

Richard L. Vail is an emeritus professor of business at Colorado Mesa University. He holds a DPhil from the University of Oxford.

ORCID: https://orcid.org/0000-0002-6165-6113

ResearchGate: https://www.researchgate.net/profile/Richard-Vail

Michael C. Gizzi is a professor of criminal justice at Illinois State University, USA. He has a PhD in political science from The University at Albany, SUNY. He is a certified MAXQDA trainer.

ORCID: https://orcid.org/0000-0002-9130-7969

ResearchGate: https://www.researchgate.net/profile/Michael-Gizzi

Using MAXQDA's Code Comments for Rapid Analysis: Writing Summaries for Analyzing and Reporting in Evaluation

Stefan Rädiker

Abstract

This chapter demonstrates how MAXQDA was effectively used in an evaluation project to analyze eight one-on-one interviews and to produce a report in just a few days. By systematically writing summaries for coded segments and storing them in code comments, I was able to speed up the entire analysis process, including development of codes, gaining insights, creating visual representations, and drafting the report. The Smart Coding Tool and MAXMaps were used to review the content covered by a code, read and cluster the written segment summaries, and develop subcodes. Furthermore, MAXMaps was used to create visualizations for the report. The techniques explained in this chapter can be applied to any project, not just evaluation, and not just when dealing with tight time frames.

Key MAXQDA features covered

- ✓ Comments on coded segments
- ✓ Smart Coding Tool
- ✓ MAXMaps: Free map
- ✓ MAXMaps: Hierarchical Code-Subcodes Model

1 Introduction

MAXQDA allows the user to write a short comment for each coded segment. These comments can be used for a variety purposes, such as storing meta-information about the coding process ("code x could also apply here"), analytical information ("this represents a key pattern in the data"), or summaries of the coded segments (Kuckartz & Rädiker, 2019; see also Schmieder & Rogers in this book). Since the comments are connected to the coded segments, they can be accessed and displayed in almost every place where the coded segments are available in MAXQDA. In this chapter, I will show how I used the comments feature in an evaluation study for the analysis and for the presentation of results.

Strategic use of comments enabled me to complete the analysis and write a thorough report in a very short amount of time. This was helpful, because evaluation projects often involve many different data sources that need to be analyzed under tight deadlines. Interviews, open-ended survey responses, and other qualitative data need to be analyzed quickly to provide helpful insights, without making compromises to methodological rigor.

Rädiker, Stefan (2024). Using MAXQDA's code comments for rapid analysis: Writing summaries for analyzing and reporting in evaluation. In: S. Rädiker & Michael C. Gizzi (Eds.), The practice of qualitative data analysis. Research examples using MAXQDA, volume 2 (pp. 71–86). Berlin: MAXQDA Press. https://doi.org/10.36192/978-3-948768188_4

The interviews were conducted as part of a large project that evaluated a three-year pilot program on ambulant caregivers in Germany. Usually, the caregivers operate within very strict time constraints and are compensated based on predefined tasks rather than the actual time spent with clients. This leaves limited room for personalized care adjustments or enhancing clients' self-sufficiency. To address these challenges, a private caregiving company introduced an *autonomous* caregiving team. Embracing the motto "more time for clients, less time for administration," this team worked independently from the main organization. Unlike the traditional compensation model, they were paid based on time, allowing them to prioritize clients' needs and to provide holistic care that taps into clients' resources.[1]

The new approach aimed to achieve several benefits: boosting team morale, making the job more appealing and less administrative, reducing absenteeism, extending clients' independence, fostering collaboration, and enhancing their social engagement. Consequently, the evaluation sought answers to pivotal questions, such as:

- How does collaboration function within the autonomous team?
- How are nursing goals put into practice?
- How are decisions reached in this setup?
- What challenges surface?
- What opportunities emerge?

2 Data collection and methodological approach

To address these questions, the evaluator of the project conducted focus groups, client surveys, and interviews at several points in time and as he needed to analyze multiple data sets at once, he requested my assistance. I was asked to analyze four one-on-one interviews that were conducted with caregivers from the autonomous team and four interviews with team members from a classical team working in the same area and having a comparable client structure. The interviews took place after the project had been running for several months and were transcribed manually by an external contractor. While the interviews with the autonomous caregivers lasted 60–100 minutes, the interviews with the traditionally working caregivers lasted only 30–60 minutes.

Because there was limited time to conduct the analysis, I needed to develop shortcut strategies to analyze the transcripts. Following the principles of qualitative content analysis and focused analysis of qualitative interviews (Kuckartz & Rädiker, 2023, Rädiker & Kuckartz, 2020), I conducted the following steps:

1 The project was inspired by the Dutch "Buurtzog" approach (www.buurtzorg.com).

1. Prepare the interview transcripts and set up the MAXQDA project including access to the audio files of the interviews.
2. Set up a coding frame in the Code System window based on the interview guide.
3. Code the first interview and adapt the coding frame to the data (together with an experienced student assistant using screen sharing).
4. Code all interviews and record short summaries of the content of each coded text passage in the code comment (done by the student assistant, using MAXQDA's TeamCloud and addressing arising questions together in two meetings via screen sharing).
5. Review the resulting 500 summaries, refining and expanding them to ensure that they accurately capture the interviewees' contributions. While reviewing the summaries, reorganize the codes[2] in the code system and reword the code names to express more accurately what they capture.
6. Analyze and visualize the summaries for each main topic, usually represented by one or two top-level codes, using various MAXQDA tools, particularly the Smart Coding Tool and MAXMaps to inductively create subcodes and write the findings and results directly into the report.

Although I knew that writing accurate summaries to capture the content of each coded segment would take time at the beginning, I hoped that it would pay off later when I analyzed the coded data and wrote the report. The idea was to focus directly on the relevant content so that I would not have to re-read the coded interview passages in detail (as they can be very long and convoluted, making it difficult to get a quick overview of the relevant content), while still having the original passage at hand if needed.

3 Data preparation and setup of the MAXQDA project

Before importing the interviews, I prepared their transcripts using Word, selecting a font and font size that would allow for easy reading on a screen, and removing unimportant meta-information at the beginning of the transcripts. I also checked that the timestamps in the transcripts were in a format that MAXQDA could read.

The four interviews were imported into two separate document groups in the Document System, one for the autonomous team and one for the traditional team (Fig. 1). Even though it was not a genuine experimental design, I labeled the document groups as "EG" (experimental group) and "CG" (control group). Along with the interviews, I imported the audio recordings to listen to the original voice later in case of uncertainty regarding the meaning

2 I will use the term "code" throughout my explanations, as it aligns with the terminology in MAXQDA, even though "category" would be more accurate for the chosen analysis methods.

of a text passage. The focus of the interview analysis was noted in the yellow project memo, located in the root of the Document System,

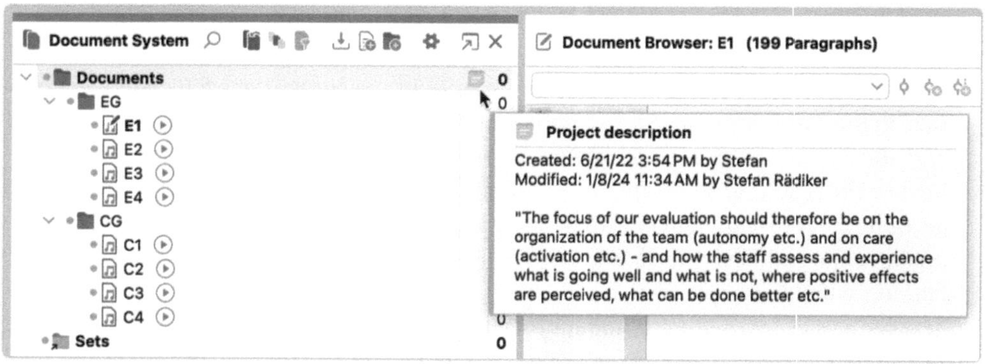

Fig. 1: Document System with two document groups, one for the "experimental" and one for the "control" group. The tooltip of the project memo shows an excerpt of the project description.

4 Coding the interviews and writing comment summaries

4.1 First coding cycle with main codes and writing summaries

Based on the interview guide, I created an initial coding frame that covered the main topics of interest, as presented in Fig. 2. The order of the codes in the Code System window followed the order of the interview guide and consisted of only 10 codes to ensure ease of application. At the end of the code list, I included a "Good quotes" code that could be applied in addition to a topic code to those interview passages that exemplified a covered aspect and could potentially be included in the report later. Please note that the analysis was conducted in German, and I translated all code names and other texts displayed in the figures of this chapter into English.

Working with a student assistant via screen sharing, we coded the first interview together to test the coding frame and to ensure consistency in the length of the coded interview passages. The assistant then coded the remaining interviews following our initial approach and ideas. For each coded segment he created, he also wrote a short descriptive summary by double-clicking on the coding stripe to the left of the text and writing the summary in the dialog box that appeared (Fig. 3). Because of the limited number of characters available for code comments (255 in MAXQDA 2022), he had to be very concise and to the point while summarizing each coded segment.

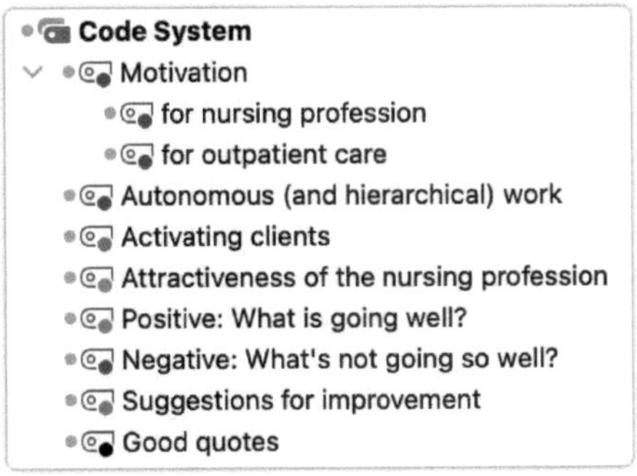

Fig. 2: Initial code system

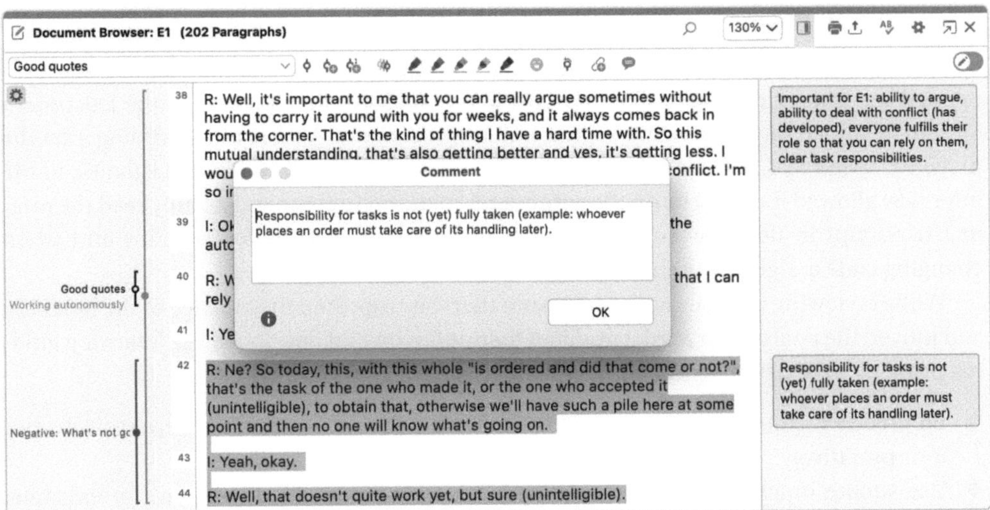

Fig. 3: Writing summaries in the code comment dialog box in the Document Browser. The existing comments are displayed in the blue boxes in the sidebar to the right.

Throughout this phase, the assistant added new codes based on insights gained during coding and summary writing. We reviewed and discussed these additions in two meetings, leading to an iterative refinement and reorganization of the code system. An important feature we utilized during the meetings was the sidebar displayed right to the text in the Document Browser, which allowed us to easily view and read existing comments (Fig. 3). In addition, the presence of a filled circle in the middle of a coding stripe left to the text was a quick visual indicator of which text passages had associated comments, which is also displayed in Fig. 3.

Using AI for creating the summaries

After my project was completed many AI features were added to MAXQDA, including the option to automatically summarize the text of a single coded segment in the Document Browser, or to summarize each coded segment of a selected code at once in the Smart Coding Tool. The summaries are stored in the code comment, just as I did in my project. These MAXQDA AI Assist feature could have greatly supported my analysis tasks: I would have asked the student assistant to identify and code relevant passages only, and I would have used AI Assist to automatically create summaries for each coded segment. Since I had to go through all the summaries to check for accuracy, this would have saved time without sacrificing quality, and there would have been much more time for analytical discussions.

4.2 Review of the coding work and the summaries

For each interview, I reviewed the assistant's coding work and his written summaries. I opened the transcript in the Document Browser and used the play icon in the Document System to launch the Multimedia Browser with the accompanying audio recording. I set the playback speed to 1.25x and used the F4 key to play and pause the audio. Listening to the interview allowed me to focus on the summaries in the code comments. I only read the original transcript in detail when dealing with complicated or complex sections and when changing code assignments and applying new codes to the interviews.

While reviewing the summaries to ensure that they captured the essence of the meaning and moved the analysis forward, I updated many of them and developed the following guiding principles to ensure consistency, efficiency, and methodological rigor:

- Be precise in your summary, focusing on the key points. Summarize descriptively, not interpretatively.
- Use square brackets for own thoughts, hints, interpretations, questions, for example: "[are hierarchies and competencies mixed up here?]"
- Use round brackets for any additional information, for example, a reference to a similar passage previously coded in the same interview: "(see par. 69-70)."
- Use double quotation marks for citations from the interview transcript and single quotation marks otherwise.

An interesting feature of MAXQDA I utilized was its ability to duplicate the summaries in the code comments when dragging and dropping an existing coding stripe from the Document Brower onto another code in the code system. That is, when I dragged a stripe "Attractiveness of care job" and dropped it onto the code "Negatives: What's not going so well?," the respective text passage was also coded with the "Negatives" code and the existing summary was automatically copied to the new code assignment. Sometimes the duplicated summary had to be adjusted; although it was written for the same passage of text, different codes necessitated unique perspectives in the summaries to reflect a different thematic focus.

It was helpful for me to not have to start from scratch with coding but instead work with the already existing codings and the written summaries, enabling me to focus on the overall analysis. While reviewing the assistant's coding work and his summaries, I reorganized some codes as it became clear that we needed more and other differentiation in the coding frame. Fig. 4 shows the code system after my review process.

Code System	528
A) Biography	0
Motivation	16
B) Work in care team	0
Working autonomously	30
Important for (autonomous) work in the care team	25
Organization of teamwork	30
Impact of the organization of teamwork	6
Co-determination and decision-making	26
Contributing competencies	12
Attractiveness of the care profession	25
Dealing with each other in the team	7
Challenges in the CG care team	7
C) Care work with clients	0
Typical situation	2
Activating clients	28
Assessment of care quality	8
Agreements regarding care services	12
Important in care work with clients/values in the ...	20
Involvement of the client's environment	37
Effects of work according to service catalog	12
Effects of work according to time budget	15
Specifics of the location	14
Comparison with classical care	26
Positive: What is going well?	28
Negative: What is going not so well?	13
Challenges	59
Suggestions for improvements by EG	24
Requirements of the caregiver	2
Good quotes	27

Fig. 4: Code system after review process

5 Using Smart Coding Tool to subdivide main codes and to write-up the report

After familiarizing myself with the interviews, summaries, and the existing coding work in the previous steps, I wanted to start writing the findings as soon as possible. Therefore, I decided to analyze the data code by code, focusing on one important topic at a time, which allowed me to create a draft of the report section by section. At the beginning of this process, I relied heavily on MAXQDA's Smart Coding Tool to gain insight into the content covered under each main code and to create appropriate subcodes to subdivide the content.

Setting up the Smart Coding Tool view

I launched the Smart Coding Tool via the ***Codes*** menu ribbon and clicked on a code in the code system displayed in the left part of the Smart Coding Tool to compile all coded interview passages covered by a code in the right part of the window (Fig. 5). By selecting the ***Display Comments*** option, I ensured that the written summaries were visible in a separate column. Since my primary focus was on the summaries, I frequently turned off the "Coded Segments" column that showed the much longer interview passages and I only turned it back on if a summary wasn't self-explanatory.

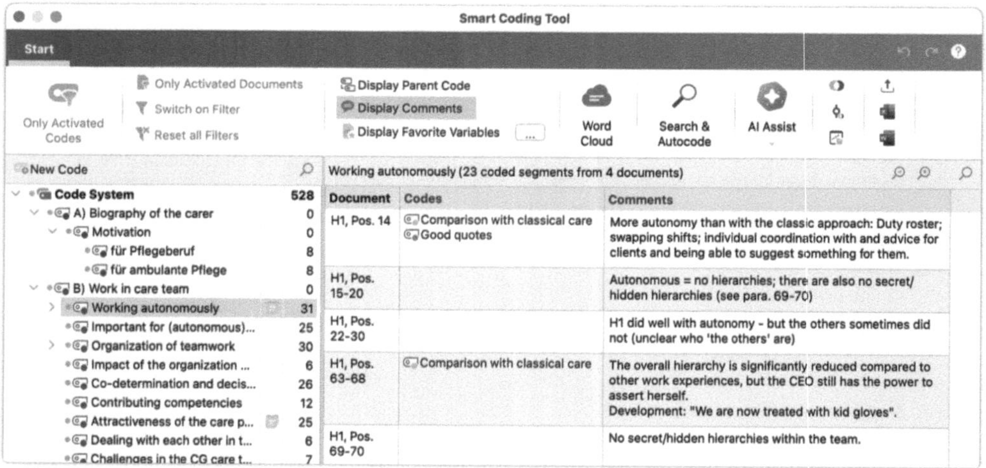

Fig. 5: Smart Coding Tool showing the summaries for a main code in the "Comments" column

The "Codes" column in the Smart Coding Tool displays all codes that are assigned to an interview segment *in addition* to the code currently selected. As Fig. 5 shows, this also applied to the "Good quotes" code, which was very helpful to identify segments suitable for inclusion in the final report as illustrations of a topic. To copy the corresponding interview segment, I needed to display the "Coded Segments" column again by right-clicking on one of the column headers and choosing the ***Select Columns*** option.

Exporting summaries and developing subcodes

For several main codes, I repeated the following steps to develop subcodes for deeper insights into a topic:

1. Export all summaries associated with a single main code from the Smart Coding Tool into a Word table.
2. Insert a column at the most right for entering suitable subcode names and writing notes.
3. Reorder, if necessary, the rows with summaries by similarity or created subcodes.
4. Insert the subcodes in the Smart Coding Tool and apply them to the segments.
5. Draft the corresponding section in the report.

For example, I used this approach to differentiate the main code "Working autonomously (and hierarchically)." Fig. 6 shows the table exported to Word with the summaries written for the corresponding coded segments. I added a column on the right for code development and employed a strategy that is known from the game show "Jeopardy": I formulated questions that encapsulated what each summary addressed, such as "What does autonomy mean?" and "Where are the boundaries of autonomy?" Based on these questions, I added and applied subcodes in the MAXDQA project while maintaining the question style (Fig. 7) and used them as chapter headings in the report.

Document	Codes	Comments [containing the summaries of coded segments]	Code development
H1, Pos. 14	Comparison with classical care Good quotes	More autonomy than with the classic approach: Duty roster; swapping shifts; individual coordination with and advice for clients and being able to suggest something for them.	What constitutes autonomy (potentially compared to classical work)?
H1, Pos. 15-20		Autonomous = no hierarchies; there are also no secret/hidden hierarchies (see para. 69-70)	What does autonomy mean?
H1, Pos. 22-30		H1 did well with autonomy - but the others sometimes did not (unclear who 'the others' are)	What are the effects of autonomy?
H1, Pos. 63-68	Comparison with classical care	The overall hierarchy is significantly reduced compared to other work experiences, but the CEO still has the power to assert herself. Development: "We are now treated with kid gloves".	What constitutes autonomy (potentially compared to classical work)? Where are the boundaries of autonomy? How has autonomy developed?
H1, Pos. 69-70		No secret/hidden hierarchies within the team.	What does autonomy mean?

Fig. 6: Excerpt of the contents for a main code exported to a Word table

I replicated this procedure of exporting to Word and developing subcodes with additional columns for some other main codes. However, instead of using the "Jeopardy Strategy" again, I employed various other techniques to create meaningful subcodes depending on the content of the summaries. For instance, I organized the rows with the summaries in Word based on similarity or utilized distinct colors to differentiate between segments from the experimental group and the control group.

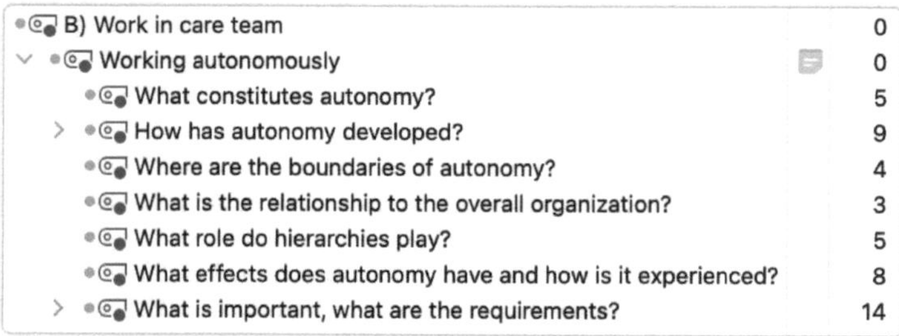

Fig. 7: Subcodes in question style, developed from the comment summaries and used as section headings in the final report

Optimizing the coding frame

While composing the results section for a main code in the report, I regularly revised the code system whenever it became apparent that the coding framework needed optimization. These adjustments were made directly in the Smart Coding Tool: codes were renamed, rearranged, and differentiated as previously described. Here are some examples to illustrate the process:

- One specific code was eliminated during report writing because all but one of its text passages were also assigned to another code. To remove the code assignments, I right-clicked on a row in the Smart Coding Tool and selected ***Remove from code 'x'***. To apply a more appropriate code to a segment, I dropped the row with the mouse on the target code while holding the Ctrl key on Windows or the command (⌘) key on Mac.
- When reading the summaries of closely related codes, it often became evident that they were not distinctly separated, or that the hierarchy needed adjustment. For instance, "Information sharing" was reclassified as a subcode of "Organization in the team." Consequently, segments were either moved from the parent code to the subcode or the subcode was additionally assigned.
- Codes were reorganized (by clicking and dragging with the mouse) to mirror the structure of the report, which was refined section by section.

Ensuring accuracy in reporting

In preparing the report, great care had to be taken not to misrepresent the statements of the interviewees. This meant occasionally going back to the original segment rather than relying solely on the summaries. To facilitate this, I sometimes reactivated the column showing coded segments in the Smart Coding Tool, as described earlier. When the entire interview segments were displayed, I sometimes clicked on a code listed in the Codes column to highlight and review the portion of the segment that was coded with that code. This proved to be very helpful for the "Good quotes" code, which was often not applied to a very long segment, but only to parts of it, as demonstrated in Fig. 8.

Document	Coded Segments	Codes	Comments
E1, Pos. 15-20	I: But how do you have to imagine autonomy/ autonomy means without hierarchies. How do you imagine an autonomous care team in the organization? R: There is no hierarchy, except one // (unintelligible). I: And // how does that work? R: Wonderful. I: (laughs) R: And if not, then we go on strike. That works, too (laughs).		Autonomous = no hierarchies; there are also no secret/hidden hierarchies (see para. 69-70)
E1, Pos. 22	R: Actually, I've been doing well with autonomy. It's just that sometimes others haven't fared so well, which has led to a few shitstorms here. I found them very exhausting. I really have to say that. That also put a bit of a strain on me.		H1 did well with autonomy - but the others sometimes did not (unclear who 'the others' are)
E1, Pos. 38-44	R: Well, it's important to me that you can really argue sometimes without having to carry it around with you for weeks, and it always comes back in from the corner. That's the kind of thing I have a hard time with. So this mutual understanding, that's also getting better and yes, it's getting less. I would say (flatly?) that we have all become a bit more capable of conflict. I'm so in need of harmony (unintelligible) (laughs). I: Okay. Good. Is there anything else that is important to you, so in the autonomy of the team? R: Well, it's also important to me that everyone fulfills their role, so that I can rely on them.	Negative: What's not going so well? Good quotes	Important for E1: ability to argue, ability to deal with conflict (has developed), everyone fulfills their role so that you can rely on them, clear task responsibilities.

Fig. 8: Column "Coded Segments" was sometimes displayed again to view the original interview text in the Smart Coding Tool. Clicking on one of the additionally applied codes listed in the "Code" column highlighted all parts coded with the clicked code.

6 Using MAXMaps to subdivide main codes and create visualizations

After working with some main codes using the Smart Coding Tool and Word, I tried an alternative method to organize the summaries, create subcodes, and gain insights for a main theme. I used MAXMaps, a workspace for creating concept maps, to visually organize the summaries. This approach showed its potential immediately, and I continued to use it for all the remaining main codes. To make the summaries of a main code available in MAXMaps, I followed these steps (Fig. 9):

1. After opening ***Visual Tools > MAXMaps***, I created a new, empty map and kept the MAXMaps window open.
2. In MAXQDA's main window, I double-clicked on a code to bring up the Overview of Coded Segments, which displays all interview segments associated with that code.
3. Using the Ctrl+A keyboard shortcut (⌘+A on a Mac), I selected all the rows in the overview table and dragged them onto the empty map.

It is important to note that when you drag a coded segment into MAXMaps, MAXQDA automatically inserts the comment instead of the segment, along with a source information (Fig. 9). This allowed me to easily insert all the summaries written for a main code into the map at once.

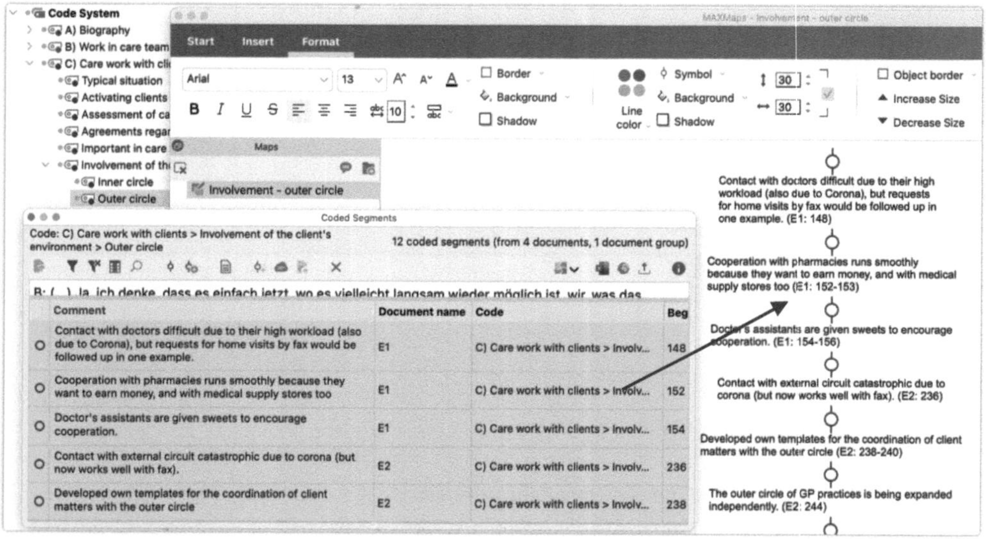

Fig. 9: Starting summary organization in MAXMaps by dragging rows with coded segments from the tabular Overview of Coded Segments window into an empty map

For most main codes, I rearranged the summaries on the map and grouped them together, often adding colored background shapes for visual distinction. I also added explanatory headings and labels to distinguish between different aspects and for ease of visual access. On some maps I kept the coding symbols for each summary, while on others I removed them by unchecking the option ***Display Symbols*** on the MAXMaps ***Start*** menu ribbon. For transparency, I kept the source information below each summary, which provided the paragraph number of the original interview. Fig. 10 shows two of the maps that I copied into my Word report as high-resolution images by using the ***Copy*** function on the ***Start*** menu ribbon.

While organizing the summaries, the interactive connection between MAXMaps and the original data proved to be very helpful: by hovering over one of the summaries, I could read the original interview text in a tooltip, which allowed me not to rely solely on the summaries for questions. If the original interview text was too long for the tooltip (which was rarely the case), I clicked on the summary in MAXMaps to display it in the Document Browser and read it there.

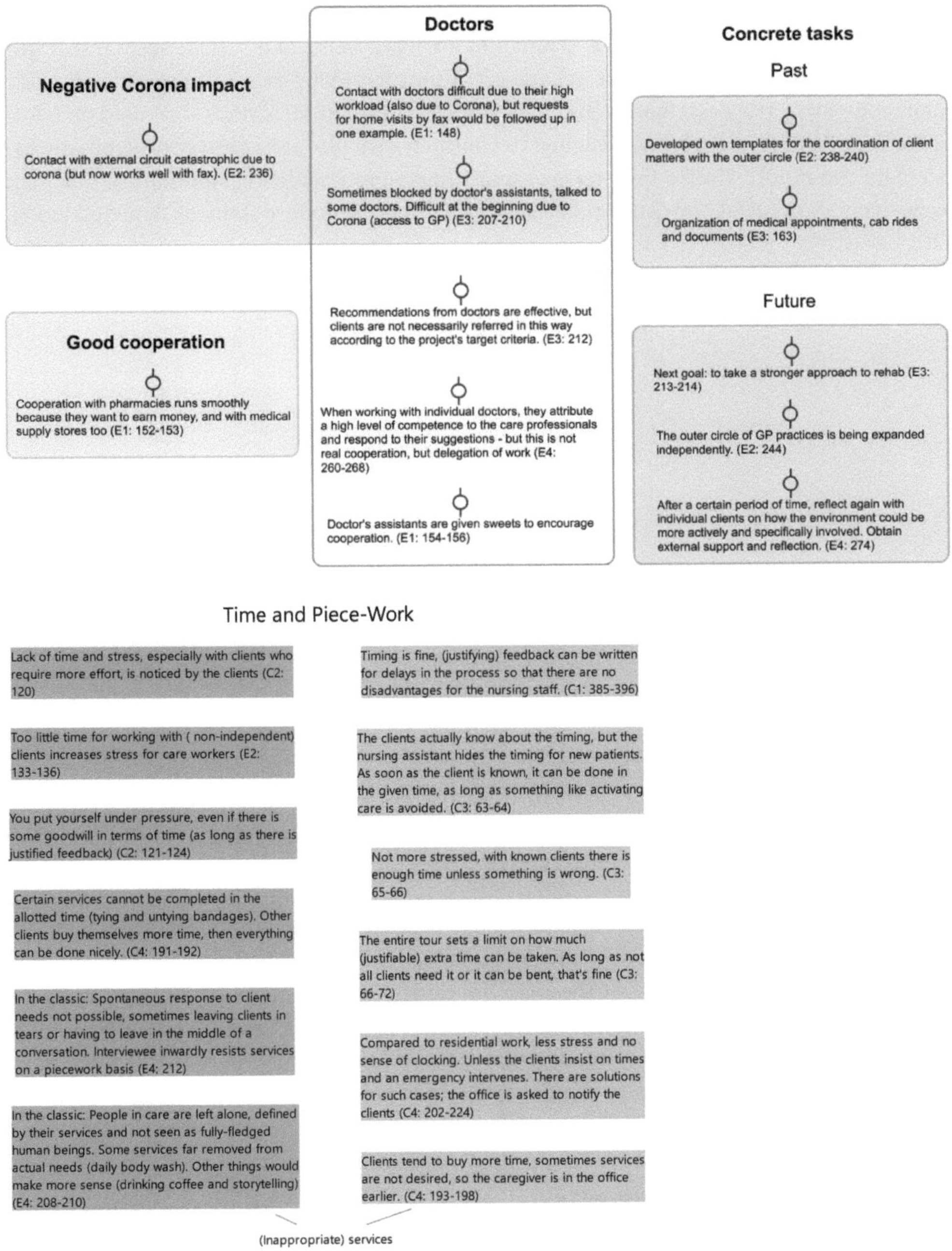

Fig. 10: Two resulting maps that have been included in the report

While creating these maps, I also refined the code system when necessary. For example, I combined the two codes "Negative: What does not work well?" and "Challenges" into a single code "Negative Aspects and Challenges." After identifying relevant subcodes for this main code using the described techniques and workflows in MAXMaps, I created an additional map. This new map was designed to concisely visualize the primary problematic aspects for the report. Unlike the previous maps that were visualizing summaries, this map exclusively showcased one code and its subcodes from the code system, as depicted in Fig. 11.

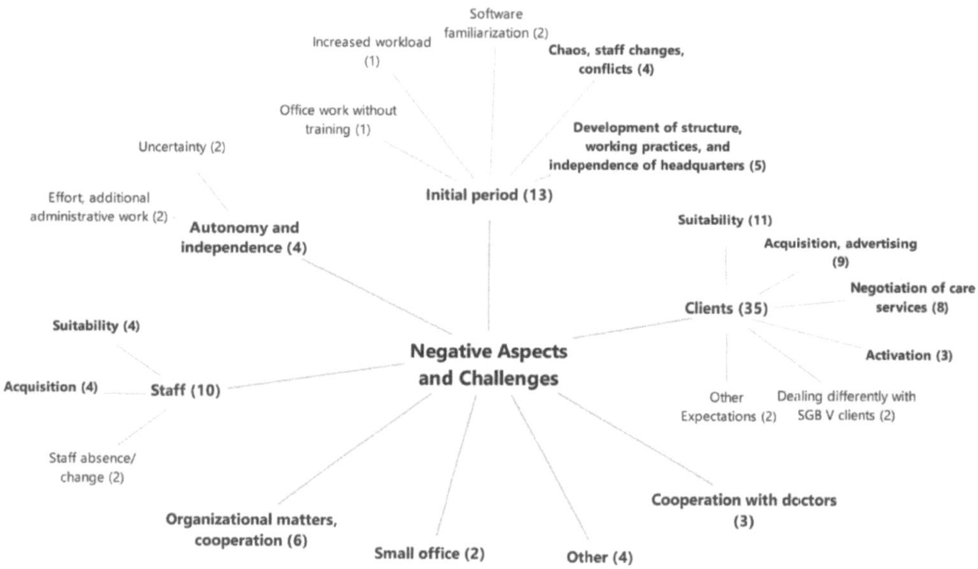

Fig. 11: Visualization of a code and its subcodes using MAXMaps

To create the map, I utilized the ***Hierarchical Code-Subcodes Model*** template in MAXQDA, accessible via ***Start > New Code Model*** in the MAXMaps menu ribbon. Once the model was created, I rearranged and optimized the map for clarity. The numbers behind the subcode names reflect the number of interview passages coded with that aspect. To emphasize the groups of problems, the direct subcodes were colored in red, while the sub-subcodes were colored in dark grey if at least three segments had been coded with it and light-grey was used for those with only one or two associated interview passages.

7 Lessons learned

The lessons learned outlined below encapsulate the research journey I undertook to analyze the interviews and to write a report for the evaluation within a very constrained time frame. In writing them, I have also taken into account the latest developments in MAXQDA, with continuing support for artificial intelligence in the analysis process and enhanced character limits for code comments. The following insights may prove beneficial for all readers, who want to utilize the code comments for writing summaries:

- *Writing summaries for each coded segment is extremely useful but relies on accuracy and consistency.* The most important lesson learned was that using MAXQDA's code comments to write summaries of the coded content aided the analysis in several ways. It sped up the process by working at the level of these summaries without having to frequently revisit the original data once the initial coding process was complete. However, crafting summaries required carefully developed guidelines, such as rules governing the usage of symbols, brackets, single and multiple quotation marks, and other elements included in the summaries.
- *Write concise and short.* Writing summaries that capture the essence of a coded segment within the strict 255-character limit of MAXQDA 2022 required a lot of thought and writing to the point. In the latest MAXQDA version, the limit has been doubled to about 500 characters. While the extra space allows more content to be included, I have found that it is still worthwhile to keep the summaries short for easy organization in later stages of the analysis.
- *Use AI Assist.* The latest developments in MAXQDA's AI features, which allow automatic summaries to be written for a single or all coded segments of a code at once, are very promising for evaluation projects. Using AI Assist would have saved time, without sacrificing quality and left more time for analytical discussions.
- *Include audio recordings.* Playing the audio files (at 1.25 speed) helped a lot to get familiar with the data and not to rely only on the written text. It also allowed me to check the possible meanings of strange passages in the data and to rule out transcription errors.
- *Use MAXMaps.* After I had started working in Word for creating subcodes based on the comment summaries, I was surprised how much more helpful it was to work with the summaries in MAXMaps. There, instead of being trapped in a linear sequence of tables and paragraphs, I could use a whiteboard to arrange summaries that belong together, and I had the ability to work more graphically, adding different types of shapes and colors.
- *Take advantage of 2 monitors if possible.* For extensive work with the summaries, it was very helpful to rely on my 2-monitor setup. While MAXQDA was running with its main window on one monitor, I often worked with the Smart Coding Tool, MAXMaps, and other tools on the second one.

Bibliography

Kuckartz, U., & Rädiker, S. (2019). *Analyzing qualitative data with MAXQDA: Text, audio, and video.* Springer Nature Switzerland. https://doi.org/10.1007/978-3-030-15671-8

Kuckartz, U., & Rädiker, S. (2023). *Qualitative content analysis: Methods, practice and software* (2nd ed.). Sage.

Rädiker, S., & Kuckartz, U. (2020). *Focused analysis of qualitative interviews with MAXQDA.* MAXQDA Press. https://doi.org/10.36192/978-3-948768072

About the author

Stefan Rädiker is a consultant and trainer for research methods and evaluation. He holds a PhD in Educational Sciences and his research focuses on computer-assisted analysis of qualitative and mixed methods data. He has worked with MAXQDA for more than 20 years and supports the VERBI team with his methodological expertise in the development of the MAXQDA software.

https://orcid.org/0000-0002-0612-1052

Using MAXQDA to Analyze Open-Ended Survey Responses: An Example From an Evaluation Project

Christina Silver

Abstract

This chapter discusses a qualitative evaluation project that analyzed free-text responses to open-ended survey questions relating to a voluntary program to support health workers in the UK through the pandemic (2020–2022) called “Coaching through Covid and Beyond.” The process of planning and undertaking the evaluation using MAXQDA is described, from preparing and familiarizing with data, through designing the analysis plan, categorizing responses, interrogating patterns and relationships, to generating engaging visualizations and preparing reports at different stages for several audiences. A variety of tools were used to accomplish the evaluation steps, including Document Variable Statistics, Word Clouds, Interactive Quote Matrix, as well as MAXMaps and Questions – Themes – Theories (QTT). The chapter illustrates the value of free-text responses to open-ended survey questions and how they can be analyzed systematically using MAXQDA. The chapter concludes with a discussion of lessons learned from this project that are transferable to other qualitative evaluations using MAXQDA.

Key MAXQDA features covered

- ✓ Survey Data: Import from Excel Spreadsheet
- ✓ Activate Documents by Variables
- ✓ Document Variable Statistics
- ✓ Interactive Quote Matrix (renamed to “Segment Matrix” in MAXQDA 24)
- ✓ Code memos
- ✓ Word Combinations
- ✓ Word Clouds
- ✓ Categorize Survey Data
- ✓ MAXMaps: Free map
- ✓ Questions – Themes – Theories (QTT)

1 Introduction

In March 2020, a call to action came for coaches to deliver free coaching to those working on the UK National Health Service (NHS) frontline during the crisis[1]. Shortly afterwards the

1 https://www.coaching-at-work.com/2021/03/01/covid-a-year-in-coaching/

Silver, Christina (2024). Using MAXQDA to analyze open-ended survey responses: An example from an evaluation project. In: The practice of qualitative data analysis. Research examples using MAXQDA, volume 2 (pp. 87–106). Berlin: MAXQDA Press. https://doi.org/10.36192/978-3-948768188_5

Coaching through Covid program was set-up, entirely run by volunteers[2]. It offered up to 6 free coaching sessions for NHS staff with coaches who offered their services for free, to help those working in healthcare with the challenges they were facing. I joined the Core Strategy Team in December 2021, to provide research and evaluation support on a voluntary basis. The team wanted to understand whether and how the program had been effective, from the perspective of both the NHS workers ("clients") who had received the coaching and the professional coaches who had provided it. This was achieved by collecting feedback via two questionnaires; one administered to clients, the other to coaches. This chapter discusses the analysis of the client feedback undertaken using MAXQDA.

The analysis began while the program was on-going, so the objectives were identified and adjusted as it progressed, in response to needs identified by the Core Strategy Team at points during the process. For example, at the outset the primary aim was to identify areas where provision could be improved, by focusing on aspects clients reported being less satisfied with. Later the focus shifted to consider lessons that could be learned from the whole process; that is, from coaches and the Core Strategy Team as well as clients, to share with others embarking on similar initiatives in the future. These shifting objectives affected how the analysis was undertaken.

2 Data collection and methodological approach

The data were collected via an online questionnaire to clients after they had received a set of free coaching sessions - usually 6 sessions, although sometimes fewer if clients chose to leave the program earlier, or more if additional sessions were arranged with the coach. The questionnaire, designed before I joined the Core Strategy Team, comprised seven open-ended questions, two closed questions, and one demographic question. Some of the open-ended questions were rephrased part-way through after it became clear that they were being understood variously by clients and were therefore not yielding directly comparative data. 82 clients completed this questionnaire between September 2020 and April 2022.

This was a pragmatic project in an applied setting and therefore the analytic method was designed specifically for it. The design was informed by principles of reflexive thematic analysis (Braun & Clarke, 2021) and evaluation methods (Patton, 2015). The way the analysis was performed, how progress was documented, and how it is discussed and presented in this chapter, is informed by the five-level QDA method (Woolf & Silver, 2018) which forefronts analytic strategies (what you plan to do) in driving software tactics (how you plan to do it).[3]

2 The program was subsequently renamed to Coaching through Covid and Beyond https://coachingthroughcovid.org/

3 For more information about five-level QDA and how it was used to plan this project, including detailed analytic overviews of the steps, see https://www.qdaservices.co.uk/post/planning-and-documenting-a-computer-assisted-qualitative-analysis

The analysis process comprised one high-level and one in-depth analysis stage. The first served to familiarize with the data and refine the evaluation questions, from those broadly specified by the Core Strategy Team. It also contained first categorization of the responses and writing a first report. The second stage provided an exhaustive in-depth analysis of client feedback and writing the final report.

3 Initial high-level analysis of client feedback

3.1 Data preparation, cleaning, and project set-up

Data preparation involved several rounds of experimentation with different ways of preparing and cleaning the data and importing into MAXQDA before settling on the most analytically meaningful structure. For example, because some questions had been changed partway through, they needed to be aligned before importing for analysis. I left the full (adjusted) questions as column headers in the Excel spreadsheet so they would transfer into MAXQDA as both code names and code memos. The code names were subsequently shortened to indicate the question, so they were easily identifiable within MAXQDA.

After some trial runs, I imported the survey data using ***Import > Survey Data > Import Data from Excel Spreadsheet.*** The import dialog box let me choose what columns from the spreadsheet I wanted to include and if I wanted them as a code, a document variable, or both. Fig. 1 shows the decisions I made:

- ❖ The unique ID did not need to become a code or a variable, because it would become the document name, referencing each individual client (shown in Fig. 2).
- ❖ There was only one closed-question in the client questionnaire, asking them to indicate on a Likert scale of 0–10 how likely they were to recommend the program. This was set to become a document variable upon import because the responses were numeric.
- ❖ The other variable created upon import captures the date and time when clients filled out the questionnaire. At this point it was not known whether this would be used within the analysis, so the choice was made to import it in case it was later decided to be used.
- ❖ All the other questions were imported as codes.
- ❖ Finally, the option ***Code empty cells*** was not checked, because I wanted a quick way to identify how many clients had answered each open-ended question.

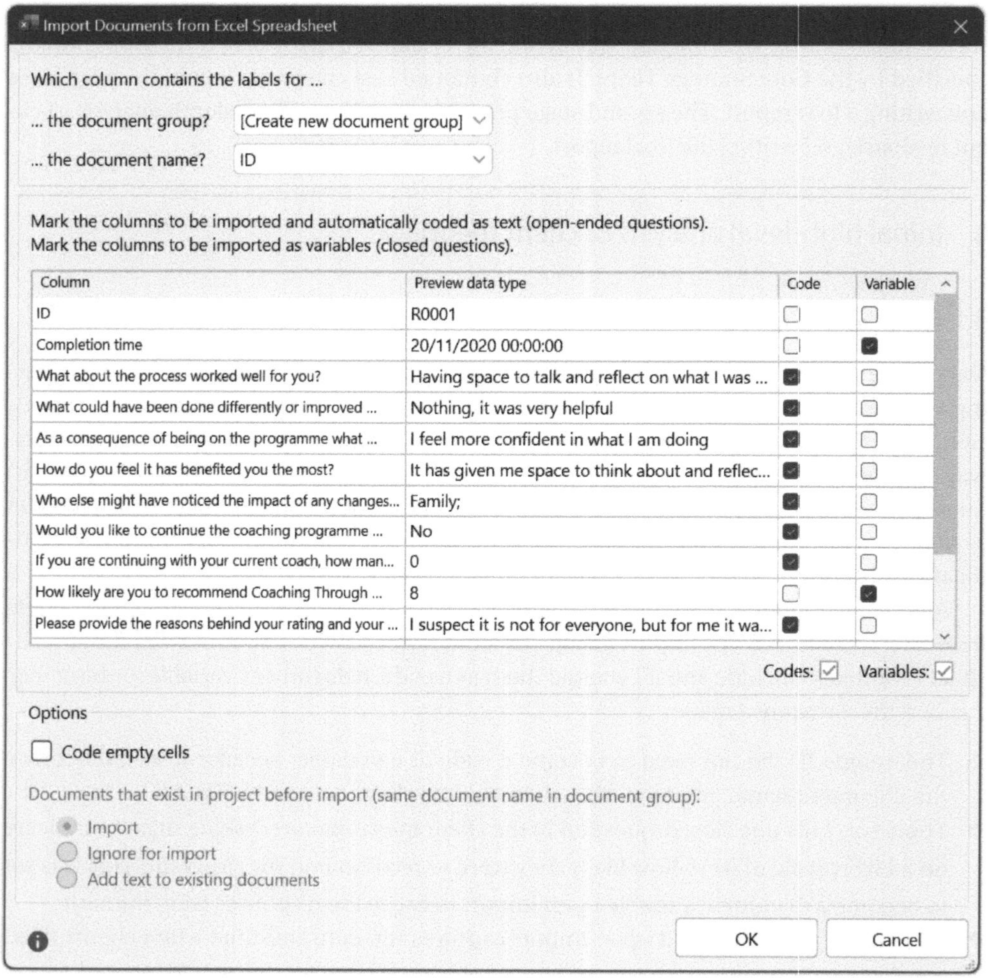

Fig. 1: Survey import process showing options chosen

After import, the data were checked to ensure everything had transferred as expected, and a few adjustments were made, most notably renaming and re-organizing the codes. The result of the import is visualized in Fig. 2, showing:

- one document per respondent, named according to the unique ID column
- each open question as a code, with very short code names for the questions and full questions in code memos
- the standardized information in two document variables (“Completion DATE” and “RECOMMEND score”)

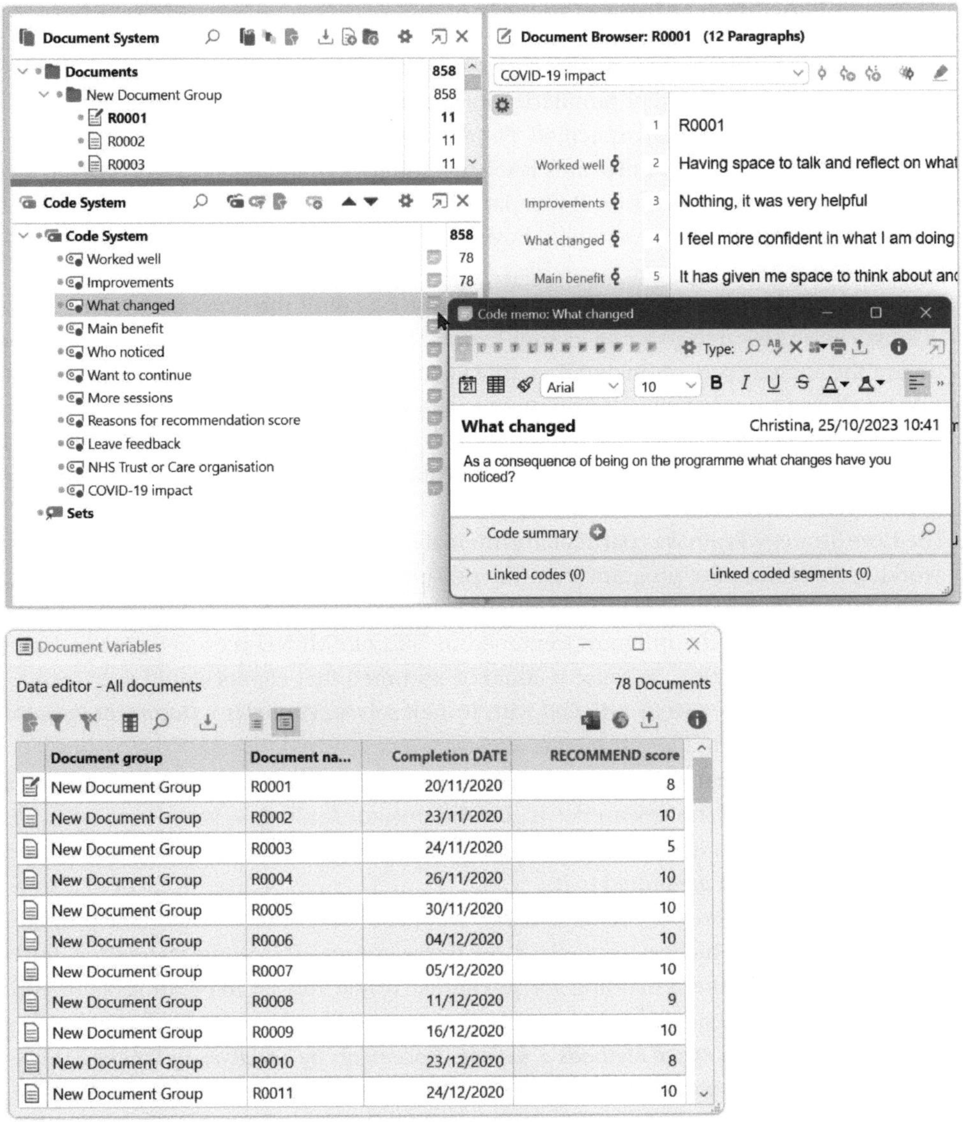

Fig. 2: Imported survey responses in MAXQDA after optimizing names of document group, codes, and variables

3.2 Data familiarization to inform analysis plan

The next task was to explore responses more systematically, and with a more analytic eye. This was informed by the earlier familiarization in Excel such that the analysis objectives could begin to be more formally specified. Familiarizing multiple times in this way is commonly advocated in qualitative methods texts, including by Braun and Clarke (2021) in describing reflexive thematic analysis. It was particularly important for this project because I did not already know the data, as I would have if, for example, I had undertaken interviews and transcribed them.

Because I was undertaking this evaluation on the behalf of the program which I knew had a longer-term vision to generate lessons learned from the endeavor, it was important to document the analytic process in detail, so that I could explain the process to the team, and it could be shared for other similar initiatives to draw upon. I used MAXQDA's logbook to note the daily tasks undertaken, the *"I did this, next I plan to do that"* audit trail, and I used in-document memos to capture reflections concerning data themselves, and the developing interpretations and findings.

The Core Strategy Team was particularly interested at this point to understand what was *not* working well about the program from the perspective of the clients, so steps could be taken to improve their experience. The responses to the closed question concerning likelihood of recommending the program (renamed to "RECOMMEND score") were used as a proxy for overall satisfaction, because it could be assumed that clients would only recommend the program if they were satisfied with it themselves. ***Variables > Document Variable Statistics*** were then used to identify clients who were less satisfied (Fig. 3).

With the QTT workspace (***Analysis > QTT: Questions, Themes, Theories***), MAXQDA provides a notebook, that allows the researcher to save important findings and write insights on them. In QTT, I created a new worksheet entitled "High Level Exploration" and transferred the table and chart views generated to it.

Because the vast majority of clients said they would be likely to recommend the program (93% gave a score of 8 or higher) it was clear that it was important to understand in as much depth as possible why the remaining 7% (6 clients) would not be likely to recommend. Therefore the "Recommend" Variable was used to group these "less satisfied" clients. This was accomplished using ***Mixed Methods > Activate Documents by Variables*** to create a document set containing 6 documents; those clients who scored 7 or less to the question (Fig. 4).

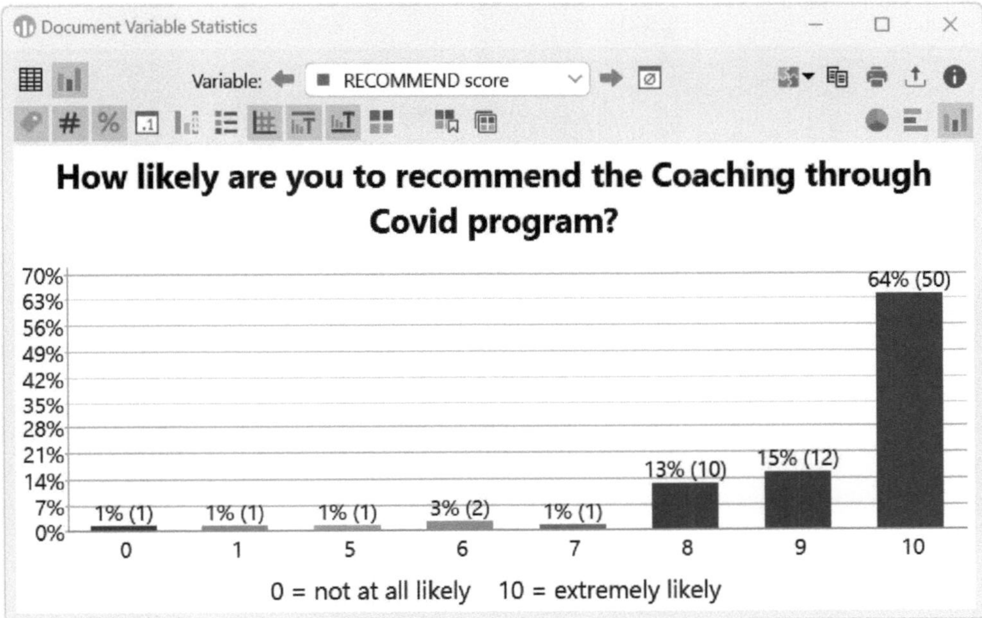

Fig. 3: Document Variable Statistics chart showing clients' likelihood of recommending the program

Another aspect of initial high-level familiarization was exploring the content of all the open-ended responses, using word frequency and word combinations tools. First, a word frequency was run on the responses to the question "*What could have been done differently or improved upon*?" by activating all documents, activating the code "Improvements" and clicking on the word cloud icon in the Retrieved Segments window. The word cloud illustrated that the most frequent word in these responses was the word "nothing" (Fig. 5). By double-clicking the word "nothing" in the cloud and looking at the search results, a quick exploration of the context showed that many clients mentioned "nothing" needed improvement. However, some clients added more information to their response. This meant that the simple "nothing" responses show satisfaction, but the detailed responses that go beyond "nothing" needed closer examination.

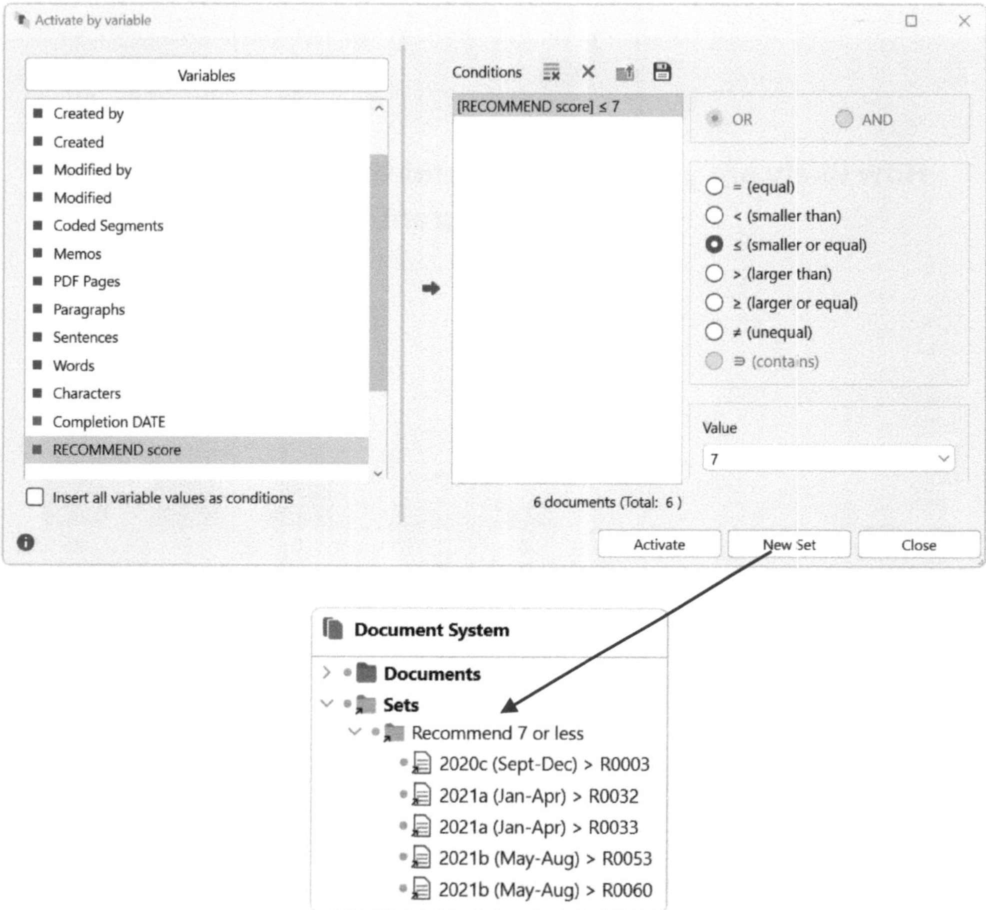

Fig. 4: Creating a document set for clients scoring 7 or less to the "Recommend" question

After exploring other frequently occurring words within these responses in the same way, common phrases were identified, using ***MAXDictio > Word Combinations***. In the resulting list of word combinations, I clicked on the word cloud icon to visualize the most frequent phrases and examine interesting ones by double-clicking on them in the cloud. I then added the word cloud visualizations to the QTT worksheet and made some notes in the insight text box about potential topics to code for arising from this exploration. I repeated this process with the other open-ended questions.

These explorations of the responses identified one client who had not completed any coaching sessions. Therefore, the document containing their responses was moved to a new document group called "Dud-responses."

Fig. 5: Word cloud visualization of responses to the "What could have been done differently or improved upon?" question

The next step was to consider how the open-ended responses differed between those with different recommendations scores, particularly focusing on those with low values. For this purpose, I used ***Mixed Methods > Interactive Quote Matrix*** and selected the option ***Include all variable values as conditions*** for the "recommend" variable. This option ensured that the Quote Matrix contained one separate column for each value. The resulting comparative display (Fig. 6) also served to further familiarize with the responses, and resulted in confirming the appropriateness of the decision to first focus on coding the responses amongst those who were less likely to recommend the program.

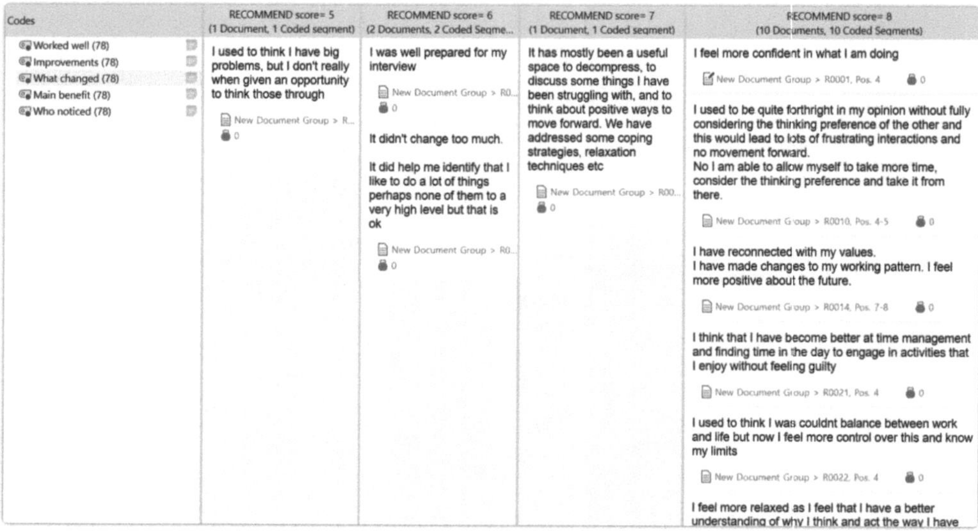

Fig. 6: Interactive Quote Matrix display generated from a Crosstab (open questions by "likelihood to recommend" scores)

3.3 Design initial analysis plan and prepare data

The next phase involved formally designing the analysis moving forward and making a few adjustments to the data to enable it, arising from the familiarization phase. First, the notes made during earlier phases were drawn upon to write up a narrative plan for the analysis in the project memo (available in the ***Memo*** menu tab). These concerned potential topics for coding and the need to first focus on open-ended responses from those who were less likely to recommend the program. A visual representation of the analysis plan was then created as a map using ***Visual Tools > MAXMaps***.

Second, a few changes to the data structure were made to facilitate the analysis. The document variables "Recommend" and "Month" were recoded using Stats, the statistical workspace in MAXQDA, to provide more meaningful bases upon which to make comparisons. In addition, the subcodes that captured the organizational unit in which the clients worked (NHS Trust) were transformed into values of a categorical document variable so they could be used later on in Crosstab queries. As mentioned earlier there was variation in the responses given, which could be solved by recoding the variable values if required.

Finally, the open-ended questions that were not going to be analyzed in-depth at this stage were moved under a new top-level code called "OEQs not being analyzed" so it was easier to focus on the core questions being analyzed. Moving these codes rather than deleting them meant they were still available should the decision be made later on to analyze them.

3.4 Categorize responses to open-questions

Now the task was to categorize all the responses to the open-ended questions being focused on. Because the main emphasis was on identifying ways in which the program might be improved, I started categorizing reasons for not recommending the program. To accomplish this, I took the following three steps:

1. Activated the document set "Recommend 7 or less" containing the clients that were less likely to recommend the program
2. Started the ***Categorize Survey Data*** tool in the ***Analysis*** menu tab and then
3. Dragged and dropped the relevant open-ended question code from the code system into the appearing dialog to start the categorization for these responses.

In the Categorize Survey Data window, I created new subcodes to categorize the comments of the seven respondents and dragged the responses to the codes. Actually, only four of the six respondents had further clarified their low rating.

I repeated this process for most of the other open-ended questions, this time with all respondents, resulting in a list of between 10–15 subcodes under each open-ended question code. Fig. 7 shows the Categorize Survey Data window for the question "*What could have been done differently or improved upon*?" For this question, the "nothing" responses re-

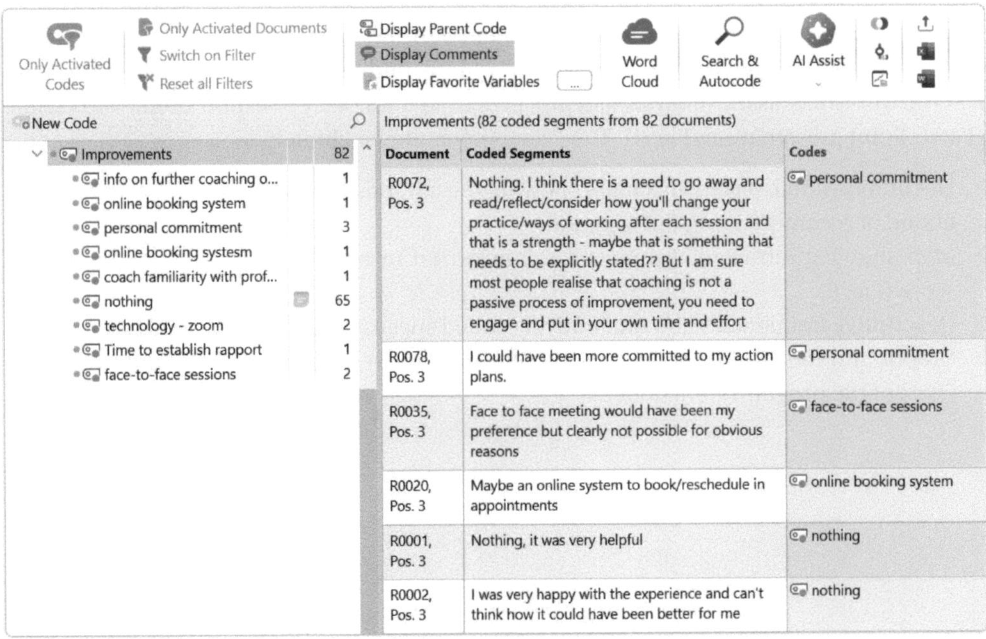

Fig. 7: Using the Categorize Survey Data tool to code all responses to each open question, one at a time

vealed themselves again. Using ***Search & Autocode*** within the Categorize Survey Data tool, these were identified, reviewed and where they did not include a qualifying statement that indicated that "nothing" actually meant "something," they were quickly autocoded to a "nothing" code.

As the responses were coded, I did not remove them from the top-level code. This enabled me to work with all the responses together and to think about and analyze each coded response separately later. I analyzed the responses question by question, which meant that I did not "cross-code" responses with subcodes to other questions created, even if they might be related to the question. But whenever I created a subcode related or similar to an existing code, I colored that code orange, so it could easily be identified in the code system later on.

The subcodes for each open-ended question generated a first descriptive overview of the topics. The next task was to review these and make relevant adjustments to ensure the coding accurately captured the breadth and depth of the responses. Taking one question code at a time, coded segments at each subcode were checked for equivalence in the Categorize Survey Data tool. Where necessary, segments were re-coded and codes merged if they captured similar content. Brief definitions were created for each code in its memo.

3.5 Prepare summary report

I was now ready to prepare a summary report detailing findings so far. This involved generating a set of visuals that provided an overview of the findings. These have been collated in the QTT worksheet as the analysis had proceeded, so it was easy to export them, and create a PowerPoint presentation (Fig. 9). The visuals generated included:

- Document variable statistic charts showing the composition of the sample and the likelihood of recommending the program.
- Map showing retrieved segments for categorized reasons for lower recommendation score (Fig. 8).
- Descriptive frequencies and qualitatively coded suggestions for improvements.
- Graphs and code clouds of categorized responses to "What Worked Well" and where impacts of the program were noticed.

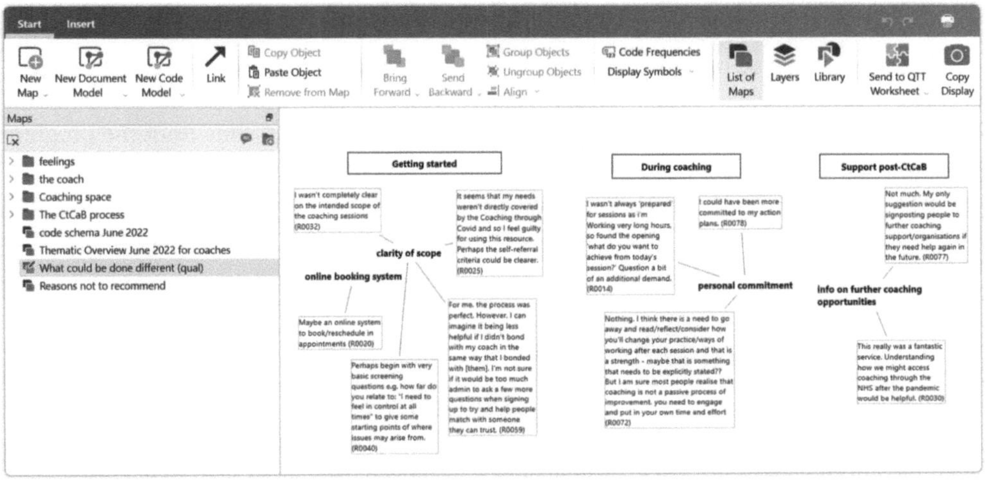

Fig. 8: Map generated in MAXMaps to illustrate the main suggestions for improving the program, organized by stage of the program

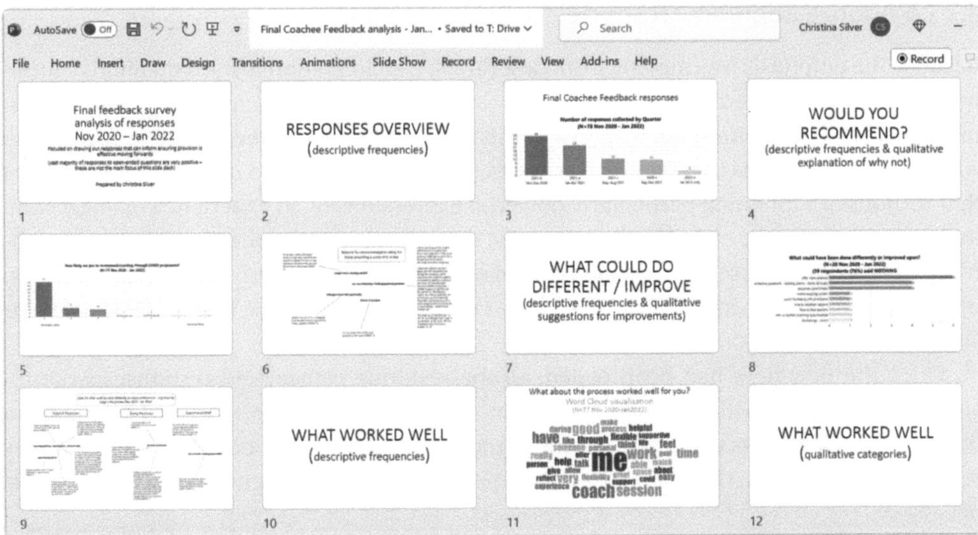

Fig. 9: Slides created for PowerPoint presentation out of visuals created in MAXQDA to summarize the first stage of the project

4 Exhaustive in-depth analysis of client feedback

The high-level analysis provided an important overview of the program from the client perspective, a general sense of what had worked well, and a detailed understanding of potential areas for improvement. However, it was also clear that to learn lessons from the program that would be useful for similar ventures in the future, more focus on the qualitative responses was required. The next stage therefore moved the emphasis in that direction and included all the feedback gathered from clients between the start of the program to its conclusion.

4.1 Prepare and import additional data

Additional data were gathered, prepared, and added to the existing MAXQDA project and using the same process as described above, the free-text responses were coded using existing question subcodes and creating new ones as required using the Categorize Survey Data tool. The remainder of this section discusses additional tasks undertaken from this point on.

4.2 Categorize additional responses into existing framework

Because the emphasis was moving from descriptive categorization toward qualitative interpretation, a code named "quotable quotes" was created to capture particularly powerful expressions of impact within the responses. This code sat at the top-level of the Code System window because it was used across responses to all the open-ended questions. This meant that responses containing particularly powerful expressions of an experience or suggestion for improvement were coded both to the code that captured the content and to the "quotable quotes" code. This set up the possibility of retrieving these powerful expressions later on in relation to other codes (using ***Analysis > Coding Query*** or ***Visual Tools > Code Relations Browser***).

Once the new data had been coded, all the resulting categorized responses were reviewed again, along with the code definitions. This involved retrieving coded segments in the Retrieved Segments window by activating each subcode in turn, along with all the survey responses documents, checking for equivalence (Fig. 10), and merging or re-coding where necessary.

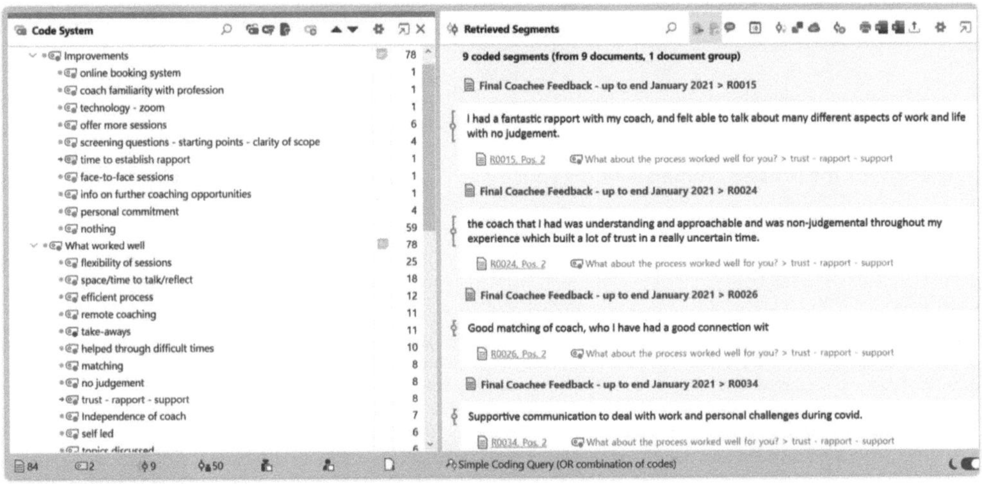

Fig. 10: Similar codes created in relation to different open questions activated and checked for equivalence in the Retrieved Segments window before merging

The review process of the code system was done in conjunction with the existing code definitions in the code memos that were also adjusted as required, to account for changes resulting from the new data (Fig. 11). In some instances, descriptive subcodes were combined to create higher-level, more abstract subcodes, but this was only done where it made conceptual sense, and was not driven by frequency. For example, codes that only referenced one or two segments were kept distinct, not merged to create a higher-level, where they captured an important personal experience or opinion. Each response was thus treated with equal weight in the analysis, even if it was uncommon.

4.3 Summarize responses per open-ended question

The next step was to summarize all the responses to each open-ended question and thus was the beginning of moving from the descriptive to the more thematic level in the interpretation. I created a new QTT worksheet for each open question being analyzed. Then, taking each question in turn, the memos relating to the subcodes were reviewed alongside the subcode statistics visuals (generated again at this point because those stored in the "High Level Exploration" QTT worksheet only referenced the responses available in the previous stage). The summaries of each open question were written in the worksheet for that question. This process brought to the fore even more than when coloring repeated codes, that there were a number of experiences and impacts that cut across the open-ended questions. This led to the need move away from the question-based analysis to consider themes more generally and thus reorganize the coding frame.

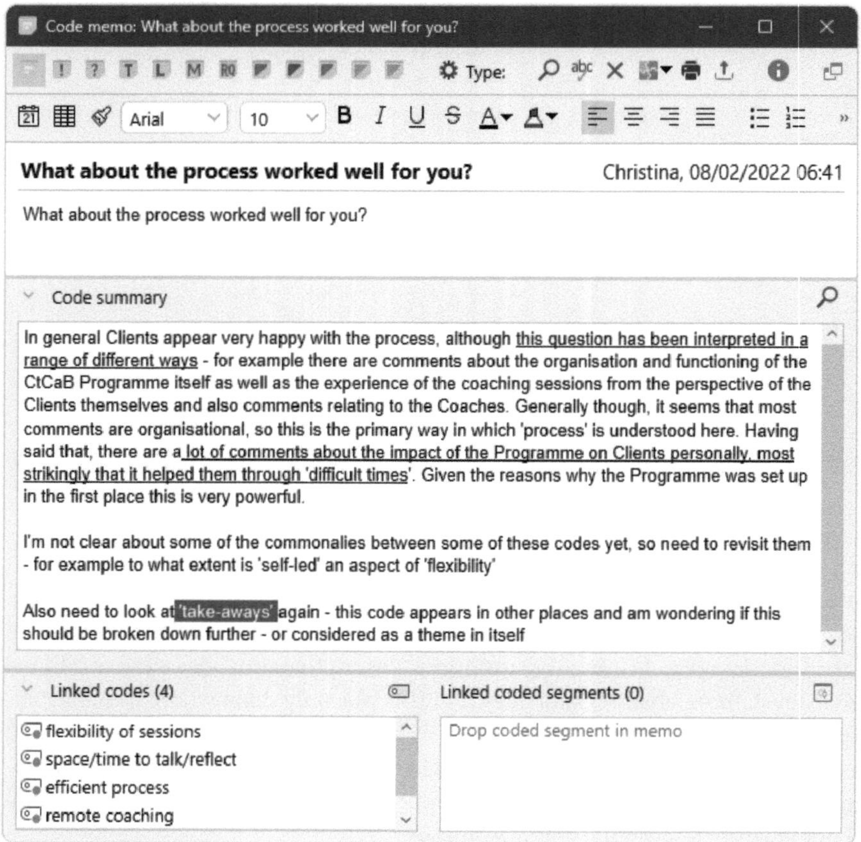

Fig. 11: Using code memos to summarize responses to open questions as new data were introduced

4.4 Reorganize codes into themes

Before reorganizing the coding frame, a back-up was created of the whole MAXQDA project, to later be able to refer back to the structure of this stage, and in case it was decided to take the analysis in a different direction. The reorganization was informed by the current analytic focus: evaluating the program by understanding clients' experiences and identifying the program's key impacts from their perspective.

The subcodes of each open-question were moved to the top-level of the Code System window and reorganized into two themes ("IMPACTS" and "WHO NOTICED") (Fig. 12). The process of checking for equivalence was facilitated by the earlier coloring of duplicated codes; the orange-colored codes could be activated to easily identify the duplications and review them before merging.

In addition, because the responses to the open-questions had not been un-coded from the top-level question codes when they had been categorized, moving subcodes out of their hierarchical position under each question code did not lose the connection between the categorized subcode and the open-question that had been answered. This is because each segment was coded at both the question code and the categorized subcode. The process of arriving at the final themes, categories, and codes was lengthy and iterative, involving several different structures until the final codebook was settled upon.

Fig. 12: The final code system after thematic reorganization

4.5 Analyze resulting themes

Once the thematically organized code system was created, it was time to interrogate patterns and relationships in the data. This involved several ways and MAXQDA features:

- Generating a series of charts illustrating the descriptive frequencies of each theme across the client responses, using ***Codes > Code Statistics > Subcode Statistics***.
- Identifying qualitative responses to illustrate them, using ***Visual Tools > MAXMaps***. A unified color scheme was created and used in these charts and maps, and when they had been generated and labelled were sent to a new QTT worksheet.
- Visually analyzing relationship between the themes and four open-questions using ***Visual Tools > Code Relations Browser***. When interrogating at the level of the themes, I switched on the option ***Count hits per document only once*** to count the number of cases, because it was useful to report how many clients expressed a view or experienced an impact, rather than the number of times a theme was mentioned. When interrogating at the code level below the themes, I ensured to switch this option off, because it was useful to report the number of segments coded because that was an indication of its relevance across clients.
- Comparing groups of clients working within different organizational units of the National Health Serivce using ***Mixed Methods > Crosstab***. To form the groups, the code for capturing the organizational unit had been transformed into a categorical document variable using the same called option in the code's context menu. This interrogation did not yield any meaningful differences, and in order to ensure clients' anonymity this information was not used further.

4.6 Produce in-depth report of findings

Once the interrogations had been generated and those to be used in the final report identified, they were exported from MAXQDA. In some instances, the visualizations created within MAXQDA were used as they were, having been edited within MAXQDA to use the color scheme—for example the subcode statistics charts and the maps. In other instances, the frequency information generated within MAXQDA was exported to Microsoft Excel and charts created there, where for example multiple MAXQDA charts needed to be combined to present the findings in the most useful way, or where different visualizations from those possible in MAXQDA at the time where needed. The result was a 40-page report that combined the analysis undertaken in the first and second stages of the project.

5 Lessons learned

This project shows that open-ended questions yield rich and useful responses for understanding impacts in evaluations. The tools within MAXQDA are well suited for surveys of any type, whatever the balance between open- and closed-questions. Through doing this project a few key lessons emerged relating to the process of qualitative evaluations:

- *Take time to plan and prepare before starting analysis in earnest.* Experimentations during planning served to help me familiarize with the data and were therefore an important part of the analytic process. The best choices vary across projects, but time spent experimenting with import options is worth it later on as they affect how data can be displayed and analyzed using MAXQDA's tools.
- *Exploration can provide meaningful insights.* A lot of data can be imported quickly from Excel; not just survey responses like those in this project, but any form of "mixed" qualitative/quantitative data. Once inside MAXQDA, a lot can also be done very quickly to explore these data. In my case time was short, and the initial focus was to generate an overview. The explorations were in themselves powerful analytically, providing meaningful high-level findings that were not only reliable but were returned to for further investigation. When doing evaluations in applied settings this is usually particularly useful because there is often an exploratory objective, and therefore it makes sense to initially understand the high-level picture, before delving deeper into particular areas. Those areas for further investigation may not only be the high-frequency clusters, but also where there are low-frequency anomalies. It is the interconnectivity between the two that MAXQDA provides which allows the relationship between quantitative and qualitative data to be explored.
- *It is important to strike a balance between reporting frequencies and meanings in telling the story of the data.* This is greatly facilitated by the mentioned interconnectivity, but also by the variety of visual tools available in MAXQDA. When reporting findings, it is important to communicate in engaging ways that are appropriate for the audience of each output. For this project, I focused on generating visualizations to communicate the findings in engaging ways that could be easily and quickly understood, rather than lengthy narrative interpretations, as are often common in academic outputs. Feedback on the outputs showed these were powerful, especially the use of MAXMaps to display qualitative responses, the Code Relations Browser, and subcode frequency charts and the tree maps (generated in Excel without outputted frequencies).
- *Document the analysis process.* This is important because being transparent is part of how the quality of an analysis can be illustrated and judged. There are several spaces in MAXQDA that can be used to generate an audit trail of process, including the logbook and the project memo. Wherever the process is documented, it is useful to structure it in such a way that it can be easily understood, and followed by others if replicability is im-

portant. Documenting the process is not just for transparency's sake, but also helps with continuity throughout a project. I've learnt the hard way that failing to keep note of where I have got to at the end of a session means I waste a lot of time getting back up to speed next time I open the MAXQDA project.

Bibliography

Braun, V. & Clarke, V. (2021). *Thematic analysis: A practical guide.* Sage.

Fielding, J., Fielding, N. & Hughes, G. (2013). Opening up open-ended survey data using qualitative software. *Quality & Quantity, 47*(6), 3261–3276. https://doi.org/10.1007/s11135-012-9716-1

Patton, M. Q. (2015). *Qualitative research & evaluation methods: Integrating theory and practice* (4th ed.). Sage.

Woolf, N. & Silver, C. (2018). *Qualitative analysis using MAXQDA: The five-level QDA method.* Routledge.

About the author

Christina Silver is Associate Professor (Teaching) in the department of Sociology at the University of Surrey, from where she runs the CAQDAS Networking Project which raises awareness and builds capacity in the use of digital tools for qualitative and mixed-methods analysis. She is also co-founder and director of Qualitative Data Analysis Services (QDAS). Christina holds a PhD in Sociology and has been using and teaching MAXQDA since 1998 in research courses, workshops, and webinars. Her interests lie in the relationship between qualitative methods and tools, and related pedagogies.

LinkedIn: https://linkedin.com/in/christina-qdas/

ORCHID: https://orcid.org/0000-0002-4614-2165

Using MAXQDA for Mixed Methods Research: An Example Integrating Interview, Survey, and Social Network Data

Sinem Toraman Turk

Abstract

MAXQDA is a useful tool for mixed methods research projects, especially when researchers aim to solve complex research problems by using multiple forms of data. In this chapter, I show how I used MAXQDA for a mixed methods research project in which I aimed to explain how recent doctorates learned about mixed methods research during their doctoral education. The example involves integrating qualitative, quantitative, and social network data. Accordingly, it provides an overview of MAXQDA functions for mixed methods research projects in four major themes: (a) organization and management of data, (b) data analysis, (c) integration, and (d) visualization and reporting. Specifically, I focus on the mixed methods functions (Crosstabs, Interactive Quote Matrix, Side-by-side Display of Results, etc.), statistical features (Frequencies and other descriptive analyses) as well as the visual tools (Code Matrix Browser, Code Relations Browser, MAXMaps) in MAXQDA to demonstrate how researchers can use these tools in mixed methods projects.

Key MAXQDA features covered

- ✓ Import Documents from Excel Spreadsheet
- ✓ Crosstabs
- ✓ Interactive Quote Matrix (renamed to "Segment Matrix" in MAXQDA 24)
- ✓ Side-by-Side-Display of Results
- ✓ Stats: Frequencies
- ✓ Stats: Descriptive Analysis
- ✓ Code Matrix Browser
- ✓ Code Relations Browser
- ✓ MAXMaps

1 Introduction

In my doctoral dissertation, I wanted to explain how recent doctorates, who adopted and used mixed methods research in their dissertations, learned about mixed methods research during their doctoral education. Specifically, my aim was to describe the sources used by recent doctorates to learn about mixed methods research in different socio-ecological contexts (for example, disciplines, institutions) and consider how these sources of learning accounted for variations in recent doctorates' levels of mixed methods research adoption. My

Toraman Turk, Sinem (2024). Using MAXQDA for mixed methods research: An example integrating interview, survey, and social network data. In: S. Rädiker & Michael C. Gizzi (Eds.), The practice of qualitative data analysis. Research examples using MAXQDA, volume 2 (pp. 107-126). Berlin: MAXQDA Press. https://doi.org/10.36192/978-3-948768188_6

dissertation was innovative, because it was an empirical example of intersecting mixed methods research with social network analysis, which was conceptually designed (Toraman & Plano Clark, 2020). In addition, my dissertation brought constant comparison technique from grounded theory (Charmaz, 2014) into the data analysis process to develop an explanation of the sources for learning about mixed methods research within the network of recent doctorates. To analyze and integrate qualitative, quantitative, and social network data, I used MAXQDA functions extensively.

The overarching research question guiding this study was: How did recent doctorates across disciplines learn about mixed methods research through sources? Specifically, the following research questions were addressed in the study:

Quantitative question

1. What was the prevalence of identified sources for learning about mixed methods research among the recent doctorates?

Mixed methods social network analysis questions

2. What sources were the most beneficial in recent doctorates' learning about mixed methods research? And why?
3. What patterns were observed among the sources for learning about mixed methods research within the network of recent doctorates?
4. What were the relationships between the identified sources for learning about mixed methods research and recent doctorates' levels of mixed methods research adoption?

Qualitative question

5. How did socio-ecological factors play key roles in identifying sources for learning about mixed methods research within the network of recent doctorates?

Mixed methods integration question

6. What were the connections among socio-ecological factors and observed patterns among the sources for learning about mixed methods research within the network of recent doctorates?

2 Data collection and methodological approach

In my study, I intersected mixed methods research with social network analysis and created a complex mixed methods research design that is outlined briefly in this section. Using a convergent design logic, I collected qualitative, quantitative, and social network data through an online survey, secondary data analysis, and qualitative semi-structured interviews. The data were collected and analyzed in three waves following the same steps (the numbers of participants refer to the final dataset):

Online survey with open-ended and closed-ended questions (qualitative, quantitative, and social network data from 81 participants)

I started the data collection with an online survey, which consisted of three closed- and two open-ended questions in addition to demographic questions to describe the study sample. The closed-ended questions asked from which source(s) the recent doctorates learned about mixed methods research and how they ranked those sources in terms of importance for learning. These questions were used for quantitative and social network analyses. I analyzed this quantitative data, using descriptive statistics (frequency, percentage, mean, standard deviation) with the statistical tools provided in MAXQDA's Stats menu. For the social network data, I created crosstabs and document comparison charts in MAXQDA and then exported the results. Then, I imported the results in UCINET software and employed multiple social network analysis strategies, including centrality measures (Borgatti et al., 2013), to examine key persons and sources in the network of recent doctorates. The open-ended questions asked about the details of the learning sources identified and why they were found to be beneficial. I analyzed the open-ended responses by using topic coding technique (Richards & Morse, 2007).

Secondary data from ProQuest Dissertations and Theses Global database (quantitative data from the same 81 participants)

This dissertation study built upon a pilot study that I conducted with my colleagues (Toraman et al., 2020) where I created a database and extracted various information about recent doctorates who used mixed methods research in their dissertations. This database included information such as each recent doctorate's publication year of dissertation, institution, the country of the graduate institution, and the type of doctoral degree earned. These four characteristics were retrieved from the ProQuest Dissertations and Theses Global database and served as additional attributes in the social network analysis performed in UCINET for my dissertation study. I used descriptive statistics and crosstabulation to explain the patterns and the connections between two or more variables.

Semi-structured interviews (qualitative data from a subsample of 10 of the 81 participants)

Based on the emerging patterns and findings from the mixed methods social network analysis, I identified and purposefully selected 10 interviewees for the qualitative part of the study. Each interview took about 60 minutes, and I used thematic analysis (Braun & Clarke, 2006) to analyze the transcripts.

To accomplish fully integrated analyses, which call for developing a holistic understanding of the phenomenon through "multiple iterative types of integration" of qualitative and quantitative analyses (Tashakkori et al., 2021, p. 283), I used constant comparison technique. By constantly comparing mixed methods social network analysis results with the qualitative findings and executing new analyses based on the integrated findings, I was able to fully integrate the quantitative, qualitative, and social network analysis results.

In my mixed methods social network analysis study, I used various functions of MAXQDA. In the following sections, I describe each of these features in four major headings: (a) organization and management of data, (b) data analysis, (c) integration, and (d) visualization and reporting.

3 Organization and management of data

The complexity of my study required me to have a thorough data analysis plan for both qualitative and quantitative components as well as integration before actually starting to collect the data. I created some mock data in a MAXQDA project to test out my data analysis plan. This strategy helped me think about how to organize and analyze my quantitative and qualitative data as well as integrate them with social network data and finally led to the organizational choices I made in the Document System as illustrated in Fig. 1.

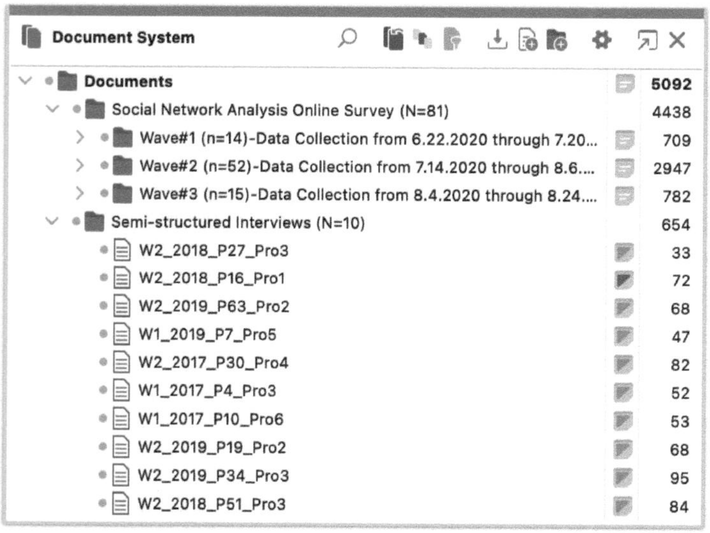

Fig. 1: Organization of the Document System by the types of data

Importing the survey data

For the survey data, I created a document group called "Social Network Analysis Online Survey (N=81)." Using the ***Import > Documents from Excel Spreadsheet*** feature, I imported the survey data collected through the Qualtrics® web-based survey tool. During the import, MAXQDA created one text document for each participant containing their responses to the open-ended questions, while the answers to the closed-ended questions were imported as document variables. To differentiate between data from the three waves, I created three second-level document groups to hold the survey answers for each wave.

For each of the 81 participants, the collected data from the ProQuest Dissertations and Theses Global database was prepared in an Excel spreadsheet. The first two columns of the spreadsheet contained the document group and document name to identify each participant (Fig. 2). The following columns contained the four variables from the database: (1) publication year of dissertation, (2) institution, (3) country of the graduate institution, and (4) type of doctoral degree earned. I imported the Excel file into MAXQDA using ***Variables > Import Document Variables***, resulting in three closed-ended questions and four variables for each participant.

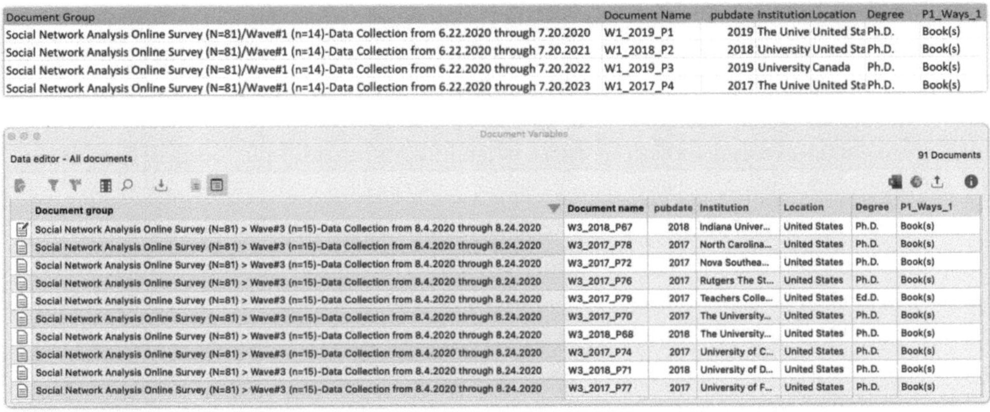

Document Group	Document Name	pubdate	Institution	Location	Degree	P1_Ways_1
Social Network Analysis Online Survey (N=81)/Wave#1 (n=14)-Data Collection from 6.22.2020 through 7.20.2020	W1_2019_P1	2019	The Unive	United Sta	Ph.D.	Book(s)
Social Network Analysis Online Survey (N=81)/Wave#1 (n=14)-Data Collection from 6.22.2020 through 7.20.2021	W1_2018_P2	2018	University	United Sta	Ph.D.	Book(s)
Social Network Analysis Online Survey (N=81)/Wave#1 (n=14)-Data Collection from 6.22.2020 through 7.20.2022	W1_2019_P3	2019	University	Canada	Ph.D.	Book(s)
Social Network Analysis Online Survey (N=81)/Wave#1 (n=14)-Data Collection from 6.22.2020 through 7.20.2023	W1_2017_P4	2017	The Unive	United Sta	Ph.D.	Book(s)

Document Variables

Data editor - All documents

91 Documents

Document group	Document name	pubdate	Institution	Location	Degree	P1_Ways_1
Social Network Analysis Online Survey (N=81) > Wave#3 (n=15)-Data Collection from 8.4.2020 through 8.24.2020	W3_2018_P67	2018	Indiana Univer...	United States	Ph.D.	Book(s)
Social Network Analysis Online Survey (N=81) > Wave#3 (n=15)-Data Collection from 8.4.2020 through 8.24.2020	W3_2017_P78	2017	North Carolina...	United States	Ph.D.	Book(s)
Social Network Analysis Online Survey (N=81) > Wave#3 (n=15)-Data Collection from 8.4.2020 through 8.24.2020	W3_2017_P72	2017	Nova Southea...	United States	Ph.D.	Book(s)
Social Network Analysis Online Survey (N=81) > Wave#3 (n=15)-Data Collection from 8.4.2020 through 8.24.2020	W3_2017_P76	2017	Rutgers The St...	United States	Ph.D.	Book(s)
Social Network Analysis Online Survey (N=81) > Wave#3 (n=15)-Data Collection from 8.4.2020 through 8.24.2020	W3_2017_P79	2017	Teachers Colle...	United States	Ed.D.	Book(s)
Social Network Analysis Online Survey (N=81) > Wave#3 (n=15)-Data Collection from 8.4.2020 through 8.24.2020	W3_2017_P70	2017	The University...	United States	Ph.D.	Book(s)
Social Network Analysis Online Survey (N=81) > Wave#3 (n=15)-Data Collection from 8.4.2020 through 8.24.2020	W3_2018_P68	2018	The University...	United States	Ph.D.	Book(s)
Social Network Analysis Online Survey (N=81) > Wave#3 (n=15)-Data Collection from 8.4.2020 through 8.24.2020	W3_2017_P74	2017	University of C...	United States	Ph.D.	Book(s)
Social Network Analysis Online Survey (N=81) > Wave#3 (n=15)-Data Collection from 8.4.2020 through 8.24.2020	W3_2018_P71	2018	University of D...	United States	Ph.D.	Book(s)
Social Network Analysis Online Survey (N=81) > Wave#3 (n=15)-Data Collection from 8.4.2020 through 8.24.2020	W3_2017_P77	2017	University of F...	United States	Ph.D.	Book(s)

Fig. 2: Importing secondary data as additional document variables (top: data in Excel, bottom: Data Editor of Document Variables in MAXQDA)

Importing and anonymizing the interviews

For the 10 interviews, I created another top-level document group and used ***Import > Transcripts*** function to load the transcripts into the MAXQDA project. As I employed a third-party transcription service, I manually reviewed each interview to ensure data quality, consistency, and accuracy after importing them into MAXQDA. Using MAXQDA's ***Edit mode*** in the Document Browser, I de-identified any information that might violate the confidentiality of the participants. I utilized document memos to categorize and label interviewees based on the total number of sources they mentioned for learning about mixed methods research in the online survey. Each interviewee was assigned a different colored memo (Fig. 1): green memo symbols were used for doctorates who named an above-average number of sources, orange memo symbols for those who identified an average number, and red memo symbols for those who identified fewer sources than the average.

Naming conventions

To organize the data efficiently, I applied naming conventions in the Document System to categorize different data types from different waves. As shown in Fig. 1, I created separate document groups for semi-structured interviews and social network analysis online survey, while adding the sample sizes in parenthesis. In addition, each transcript name followed a specific structure. For example, the semi-structured interview labeled "W2_2018_P27_Pro3" represents a participant in the second wave (W2) who graduated in 2018 (2018), was the 27th participant (P27) in the survey and falls into the Profile 3 category (Pro3) based on the social network analysis results (how I came up with the profiles is explained in section 5 "Integration"). Applying this convention for each participant allowed me to easily know and track whose data I was working with when coding the qualitative data. Similarly, I created a convention for the social network analysis online survey data for each wave. It began with the wave number (Wave#1), followed by the sample size for each wave (n=14), and concluded with the date range for data collection. This approach allowed me to holistically look at the data from each wave and across the waves when integrating multiple forms of the data.

Organization of the code system

Similar to the organization of the Document System, I organized the Code System by different types of data analysis strategies used in the study. As seen in Fig. 3, I created a major code for each type of data in the data analysis process.

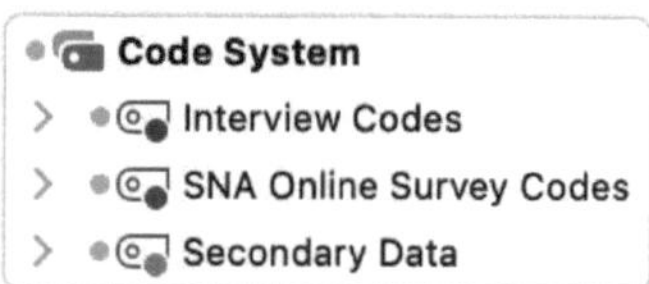

Fig. 3: Organizing the codes for different types of data analysis

Regularly writing logbook entries

From the very first day of developing my database, I used ***Home > Logbook*** function to stay organized and track my progress in my dissertation. As mixed methods research projects take more time due to their complexity and the volume of multiple forms of data collection and analyses, it is important to take some actions during the process and track our progress as detailed as possible to ensure quality in mixed methods research (Fetters, 2020; O'Cathain, 2010; Plano Clark & Ivankova, 2016).

Regularly creating backups

MAXQDA has preferences for ***Automatic Backups*** function that allows researchers to set time intervals in days to create a backup of their MAXQDA file in a specific folder that can be identified. This function not only allows researchers to be protected in case of a system failure but also gives researchers an opportunity to revisit earlier versions of their data analysis files if needed. As mixed methods research involves iterative data collection, analysis, and integration, I found this function extremely useful. Especially when I examined patterns and explored the context-dependent information using constant comparison technique, this function helped me given that the iterative nature of the qualitative coding and integration process required me to revisit or change some of the emergent codes, themes, or integrated findings.

4 Data analysis

To address my first, quantitative research question—*What was the prevalence of identified sources for learning about mixed methods research among the recent doctorates?* —I used MAXQDA Stats. After activating the social network analysis online survey documents in the Document System, I selected ***Stats > Start with Activated Documents*** from the main menu to open the Stats workspace. I first used ***Descriptive Statistics > Descriptive Statistics*** menu to examine the mean and standard deviation in the study sample for the total number of sources used in learning about mixed methods research among the recent doctorates. Then, I followed ***Descriptive Statistics > Frequencies*** menu to examine the prevalence of identified sources for learning about mixed methods research among the recent doctorates. After selecting the variables (that is, sources for learning about mixed methods research) that were of interest, I created a frequency table for each variable in MAXQDA (Fig. 4) and then combined them into a single table for all variables (see Toraman, 2021, p. 113).

Similarly, I used ***Descriptive Statistics > Frequencies*** menu to address the second, mixed methods social network analysis question—*What sources were the most beneficial in recent doctorates' learning about mixed methods research? And why?* —Then, I created figures to present the frequencies and percentages of the most beneficial sources in learning about mixed methods research with a bar chart (Fig. 5). It is important to note that MAXQDA can show absolute and relative frequencies together on the top of the bar charts. I qualitatively analyzed the open-ended follow-up questions in the online survey to address the "why" question and explained the participants' reasons about the importance of these beneficial sources to describe the patterns.

	Frequency	Percent	Percent (valid)	Percent (cum.)
Book(s)	66	81.5	100.0	100.0
TOTAL (valid)	66	81.5	100.0	
MISSING: System	15	18.5		
TOTAL	81	100.0		

Fig. 4: Frequency and percentage table for one of the variables ("Books")

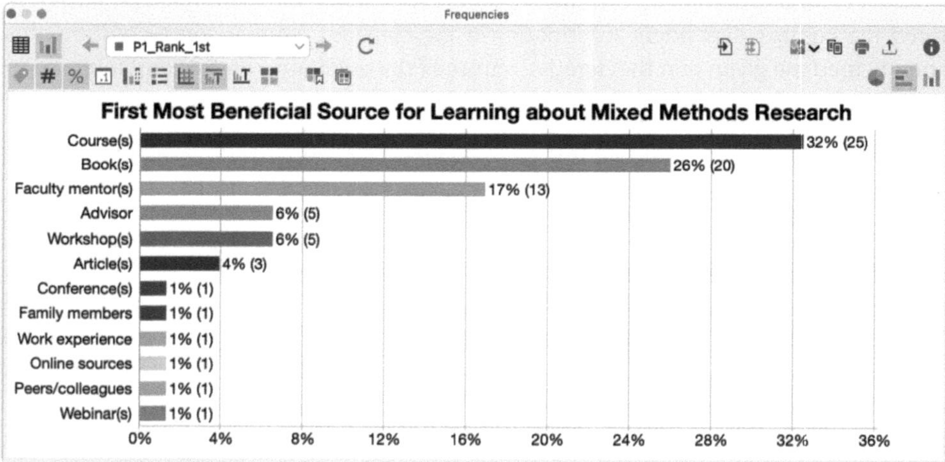

Fig. 5: A bar chart for the frequencies and percentages for the first most beneficial source for learning about mixed methods research

My third and fourth, mixed methods social network analysis questions called for the use of a combination of various social network analysis strategies, quantitative descriptive statistics, and qualitative thematic analysis. To address these research questions, I employed various exploratory social network analysis strategies using UCINET data analysis tool (to learn more about these analyses, see Toraman, 2021). After completing the analysis in UCINET, I brought the resulting social network maps into MAXQDA for the integration of qualitative, quantitative, and social network data at the interpretation and reporting level of the integration (see section 5 "Integration" below). Analysis of the open-ended questions in the online survey helped me explain the patterns explored through the third and fourth mixed methods social network analysis questions.

To address my fifth, qualitative research question—*How did socio-ecological factors play key roles in identifying sources for learning about mixed methods research within the network of recent doctorates?*—I used thematic analysis following the recommended steps by Braun and Clarke (2006). I analyzed the 10 interviews to gain a deeper understanding of recent doctorates' experiences of learning about mixed methods research. I inductively coded the interviews and used conceptual memoing throughout my data analysis due to the nature of the data collection in three waves. Conceptual memoing is defined as a technique that facilitates the process of coding and helps researchers reflect on the emerging codes and ideas (Charmaz, 2014). To accomplish this, I actively used MAXQDA's ***Memos*** function and created free memos that were about emerging ideas and my reflections in the process of coding.

As a result of these processes, my coding system constantly evolved over the course of my data collection and analysis. I used code memos to define each code and as they changed, I revised the definition if needed. I also used color coding strategy for my interview codes and added comments on the coded segments to include any of my takeaways from the coded segment or my notes from the interview related to the information coded in that segment. When I completed the third round of qualitative data collection, I went through all the interview documents to review the coded segments. By activating the codes in the Code System and interviews in the Document System, I used the Retrieved Segments window to focus on addressing my qualitative research question through the lens of socio-ecological factors. The Retrieved Segments helped me read through the codes that I thought that were related to each other. To holistically review the coded segments and group my codes to develop categories and themes, I used ***Codes > Smart Coding Tool*** function where I could see the intersections of multiple codes and review the coded segments, which helped me develop themes (Fig. 6).

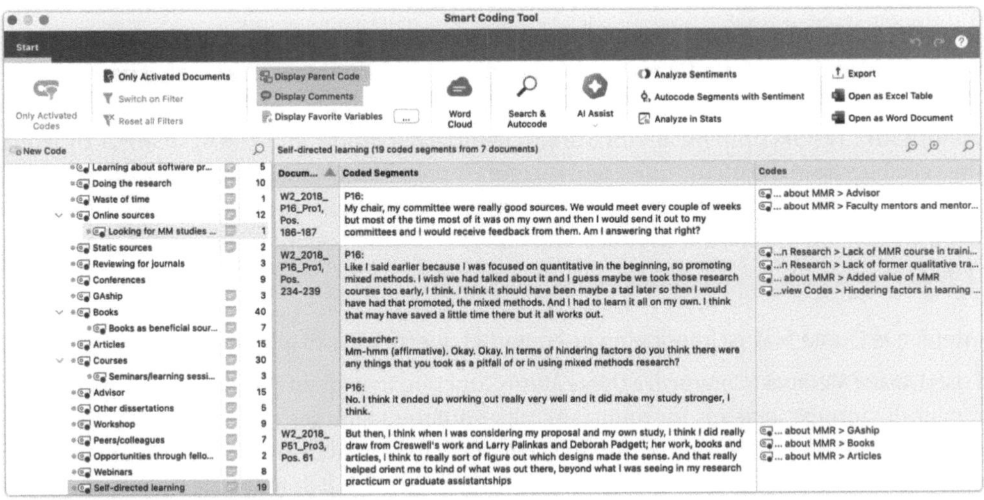

Fig. 6: Using Smart Coding Tool for examining the intersection of the "self-directed learning" code with the other codes when developing themes

5 Integration

To address my sixth, mixed methods integration question—*What were the connections among socio-ecological factors and observed patterns among the sources for learning about mixed methods research within the network of recent doctorates?*—I employed mixed methods integrative analysis (Creswell & Plano Clark, 2018; Fetters et al., 2013; Kuckartz & Rädiker, 2022; Tashakkori et al., 2021). This involved using joint displays and narrative techniques along with the social network maps that were produced based on my mixed methods social network analysis research questions. Joint displays are defined as visual tools that bring the qualitative and quantitative data together to gain insights beyond these methods separately (Fetters et al., 2013).

To integrate qualitative, quantitative, and social network findings, I used various features from MAXQDA's ***Mixed Methods*** menu tab and conducted constant comparison technique to accomplish fully integrated analyses.

Activate documents via variable: Identifying number of sources per interviewee and creating document sets for the learner profiles

To explain the patterns observed among the recent doctorates in their learning about mixed methods research through sources, I started my analyses with ***Mixed Methods > Activate Documents by Variables*** function. I chose total number of source variables as a reference point and activated the documents for those recent doctorates who identified total number of sources more than the average, at average, and below the average. Thus, I could examine how these recent doctorates' experiences of learning about mixed methods research differed based on their socio-ecological contexts. In addition, I created document sets when I merged quantitative, qualitative, and social network data for the integration when interpreting the mixed methods findings. The profiles of recent doctorates were created based on the mixed methods social network analysis results by integrating social network analysis and quantitative results from the online survey. I employed profile analysis in UCINET by using the variables from the quantitative and secondary data as previously explained. Accordingly, I used document sets for organizing the interview data for those profiles of recent doctorates to better explain the context in which and how they learned about mixed methods research (Fig. 7).

Interactive Quote Matrix: Integrating open-ended questions with interviews

I used ***Mixed Methods > Interactive Quote Matrix*** function to explain the contextual meaning of recent doctorates' reasons for their ranking of different sources (retrieved from the open-ended questions in the online survey) and their experiences of learning through those sources (retrieved from the semi-structured interviews). Fig. 8 demonstrates an example for books as the source of learning about mixed methods research for the recent doctorates who were identified as Profile 2.

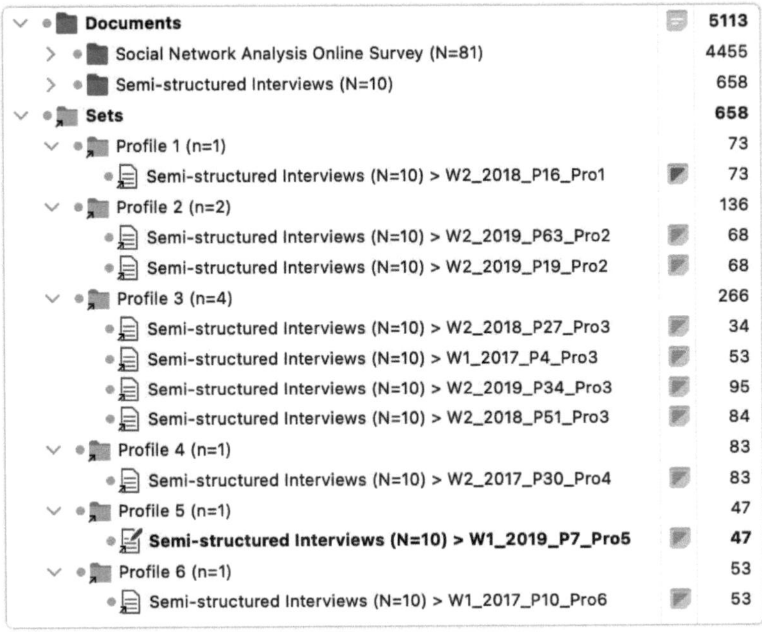

Fig. 7: Creating document sets for the learner profiles

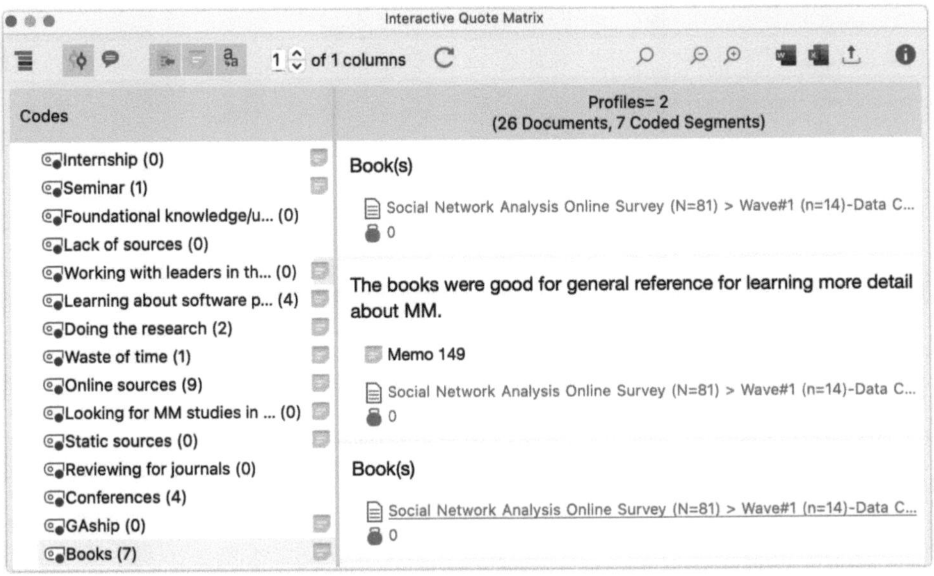

Fig. 8: Interactive Quote Matrix for integrating qualitative open-ended responses from the survey and qualitative interviews for Profile 2 participants

Crosstab: Comparing code frequencies

To do a comparison between the identified sources of learning about mixed methods research and their ranking, I used ***Mixed Methods* > *Crosstab*** function. As seen in Fig. 9, this crosstab allowed me to do a comparison numerically. In addition, by double-clicking on each number in the table, MAXQDA compiled the relevant segment in the Retrieved Segments window, and I could quickly review which participants identified which sources. In addition to the opportunity of comparing these two aspects of the research, I could extract this information as an Excel spreadsheet to use the matrix for further social network analyses.

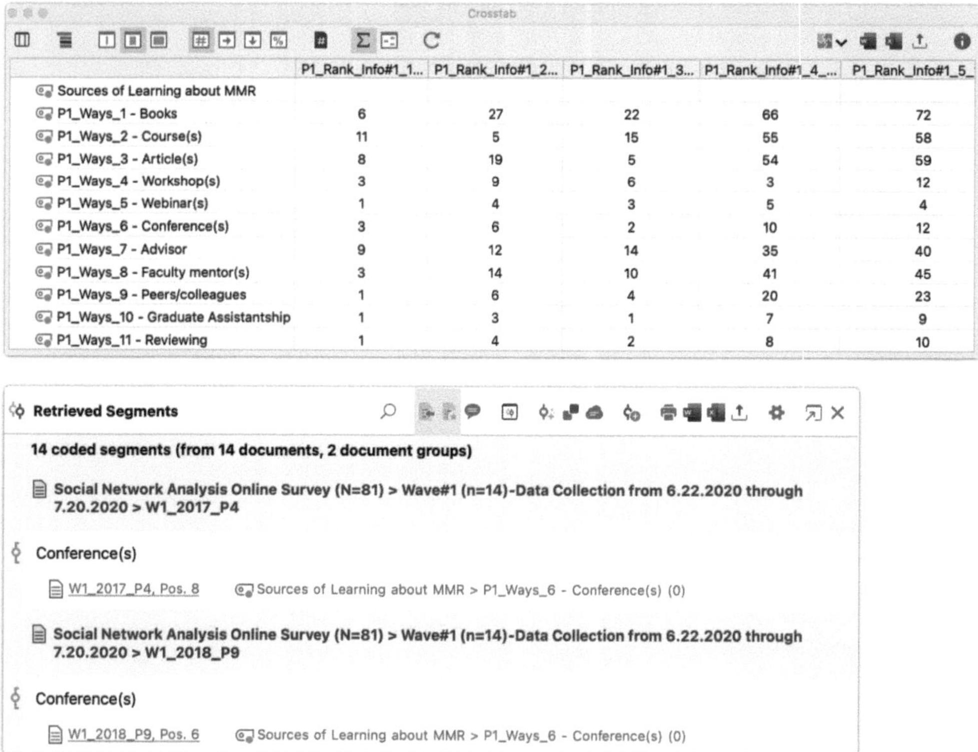

	P1_Rank_Info#1_1...	P1_Rank_Info#1_2...	P1_Rank_Info#1_3...	P1_Rank_Info#1_4_...	P1_Rank_Info#1_5_
Sources of Learning about MMR					
P1_Ways_1 - Books	6	27	22	66	72
P1_Ways_2 - Course(s)	11	5	15	55	58
P1_Ways_3 - Article(s)	8	19	5	54	59
P1_Ways_4 - Workshop(s)	3	9	6	3	12
P1_Ways_5 - Webinar(s)	1	4	3	5	4
P1_Ways_6 - Conference(s)	3	6	2	10	12
P1_Ways_7 - Advisor	9	12	14	35	40
P1_Ways_8 - Faculty mentor(s)	3	14	10	41	45
P1_Ways_9 - Peers/colleagues	1	6	4	20	23
P1_Ways_10 - Graduate Assistantship	1	3	1	7	9
P1_Ways_11 - Reviewing	1	4	2	8	10

Fig. 9: Crosstab for comparison of ranking and identified sources for learning about mixed methods research

Side-by-side Display of Results: Comparing qualitative and quantitative data

When using constant comparison technique for my mixed methods integrated analysis, I also used ***Mixed Methods > Side-by-side Display > Side-by-side Display of Results (Coded Segments)*** function to compare how each participant described their experiences of learning about mixed methods research for the source they identified in the online survey. As seen in Fig. 10, I chose the semi-structured interview and the survey document for the same participant (P16). Then, I reviewed the participant's description of sources and how they were beneficial in their learning about mixed methods research.

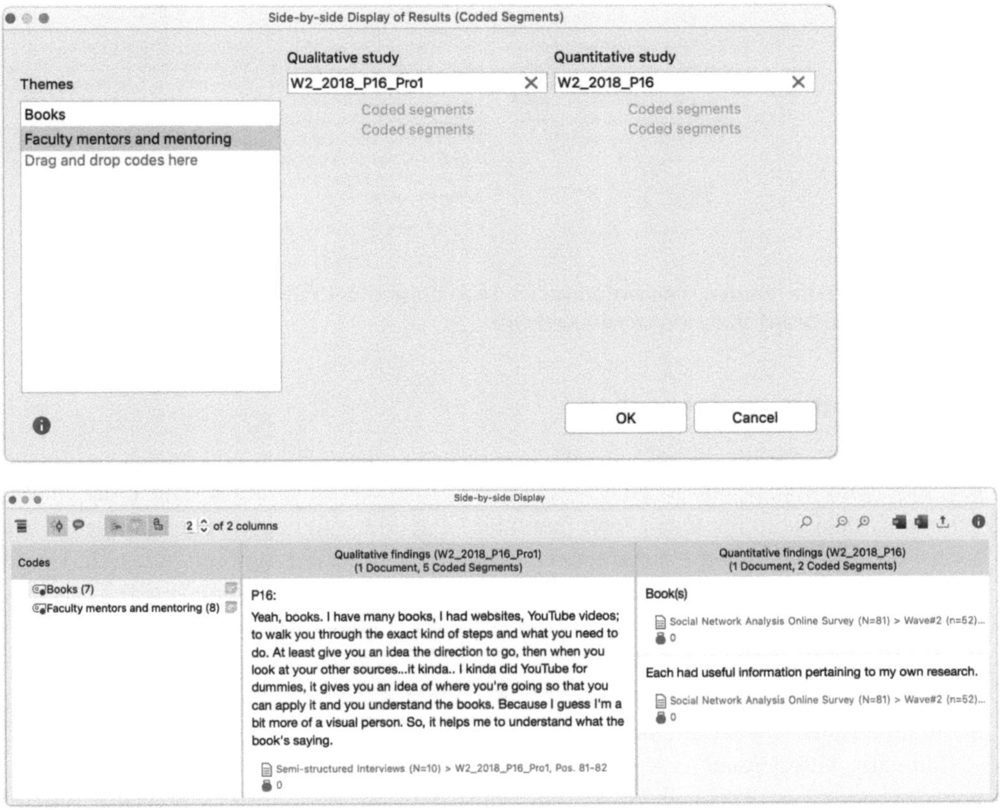

Fig. 10: Side-by-side Display of Results

QUAL Themes by QUAN Groups: Comparing doctoral degrees

In addition to these tools, I used ***Mixed Methods > QUAL Themes by QUAN Groups*** function to explain the role of the socio-ecological context factors in recent doctorates' learning about mixed methods research. For example, as seen in Fig. 11, I reviewed the qualitative themes from the open-ended survey questions for the participants' description of learning about mixed methods research by their doctoral degree type (that is, Ph.D., Ed.D., and D.A.).

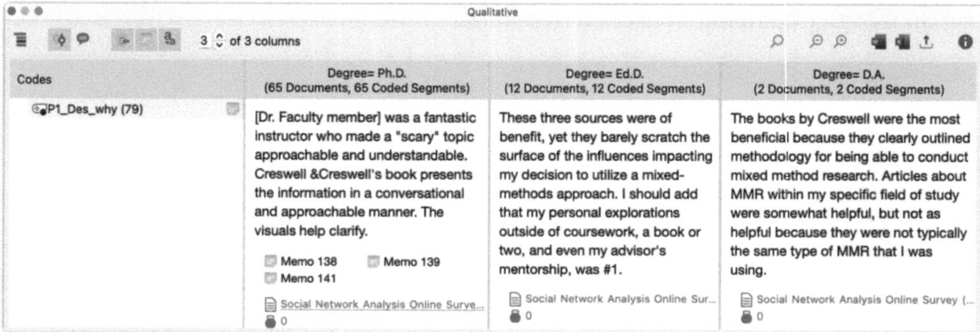

Fig. 11: Qualitative themes by quantitative groups for the participants' description of learning about mixed methods research by their doctoral degree type

6 Visualization and reporting

MAXQDA offers various visual tools that support the presentation and analysis of mixed methods data and results as well as for mixed methods integration. The Code Matrix Browser (available in the ***Visual Tools*** menu tab) helped me to compare the profiles of the recent doctorates by their experiences of learning about mixed methods research. I used this function by choosing document sets as shown in Fig. 12. After exploring the visual in the Code Matrix Browser, I clicked on the first icon to the left to compare the responses in the ***Interactive Quote Matrix*** for each recent doctorate's experiences. This allowed me to better understand how individuals from the same profile had different experiences of learning about mixed methods research.

Similarly, I used ***Visual Tools > Code Relations Browser*** function to explore the relationship between codes. Fig. 13 displays an example from exploring relationships among disciplinary norms and promoting factors in learning about mixed methods research code along with the sources for learning about mixed methods research (that is, conferences, graduate assistantship, books, articles, courses, advisor, workshop, peers/colleagues, and webinars). This function allowed me to understand the role of socio-ecological factors such as disciplinary norms in identifying sources for learning about mixed methods research within the network of recent doctorates.

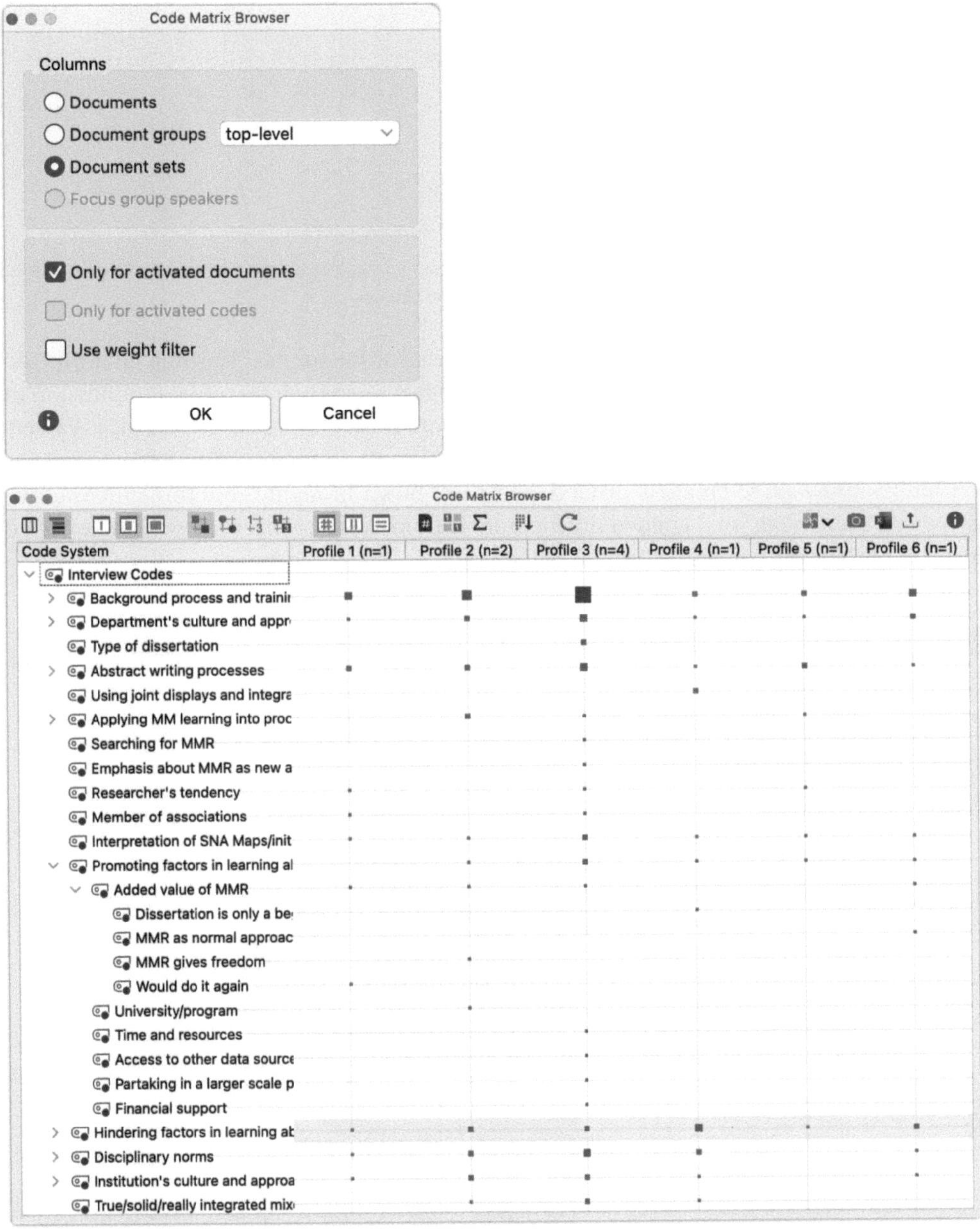

Fig. 12: Using Code Matrix Browser for comparing different document sets in the columns showing the profiles of mixed methods research learners

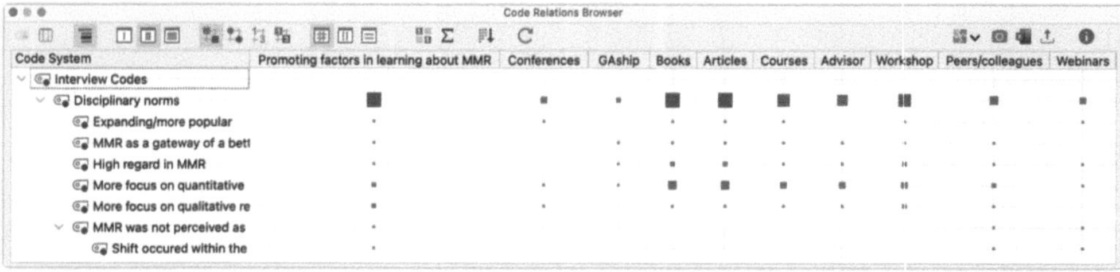

Fig. 13: Code Relations Browser for exploring relationships among disciplinary norms and promoting factors in learning about mixed methods research along with the sources

In my study, I used three theories to explain the recent doctorates' learning about mixed methods research and the role of socio-ecological factors in their learning: (a) diffusion of innovations theory (Rogers, 2003), (b) social network theory (Borgatti et al., 2013; Wasserman et al., 2005), and (c) ecological systems theory (Bronfenbrenner, 1979, 2005). I used ***Visual Tools > MAXMaps*** to create a visual depiction of how I brought these three theories together. As seen in Fig. 14, I created my theoretical framework by inserting shapes, text, and icons to present my conceptualization of integration of the three theories.

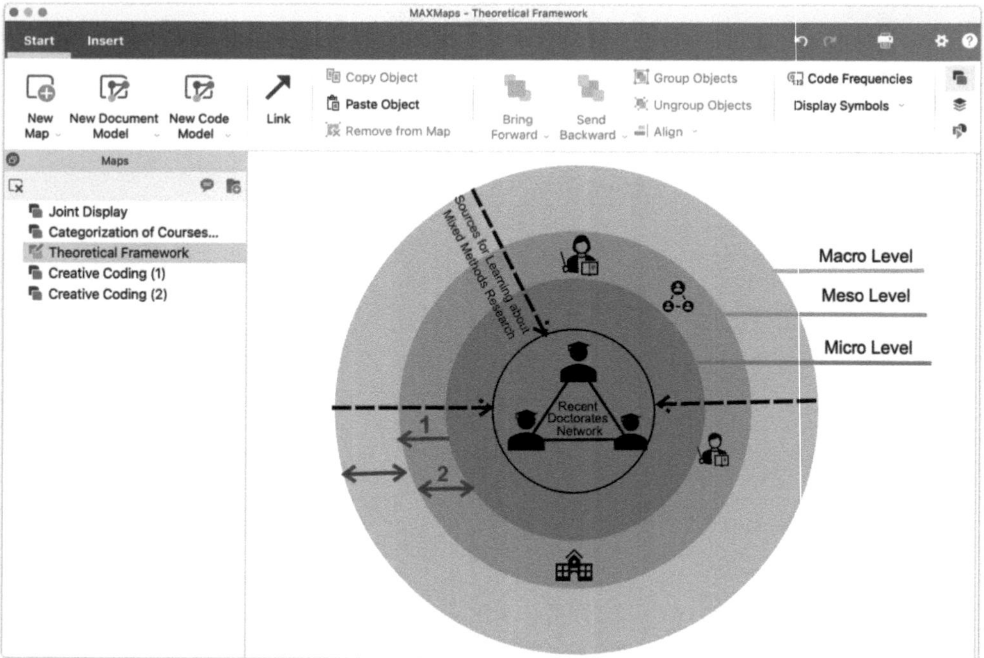

Fig. 14: Using MAXMaps to develop a conceptual framework for the recent doctorates' learning about mixed methods research

I also used ***Visual Tools > MAXMaps*** function to create categorization of courses by recent doctorates' doctoral degree type after inserting the social network map from the UCINET as an image. After inserting shapes to capture clusters of recent doctorates within the network, I clicked on the ⊘ icon on the background spectrum to make sure the network map appears in the back. After adding the relevant text and choosing a color for each group, the map was created and used in the final dissertation as seen at the bottom of Fig. 15.

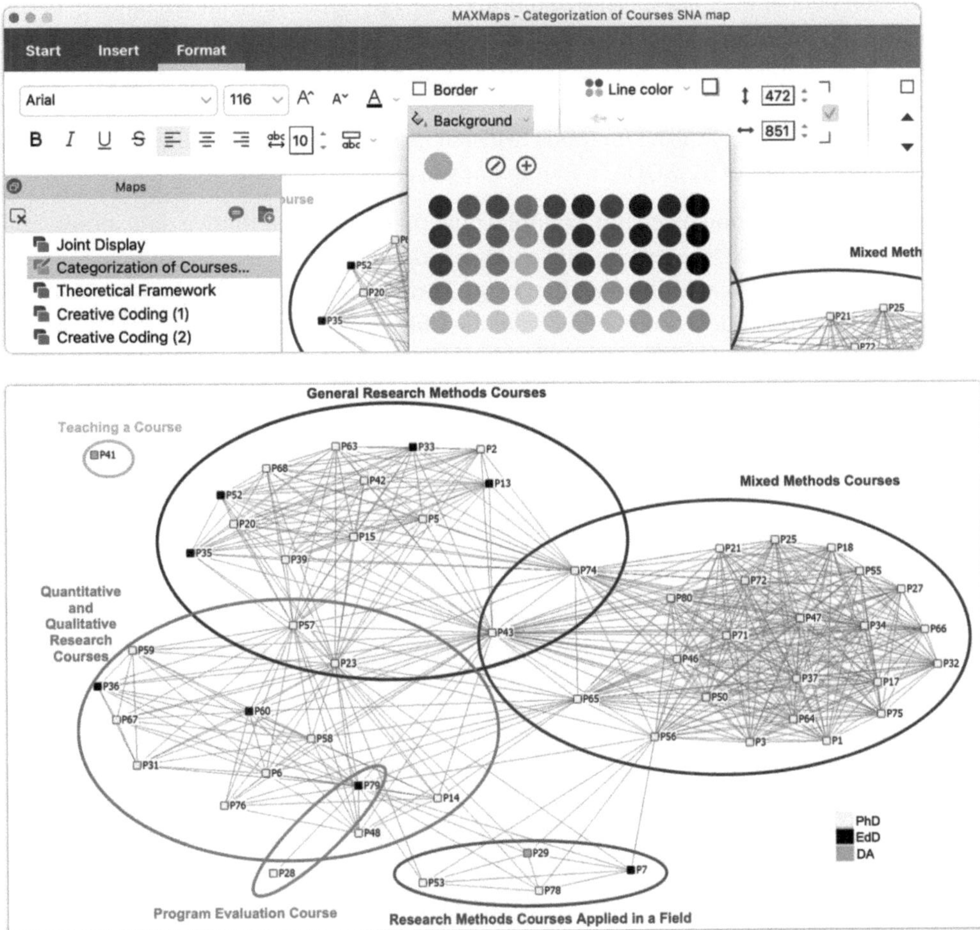

Fig. 15: Using MAXMaps for the categorization of courses by recent doctorates' doctoral degree type

7 Lessons learned

Due to its iterative nature, mixed methods research studies can be very complex and often even overwhelming. In fact, each mixed methods research project is unique and specific to the context in which the phenomenon of interest is studied. Despite the challenges and complexities of this methodology, a well-designed and thoroughly conducted and reported mixed methods research study may help researchers address some complex research problems in their field or area of expertise and bring a new perspective to understanding of the phenomenon. Therefore, rather than hesitating about using mixed methods research, I recommend harnessing various functions of the MAXQDA qualitative and mixed methods data analysis tool to accomplish integration.

When conducting my mixed methods research dissertation study, I benefited from and learned about the use of MAXQDA in four major ways:

- First, having all in one place (for example, qualitative and quantitative data, notes, and memos) made MAXQDA very helpful and user-friendly.
- Second, MAXQDA is a flexible tool that helped me develop naming conventions, organize the data and code system, and create data files (for example, matrices) for further analyses in different programs and tools such as social network analysis and UCINET.
- Third, regularly creating backups with MAXQDA is beneficial, which worked well for me as I was interested in reviewing different versions of my dataset when integrating different types of data through three waves of data collection and comparing the results from different types of data.
- Fourth, various mixed methods research functions in MAXQDA are useful in addressing complex mixed methods research questions.

There are multiple possible ways of using MAXQDA for a mixed methods research project. I conclude with three recommendations for how researchers can improve their use of MAXQDA in future projects:

- *Explore the tool.* MAXQDA is a user-friendly tool that helps researchers choose from a set of menu options that is available to its users. However, it is not limited to those functions but researchers' imagination in ways to organize and analyze their data. Before I started my dissertation data collection, I created a mock dataset to really explore different ways to test the utilities of the tool's functions. One of the examples was that MAXQDA allowed me to create crosstabs and export them in Excel spreadsheets. Using those spreadsheets, I could easily import them to UCINET as matrices for social network analysis. Another creative way of using MAXQDA in my dissertation was the development of the theoretical framework as an integration of three theories as described in the chapter. When exploring MAXQDA, rather than focusing on what it offers, I recommend thinking about what you, as a researcher, want to accomplish with your mixed methods research project and how you can harness those MAXQDA functions to achieve the goals and objectives of your mixed methods project.

- *Develop an optimal organization system.* MAXQDA offers different windows such as Document System and Code System to help researchers organize their data and analysis. When multiple forms of data collection are used in a mixed methods study, it is important to organize them by some forms of categorization or system for both of these windows to easily navigate in MAXQDA when analyzing and integrating multiple forms of data. I recommend not only creating a system of categorization but also some naming conventions to help researchers easily find some important characteristics of those study participants for different forms of data collected in a mixed methods study. Developing an optimal organization system that is unique to each mixed methods research project can ease the mental burden on researchers while they are paying attention to addressing their research questions.
- *Keep a journal.* Because there are best practices for qualitative (Kuckartz, 2014), quantitative (Osborne, 2007), social network (Borgatti et al. 2013), and mixed methods (Creswell et al., 2011) data analyses, it was important for me to implement these practices in my mixed methods research project to ensure the quality of the study. As each methodology has its own set of practices, I personally found keeping a journal as a beneficial strategy throughout the process. Taking reflexive memos along with free memos about the project helps flesh out the ideas while researchers have hard time zooming out in their project to see the big picture. MAXQDA offers a logbook (in the ***Home*** menu tab) in addition to various memo options. I recommend researchers being intentional about their research journey and keeping a journal to accurately report their mixed methods research projects.

I hope that these lessons learned and recommendations help researchers think creatively about their use of MAXQDA for their mixed methods research projects and engage in conversations about different ways of using the tool.

Bibliography

Braun, V., & Clarke, V. (2006). Using thematic analysis in psychology. *Qualitative Research in Psychology, 3*(2), 77-101. https://doi.org/10.1191/1478088706qp063oa

Bronfenbrenner, U. (1979). *The ecology of human development.* Harvard University Press.

Bronfenbrenner, U. (2005). *Making human beings human: Bioecological perspectives on human development.* Sage.

Charmaz, K. (2014). *Constructing grounded theory* (2nd ed.). Sage.

Creswell, J. W., Klassen, A. C., Plano Clark, V. L., & Smith, K. C. (2011). *Best practices for mixed methods research in the health sciences.* Bethesda, MD: National Institutes of Health. https://obssr.od.nih.gov/sites/obssr/files/Best_Practices_for_Mixed_Methods_Research.pdf

Creswell, J. W., & Plano Clark, V. L. (2018). *Designing and conducting mixed methods research* (3rd ed.). Sage.

Fetters, M. D. (2020). *The mixed methods research workbook: Activities for designing, implementing, and publishing projects.* Sage.

Kuckartz, U. (2014). *Qualitative text analysis: A guide to methods, practice, & using software.* Sage.

Kuckartz, U. & Rädiker, S. (2022). Using MAXQDA for integration in mixed methods research. In J. H. Hitchcock, A. J., Onwuegbuzie (Eds.), *The Routledge Handbook of advancing integration in mixed methods research* (pp. 540-562). Routledge.

O'Cathain, A. (2010). Assessing the quality of mixed methods research: Towards a comprehensive framework. In A. Tashakkori & C. Teddlie (Eds.), *SAGE Handbook of mixed methods in social & behavioral research* (2nd ed., pp. 531-555). Sage.

Osborne, J. (2008). *Best practices in quantitative methods.* Sage.

Plano Clark, V. L., & Ivankova, N. V. (2016). *Mixed methods research: A guide to the field.* Sage.

Richards, L., & Morse, J. M. (2007). Coding. In L. Richards & J. M. Morse (Au), *Readme first for a user's guide to qualitative methods* (2nd ed., pp. 133-151). Sage.

Rogers, E. M. (2003). *Diffusion of innovations.* Free Press.

Tashakkori, A., Johnson, R. B., & Teddlie, C. (2021). *Foundations of mixed methods research: Integrating quantitative and qualitative approaches in the social and behavioral sciences* (2nd ed.). Sage.

Toraman, S., Cox, K., Plano Clark, V. L., & Dariotis, J. K. (2020). Graduate students' current practices for writing a mixed methods research study abstract: An examination of doctoral dissertation and master's thesis abstracts in the ProQuest Dissertations and Theses Global™ database. *International Journal of Multiple Research Approaches, 12*(1), 110-128. https://doi.org/10.29034/ijmra.v12n1a4

Toraman, S., & Plano Clark, V. L. (2020). Reflections about intersecting mixed methods research with social network analysis. In D. E. Froehlich, M. Rehm, & B. Rienties (Eds.), *Mixed methods social network analysis: Theories and methodologies in learning and education* (pp. 175–188). Routledge. https://doi.org/10.4324/9780429056826

Toraman, S. (2021). *How Recent Doctorates Learned About Mixed Methods Research Through Sources: A Mixed Methods Social Network Analysis Study* [Doctoral dissertation, University of Cincinnati]. OhioLINK Electronic Theses and Dissertations Center. http://rave.ohiolink.edu/etdc/view?acc_num=ucin1637150105919799

Wasserman, S., Scott, J., & Carrington, P. J. (2005). Introduction. In P. J. Carrington, J. Scott, & S. Wasserman (Eds.), *Models and methods in social network analysis* (pp. 1-8). Cambridge University Press.

About the author

Sinem Toraman Turk, PhD is a research methodologist specializing in qualitative and mixed methods and Associate Research Scientist at the Yale Global Health Leadership Initiative and in the Department of Health Policy and Management in the School of Public Health at Yale University. Dr. Toraman Turk was the recipient of the 2023 American Educational Research Association Mixed Methods Research Special Interest Group Outstanding Dissertation Award, which was the exemplar study used in this chapter. Dr. Toraman Turk has used MAXQDA since 2012 in numerous research and evaluation projects, and she teaches MAXQDA courses as well as delivers workshops and webinars for qualitative and mixed methods researchers across the world.

ORCID: https://orcid.org/0000-0002-5837-4414

ResearchGate: https://www.researchgate.net/profile/Sinem-Toraman-Turk

Using MAXQDA for a Large Qualitative Dataset: Identifying Relevant Data and Analyzing It With Thematic Analysis

Christian Schmieder, Allison Rogers

Abstract

In this chapter, we show how MAXQDA's automatic text searches, document groups, and complex coding queries were used to identify and manage relevant data in a large qualitative dataset of over 6,000 records. We illustrate how we iteratively coded and re-coded the identified data with the goal of generating an overview of our organization's work with First Nations in Wisconsin. To this end, we show how generic analytic steps common in thematic analysis (familiarization with data; development of codes; writing analytic notes; iteratively refining codes, coding, and code definitions) can be conducted in MAXQDA. Specifically, we show how we procedurally combined functions for sorting of data (codes), annotation (code comments), and summation (code memos) to bring this iterative process to life.

Key MAXQDA features covered

- ✓ Import Documents from Excel Spreadsheet
- ✓ Text Search & Autocode
- ✓ Activate Documents Containing This Code
- ✓ Complex Coding Queries
- ✓ Project memo
- ✓ Code memos
- ✓ Comments on coded segments
- ✓ Overview of Coded Segments

1 Introduction

In this chapter, we use the example of an analysis of educational and outreach activities of about 500 professional community-based educators, outreach specialists, and faculty in the Division of Extension at the University of Wisconsin – Madison. The goal of our analysis was to better understand the scope and nature of our organization's work with First Nations (that is, communities and groups whose ancestors were the original peoples of North America). A secondary goal was to explore how this work connected to the broader goals outlined in university-wide strategic planning. Our deliverable consisted of an overview that described areas of educational focus which included frequency assessments (total initiatives, initiatives by programmatic area, development over time, distribution of actions to expand

Schmieder, Christian & Rogers, Allison (2024). MAXQDA for a large qualitative dataset: Identifying relevant data and analyzing it with thematic analysis. In: S. Rädiker & Michael C. Gizzi (Eds.), The practice of qualitative data analysis. Research examples using MAXQDA, volume 2 (pp. 127–147). Berlin: MAXQDA Press.
https://doi.org/10.36192/978-3-948768188_7

access/provide equitable programming across educational foci). In addition, we created annotated lists of educational activities structured by themes to support strategic planning efforts in our organization.

2 Data collection and methodological approach

The data used in this chapter consists of over 6,000 written educational activity reports that describe the educational and outreach efforts of about 500 professional community-based educators, specialists, and faculty in the State of Wisconsin. Each record includes brief narratives related to the audience being served, the type of education, what participants learned or did, and how the learning outcomes connect to broader societal issues. In addition, each record contains information on strategies to expand access to under-served and under-represented audiences, information related to the geographies served, and information related to institutional educational outcomes and institutional program affiliation. These records are collected monthly in our internal reporting system, and employees in educational roles annually share about 3,000 of these records. The records are used by evaluators, program managers, educators, and communications staff to evaluate the outcomes and direction of our work, and to communicate its scope and impact to partners, funders, and the general public.

We utilized a series of generic analytic steps that are commonly found in many qualitative approaches and that have been closely associated under the umbrella of thematic analysis (for example, Braun & Clarke, 2006, 2022; Boyatzis, 1998; Guest et al. 2012)[1] or qualitative content analysis (for example, Kuckartz & Rädiker, 2023; Mayring, 2021). The key procedural tasks of our analysis involved: (1) familiarizing ourselves with the data; (2) utilizing existing broad areas of interest as starting points for coding; (3) engaging in an iterative process of searching, reviewing, and modifying clusters of data; (4) generating a report for our stakeholders.

In this chapter, we focus on the concrete implementation (the "how to") of these generic steps, rather than anchoring common techniques in any specific tradition of thematic analysis. However, we believe that the demonstrated workflows, due to their generic nature, can be transferred to various analytic workflows or methods.

1 Please note that there are different ways of framing thematic analysis, and our framing is more in line with Boyatzis (1998) and Guest et al. (2012) than with reflexive thematic analysis proposed by Braun and Clarke (2006, 2022).

3 Importing a large qualitative dataset into MAXQDA

We first exported the data from our internal reporting system into a Microsoft Excel file (Fig. 1). To reduce the number of records being imported into MAXQDA, we filtered out reports that had not received approval through our internal quality control processes. Other pre-import steps included:

- Making sure the headers of our Excel columns were descriptive for each component of the record, without being too long, because MAXQDA uses this information to create the code and variable names upon import.
- Identifying one column in the Excel spreadsheet to serve as distinctive identifiers for each record, which later became the document name in MAXQDA. We used record IDs from our reporting system; in other analyses based on online survey data, we typically use the response ID created by default in online survey software. We changed the heading for the record ID column in Excel to "Document Name" to facilitate the import in MAXQDA. We also created a new column in the Excel file named "Document Group" and specified a group name for every document (in our case "First Nations"). This way all data would be imported into one specific document group in MAXQDA.

	A	B	C	D	E	F
1	**Document Group**	**Document Name**	**Abstract Sentence**	**Type of activity**	**Outcome Statement**	**Report Year**
2	First Nations	4829	A series of presentations for Native Americans where they learn how cultural knowledge and water science can connect on water topics. This effort was designed to increase Native American confidence to be local advocates for water.	Programming/work that occurred/is occurring	Tribal Nations have been stewards of the local water resources in the area for a very long time. Cultural knowledge gained from this long relationship with the nature, also known as traditional ecological knowledge, is a needed perspective when addressing water issues. Roberts created and delivered a series of presentations, titled Izhi-Nibi: Water Ways, at the Lac Courte Orielles Ojibwe College St. Croix Outreach Center to community members. Topics included watersheds, manoomin (wild rice), and fish including ogaa (walleye) and name (lake sturgeon). The program was designed with input from the outreach center coordinator and an educator. The goal was to build connections between traditional ecological knowledge and western science. By building connections between cultural knowledge and science, Ojibwe community members will gain confidence in bringing their perspective to local water issues.	2021
	First Nations	5195	Technical assistance for a retreat for Community Leadership Alliance (CLA) of	Programming/work that occurred/is occurring	Developed a outline for a board retreat which would enable the board of directors to collectively evaluate the current status of the leadership	2021

Fig. 1: Sample of data prepared in Excel for import into MAXQDA

We imported the data into a new MAXQDA project using ***Import > Documents from Excel Spreadsheet***. This feature creates a text document for each record, containing the qualitative text data, and document variables with standardized information for each record. MAXQDA will take some time to import several thousand records at once. Therefore, we tested the import process with a small test file of about two dozen records to ensure the data was imported in a way that was conducive to our analysis. This helped us confirm which data should be imported as variables, as codable text, as both, or not at all. Then we moved forward with importing all our data into MAXQDA (Fig. 2).

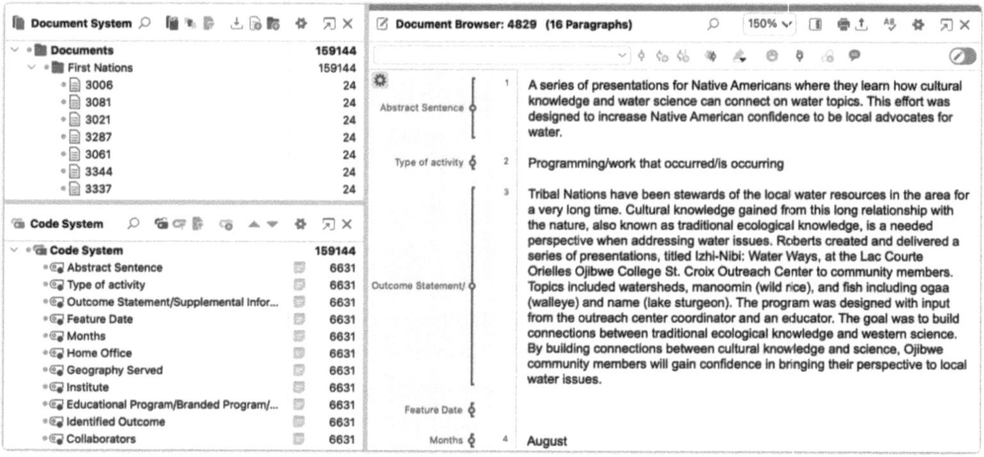

Fig. 2: Data upon being imported into MAXQDA from Excel

4 Identifying relevant data in the large dataset

We had imported about 6,000 reports into MAXQDA, but this included educational work from all communities we serve in Wisconsin. Thus, we needed to start identifying the records that were relevant to our analysis—that is, those that related to work with First Nations communities in Wisconsin.

4.1 First step: Text searches

To filter our dataset, we utilized a list of terms and names related to the First Nations of Wisconsin (for example, *Bad River, Chippewa, Lac du Flambeau, Oneida,* as well as general terms like *tribal nation, indigenous, First Nation,* etc.) that had been developed in a similar previous analysis, and with additional input from our educators and outreach specialists. These terms helped us cast a wide net for outreach work related to First Nations. We deliberately aimed to include more records at this early data management stage, rather than prematurely excluding relevant results. We started the ***Text Search & Autocode*** tool from the ***Analysis*** menu tab, entered all search items into the search dialog (Fig. 3), and ran a search in all documents.

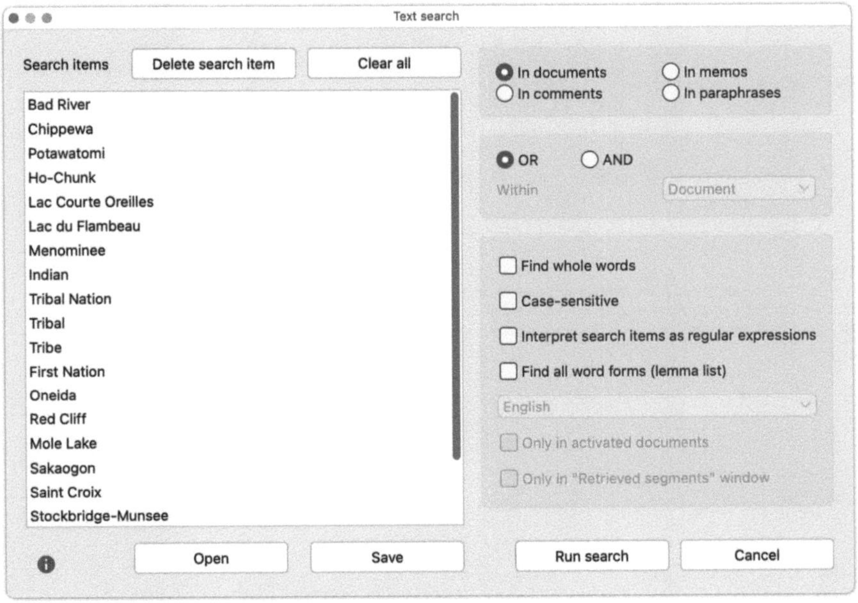

Fig. 3: Text search dialog with all search items for broad screening

The search resulted in more than 3,000 text segments across more than 1,300 documents. By scanning through a random sample of search hits in the search results window, we confirmed that the search results provided relevant results. We used the ***Autocode search results with new code*** icon in the results window to code all search results into a new code ("Autocode - First Nations"). We chose to code the entire paragraph in which the term was found (Fig. 4), which was important for complex coding queries we describe in steps that follow.

In our projects, we typically call such codes "helper codes," because they help us sort documents and organize data on a managerial level (rather than serving as a node for data connected to a thematic area). From here on out, we used this new helper code to sort relevant documents and create document groups based on relevance.

4.2 Second step: Using document groups to re-scope the dataset

The dataset we imported into MAXQDA contained over 150,000 coded segments created automatically upon import. A file this big was unwieldy to manage, because both routine coding operations (coding data, moving coded segments, ad-hoc retrievals, etc.) and complex analysis features (such as crosstabs, complex retrievals, etc.) were slow. Our next step was therefore to delete all data that we had identified in the previous step as not containing information related to First Nations audiences.

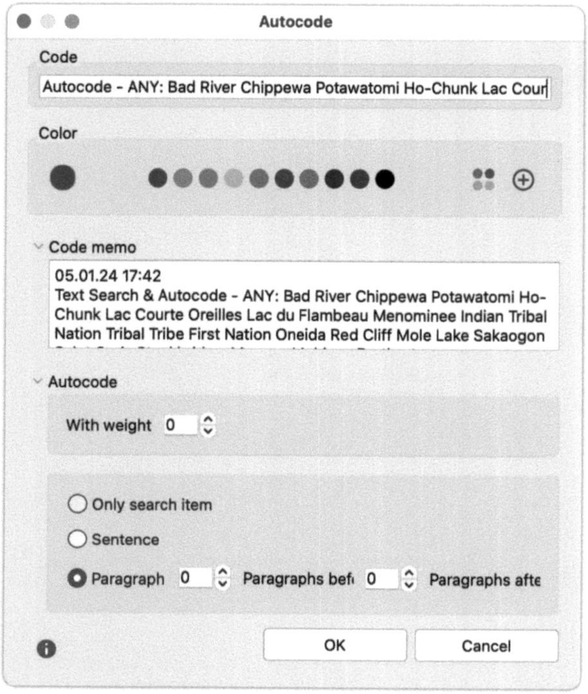

Fig. 4: Autocoding of relevant search hits, specifying the paragraph as the unit of code length. When creating new codes via the auto code function, MAXQDA automatically documents the search terms in the code memo.

To do this, we created a new document group that contained only the records that we had identified as possibly relevant via our earlier autocoding. To create this document group, we first right-clicked on the helper code in the Code System and selected ***Activate Documents Containing this Code***. In the Document System, we then created a new document group, right-clicked on the new document group, and selected ***Move Activated Documents Here*** (Fig. 5). This moved all documents that contained our helper code into one document group. We named this group "potentially relevant" to indicate that more sorting needed to be done with these documents (see following steps).

The remaining documents (those not coded during the previous text search) were left in the initial import document group. We decided to delete these documents to improve software performance. Before the deletion, we first randomly selected 100 documents via the ***Activate Documents by Random*** function (accessible in the Document System root context menu). We then read through the 100 documents to be sure we were not missing relevant documents that for some reason were not found by the search (for example, if a relevant term was accidentally omitted from the search). We created a backup of the file in case we needed to get back to the full dataset and then deleted all records that did not contain our helper code "Autocode - First Nations." Deleting over 4,500 documents from the file greatly helped with software performance during subsequent searches and coding.

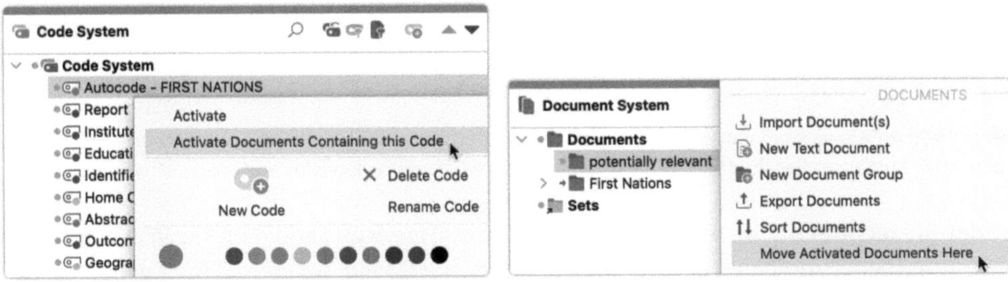

Fig. 5: Activating documents coded with our helper code in the Code System (left) and creating a new document group in the Document System (right)

4.3 Third step: Using complex coding queries to further specify relevant data

We had already narrowed down our dataset from over 6,000 records to about 1,300 records, but we were aware that several records did not provide specific information to answer our question. Our goal was to create a dataset containing every record either focused solely on First Nations audiences or explicitly mentioning a First Nations audience as part of the report narrative (regardless of whether the First Nations audiences were the only targeted audience or one of many). To identify these records, we performed a series of complex coding queries.

Our first task was to identify records that indicated First Nations audiences and communities as the only underserved or underrepresented audience reached. We collect this information in our reporting system using a controlled multi-select field. This information was coded automatically with "Audiences Reached" when we imported the data into MAXQDA. Now, we needed to sift the dataset for records where the *only* selected audience reached consisted of persons who identify as American Indian or Alaska Native (which is one of the multi-select options in the reporting form).

To provide an illustration, documents we wanted to include in our analysis were coded like this:

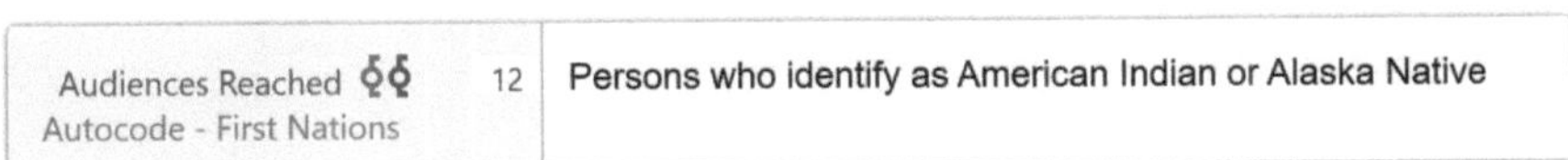

A record where "American Indian or Alaska Native" was the only selected Audience Reached. Based on our earlier autocoding, the two codes "Audiences Reached" and "Autocode - First Nations" overlap completely.

Documents we wanted to exclude from our analysis were coded like this:

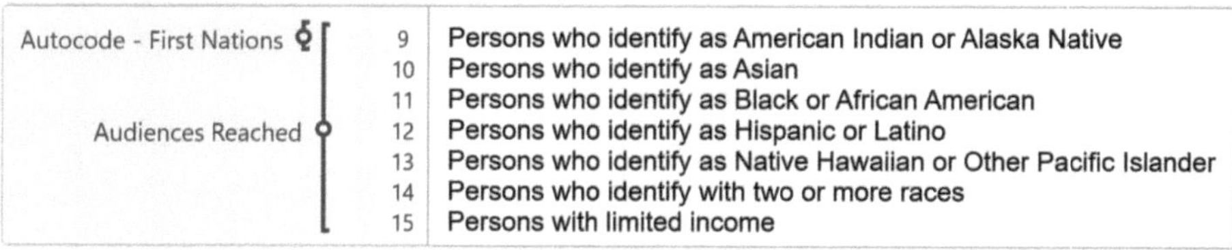

A record where "American Indian or Alaskan Native" was not the only selected Audience Reached, so that text coded with "Audiences Reached" was not the same text as what was coded with "Autocode - First Nations."

To identify records where "Persons who identify as American Indian or Alaska Native" was the only audience indicated in the "Audiences Reached" field, we started the ***Analysis > Complex Coding Query*** tool. In the dialog, we selected the "If inside" query function, and then dragged the "Audience Reached" code into field A and the "Autocode - First Nations" code into field B (Fig. 6). This allowed us to reveal all coded segments with complete congruency between both codes as displayed in the screenshot before, while ignoring all documents where "Audience Reached" was larger than the "Autocode - First Nations" code.

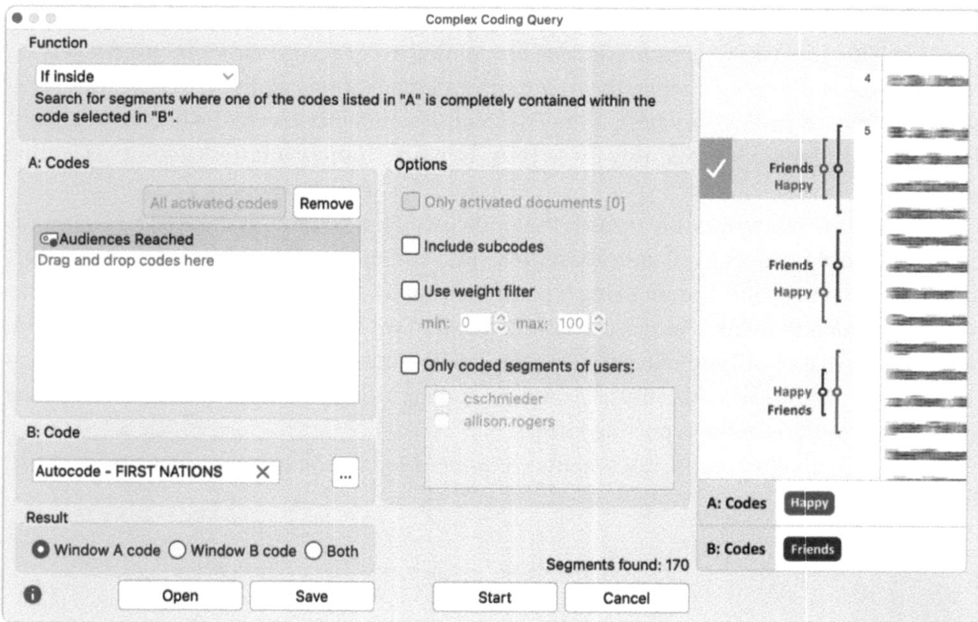

Fig. 6: A complex 'If inside' query in MAXQDA

This query yielded 170 hits from 170 documents. We coded these retrieved segments with a new code, “Audience Served = FN only,” and we then moved these documents to a new document group named “Analysis,” using the same steps as explained in section 4.2. However, at this point we did not delete any data, since we needed to run another query identifying all records where our search terms related to First Nations were present in any of the reports’ narrative fields.

In our data, these fields are the “Abstract Sentence,” where educators briefly describe the work that took place, and the “Outcome Statement,” where educators describe the impact or outcomes of their work in more detail. Educational efforts that explicitly engaged with First Nations would use terms present in our broad text search. To filter for those records, we used another complex coding query. This time, the goal was to find where the First Nations terms, coded with “Autocode - First Nations,” were found in the “Abstract Sentence” or “Outcome Statement” fields. Under the ***Analysis*** tab, we once more selected the ***Complex Coding Query*** function and used the “If inside” function. We selected the helper code “Autocode - First Nations” for field A, and the code “Abstract Sentence” for field B to find segments where both code A and B were present. This turned up over 160 hits, which we coded with a new helper code “FN in Abstract Sentence,” then repeated this complex query with the code “Outcome Statement” which was also created during import. We coded these results with a new helper code “FN in Outcome Statement.”

We then merged our helper codes into one helper code, “FN in Abstract Sentence/Outcome Statement,” containing over 250 coded segments from over 250 documents (the number is smaller than the sum of the three queries, because some records were caught in multiple complex queries). We then activated all documents that contained the helper code and moved the activated documents into our previously created “Analysis” document group. Because we had done several iterations of searching, sifting, and winnowing documents down from initial import, we were reasonably sure we had not left any relevant documents behind in the “potentially relevant” document group. However, we decided to not further delete these documents because the MAXQDA file ran smoothly, and because we wanted the option to go back to the data if necessary.

5 Iterative development of themes

5.1 Creating thematic collections of data through a core analysis loop

Now that we had identified the key data for our analysis, we were ready to begin the process of developing themes. We did this through an analysis loop (Fig. 7) that focused on collaborative and iterative development.

In every analysis session, we would (1) continually anchor our analysis in the session's key analysis question; (2) document in comments how each segment of data related to or answered this question/anchor; (3) review both our comments and coded segments to develop and modify possible themes; (4) "try on" emerging themes by doing additional coding of new data or by re-coding previously coded data and (5) continually review themes for internal consistency and external difference. In the remainder of this chapter, we will describe in more detail how each one of the steps played out.

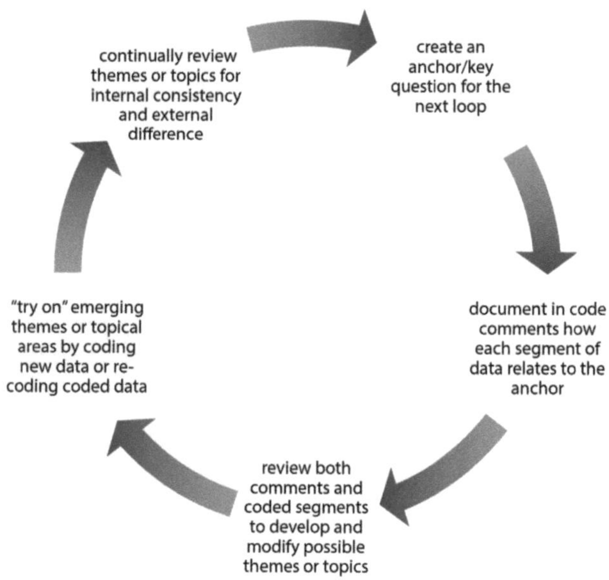

Fig. 7: Key analysis loop for theme development

Whenever possible, we analyzed data together, by either working in the same room, or by screensharing via online call. This was a key mechanism to establish "social reliability" (Sanders & Cuneo, 2010): team analysis practices that foster and require consensus and discursive agreement. Analyzing data together ensured that we checked and called out each other's biases and "voices of preoccupation" (Lawrence-Lightfoot & Davis, 1997), and that we created and maintained a shared understanding of the data, the analysis process, our interpretations, and the goal of our analysis.

During the lifespan of a project, we work through the analysis loop many times. In this example, we will first illustrate how we used the analysis loop during the initial familiarization with the data and initial code development. We then show how we used this loop to iteratively develop our themes with the goal of understanding the nature and scope of our organization's work with First Nations in Wisconsin.

Step 1: Anchoring how we read the data in a concrete analysis question

We make an explicit effort to ground every analysis session—and every key task of the analysis—in a concrete question. This fosters alignment between analysts and supports goal setting during a co-analysis session. Throughout an analysis session we typically remind each other of the key analysis question whenever we lose focus, or when we work through tough decisions.

The analysis question continually changes, based on the analytic task at hand. For example, during initial familiarization with the data, the analysis question will be very broad. We started with "What is the nature and scope of Extension's educational work in and with First Nations?" When working on specific themes or aspects of the data, the analysis question became more concrete. For example: "What are different approaches to food security education in First Nations?" The analysis question is a heuristic to make explicit the goal and focus of our analysis; it provides direction to each analytic task.

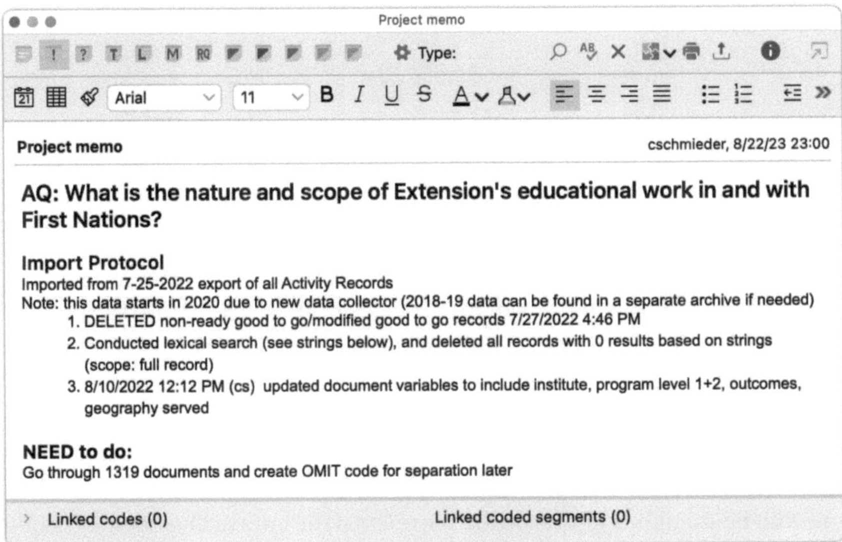

Fig. 8: Anchoring memo with import protocol and to-do list

We documented our analysis questions in a top-level document memo so that we could quickly access them; occasionally, we kept the memo open as a reminder while we analyzed. Typically, we also use the same memo to save our import protocol and to-do lists (Fig 8). Revisiting this memo at the beginning and end of each analysis session helped us to stay focused and on track with the project over time, particularly when we had not looked at the data for several days.

Step 2: Writing how each segment of data relates to the anchoring question

To familiarize ourselves with the data, we explored how our colleagues' reports could help us answer our analysis question. We decided to read 30–40 random records to get started. We focused on the more information-dense part of our data, the "abstract sentence." We created a helper code called "Abstract Sentence Theme," opened a document, read the abstract out loud, and coded it with our helper code. Next, we discussed how the information connected to our question, and we added a rephrased summary of the relevant information into the code comment for the segment we just coded (Fig. 9).

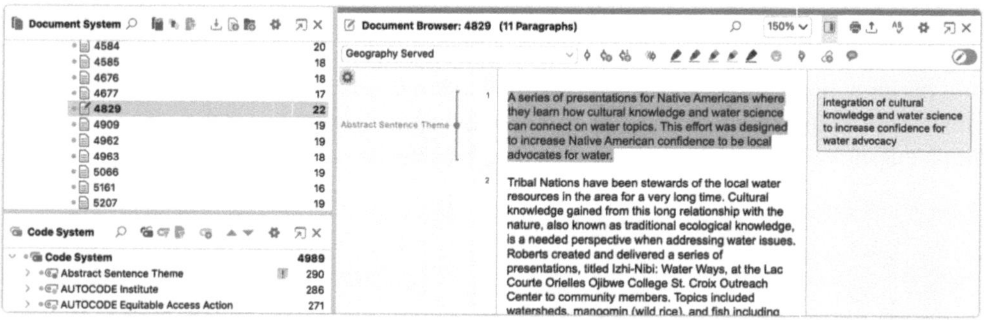

Fig. 9: Coding and annotating data during the first round of coding. The code comment is displayed on the right of the screen.

After coding a document, we changed its color in the Document System to keep track of which data we had already analyzed. Since our analysis process consisted of multiple rounds of coding and re-coding, we used different colors for different coding cycles. This ensured that no data was overlooked in any coding round.

Step 3: Developing initial themes by reviewing coded segments and comments

After about an hour of relating abstract sentences to the analysis questions (via code comments), we began to develop initial themes that could help us understand the nature of our colleagues' work with First Nations in Wisconsin. We opened the tabular Overview of Coded Segments by double-clicking on our helper code "Abstract Sentence Theme" to list all code comments. We then discussed which educational topic areas we repeatedly saw reflected. During this scan, we looked at our code comments and the corresponding data that was coded.

Step 4: Testing a coding scheme

During the initial familiarization, we noticed some overlap between our code comments and the broader strategic plan that was jointly developed by First Nations leaders and the University of Wisconsin. This plan scoped out broad areas of interest, such as "Health," "Environment and Natural Resources," "Language and Culture," "Education Pathways." We decided to first group the data into the areas of interest. This would help us understand how our organizations' work related to these broad strategic areas, and it would help identify where we had to develop a more intricate coding scheme to better represent the data (in other words: to adequately reflect the work of our colleagues in relationship with this broader framework).

To do this, we "tried on" the categories from the strategic plan. We started to code the segments we had previously annotated, using the pre-existing, broad thematic areas of interest. Whenever we were unsure whether a piece of data would fit into these categories, we assigned it a helper code that we called "Unsure." The goal was not to "force" data into these tentative categories but to scope out and try on to what extent this coding scheme needed to be modified.

Throughout the process, our goal was to make consensual decisions. Whenever we could not agree, for example, on the scope or meaning of a theme or how a set of data should be coded, we typically "shelved" the issue by documenting it. For disagreements on the segment level, we typically coded the segment with our "unsure" helper code, and we used the respective code comment to document our positions or conflict. For broader, or more conceptual disagreements, we typically noted the disagreement as short narratives in code memos.

Step 5: Continually reviewing codes for internal consistency and external difference

After re-coding our initial subset of data, we examined all coded segments and comments in our "unsure" helper code. We typically did this by either opening the Overview of Coded Segments with a double-click on the code (Fig. 10) or by compiling them in the Retrieved Segments window, activating all documents and the helper code. We then carefully reviewed and discussed the segments to identify any patterns indicating the need for additional codes. Early on, we found that a major topical area mentioned in our data ("Organizational development support and community development support") was not explicitly outlined in the list of priorities that served as our initial reference point.

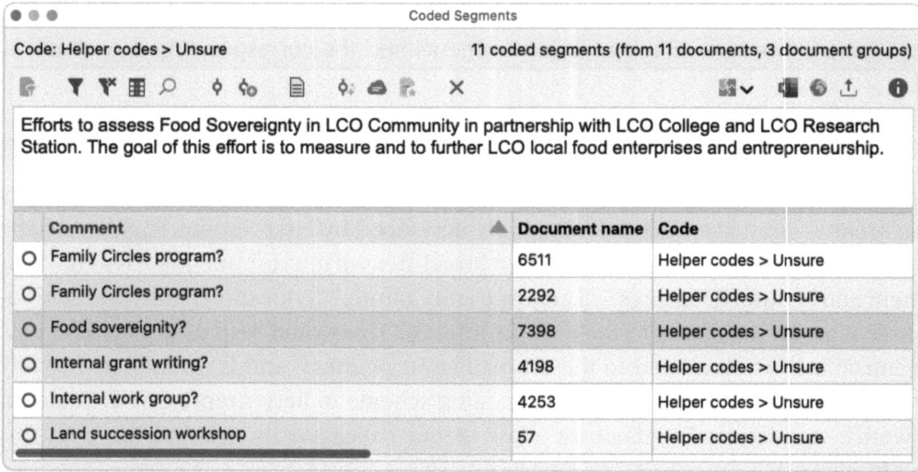

Fig. 10: Overview of Coded Segments, listing coded segments with comments in the *'Unsure'* code. In each analysis loop, we reviewed all segments in the *"Unsure"* category to determine if they could be assigned to existing codes or if they formed clusters that justified the creation of new emergent codes.

To accommodate this, we created a new code, "Community/Organizational Development Support" and documented our discussion and tentative definition in the code memo (Fig. 11). Subsequently, we moved the respective segments from the "Unsure" code to the new code. In a sense, we returned to the previous step—trying on adaptations—for a few minutes, testing our ad hoc modification to the coding system.

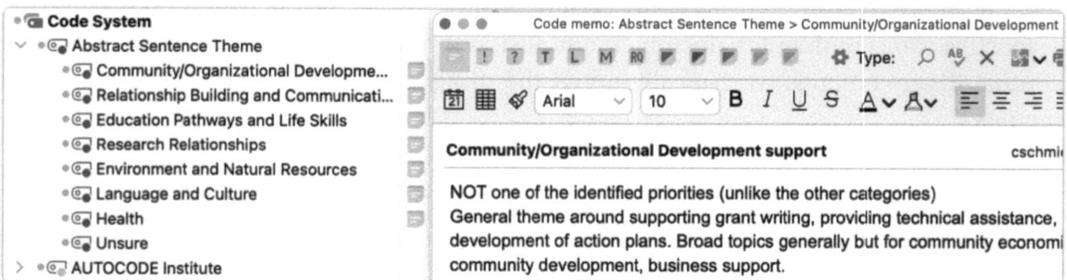

Fig. 11: An initial set of codes based on our first scan of the data, including code memos. The memo corresponds to the code *"Community/Organizational Development support,"* which was a newly created code.

We repeated this review process for every code to gain a deeper understanding of the clusters formed around those major areas of educational work—and to critically assess to what extent they would be useful for subsequent coding. For example, we found that we had clustered a lot of different information in the "Health" code. This code needed to be divided into more specific subcodes to be useful (that is, to be representative of our organization's work).

This concluded our initial analysis loop, and our first co-analysis session. We wrapped up by documenting any significant hunches, tensions, discussions, and next steps in a memo and stepped away from the project until the next day. Moving forward, we structured our time together around completing one (or more) analysis loops. This prevented analysis sessions from stopping abruptly mid-process, which would have required additional investment of time and mental energy for analysts to re-orient themselves.

5.2 Repeating the process to flesh out subcodes and create emergent codes

We repeated the core analysis loop to further develop our coding scheme. First, we changed the anchor of our analysis to reflect that we were looking at data at a more granular level. One tentative theme (that is, top-level code) at the time, we reviewed both our comments and coded segments to develop and modify the scope and meaning of the code. For example, we first re-reviewed, re-discussed, and re-commented data we had sorted into the "Health" code. We then re-wrote all code comments to focus on the more specific types of work related to health (or health-adjacent topics) such as mental health, COVID support, and substance use prevention. We effectively began to identify possible subcodes (that is, clusters of educational topics). This was an important mechanism to better understand and make explicit what should and should not be coded under "Health" when we would code additional data from our dataset (see section 5.3).

In our initial discussion and comment-writing the day before, we did not focus on creating comments that resembled each other; they were more or less "wild" annotations of the data based on the analytic anchor. In this next stage, we tried to standardize our comments, so that we could create the foundation for additional codes and subcodes (Fig.12).

We prefer to use comments for this type of code development, rather than immediately creating subcodes. We have found it easier to "play" with different ideas and perspectives by writing and re-writing code comments, rather than creating static "code" objects too early. In our experience, creating "code" objects in the software can lead to very early fragmentation of the data, and an overwhelming proliferation of codes. Instead, we prefer to "mature" potential sub-themes first by constant comparison of coded content and code comments in the context of a broader thematic category.

We repeated this refinement process for each of our initial codes and compared the subcodes across different themes. This further fostered internal consistency and external difference. This also helped us build continued shared understanding of the structure that emerged through this process. During this phase, we also assessed whether some of the new subcodes should become their own top-level code or if they were better suited under established codes. We also examined the extent to which the initial top-level codes reflected our colleagues' work and identified areas where we needed to more significantly expand or modify the initial coding structure.

Comment	Document name	Code	Beginning
Facilitated planning process related to grant development	3653	Helper codes > Abstra...	1
Development of leadership model that integrates indegenous leaderhip perspectives	4015	Helper codes > Abstra...	1
Facilitation/Planning support for FN leadership based on indegenous culural teachings	4501	Helper codes > Abstra...	1
Creation of website to integrate Ojibwe traditional ecological knowledge into lakeshore climate assessmenty	6296	Helper codes > Abstra...	1
Facilitation of strategic planning process to support FN agriculture department	8033	Helper codes > Abstra...	1
Planning (and facilitation?) support for data collection policy	8397	Helper codes > Abstra...	1
Grant development support (?) with the goal of improving organizational capacity	8398	Helper codes > Abstra...	1

Comment	Document name	Code	Beginning
Organizational development / building org capacity	3653	Helper codes > Abstra...	1
Leadership Development (and connection with indegenous leadership models)	4015	Helper codes > Abstra...	1
Leadership Development (and connection with indegenous leadership models)	4501	Helper codes > Abstra...	1
Integration of Science and Indigenous knowledge	6296	Helper codes > Abstra...	1
Organizational development / building org capacity	8033	Helper codes > Abstra...	1
Organizational development / building org capacity	8397	Helper codes > Abstra...	1
Organizational development / building org capacity	8398	Helper codes > Abstra...	1

Fig. 12: The image on the top shows the less structured, "wild" annotations from our first coding step. The image on the bottom shows how we standardized these comments in our second reading of the data.

Broadly speaking, we continually made explicit to ourselves—at this early stage of analysis—how we envisioned our emergent codes, and how we grounded them in the data. To document and utilize this shared understanding, we crafted our stabilized code comments into tentative code memos (Fig. 13). This set us up with an initial decision-framework to finally look at more, fresh data, with the goal to further "try on" our coding scheme.

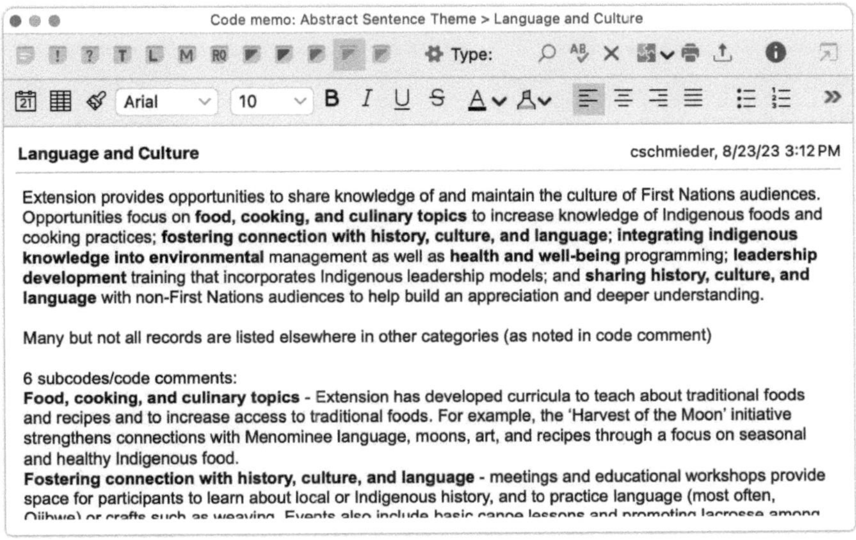

Fig. 13: A tentative code memo with a list of subcodes describing the data currently sorted into this code. These code memos would later be used as the basis for summaries in the final report.

5.3 Repeating the process with additional data

We were now equipped to analyze the next batch of uncoded data with the goal of testing our current coding and commenting scheme. Again, we decided to analyze approximately 30 more documents. This time, we not only used our top-level codes to code the data but also used the phrases from our more established code comments to annotate the newly coded data in a more structured way. This allowed us to quickly evaluate the appropriateness of our current code comments (Were they too narrow? Too broad? Not distinct enough from each other?). It also revealed any gaps in our current code and comment system. Whenever it was not possible to use an already established comment, we wrote a more free-form comment connected with the code. We also added an asterisk at the beginning of the comment to highlight coded segments that aligned with the broader code but not the emergent subcodes; this made them visually stand out during subsequent reviews of the coded data (Fig. 14). Afterwards, we reviewed all free-form comments to assess whether a new sub-aspect of the data was emerging.

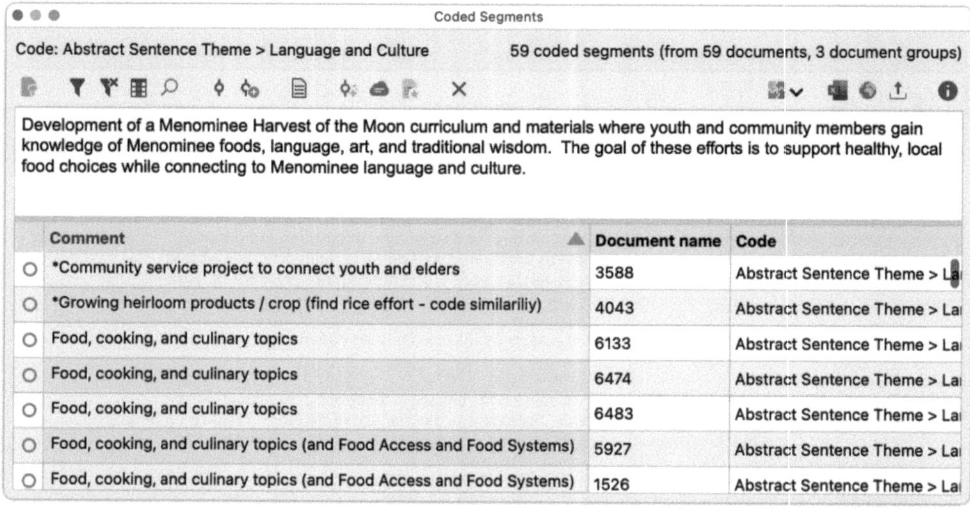

Fig. 14: Segments coded with "Language and Culture." Comments starting with an asterisk indicate data that could not be annotated with already existing thematic comments.

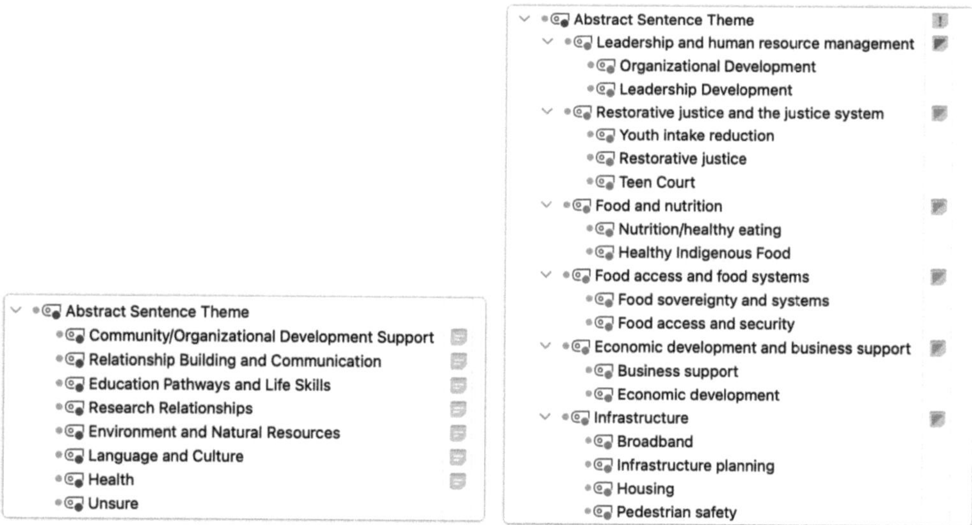

Fig. 15: The screenshot on the left is the initial coding scheme after a first scan of the data, containing a set of initial topics. The one on the right is an excerpt of the final coding scheme, including subcodes that are defined and discussed in the parent-level code memos.

We repeated this process multiple times with batches of about 30 documents. After having analyzed about half of our data, we reached a point where our coding frame stabilized, and major modifications where no longer necessary (Fig. 15). At this point, we stopped coding new data as a team. Instead, Allison used the established code system and comments to sort remaining data. Whenever Allison was not sure about a coding decision, she either indicated this via a "?" in the code comment or by coding the piece of data with our "Unsure" helper code. Later, we discussed the data in question during co-analysis sessions.

5.4 Writing up and communicating findings

As we worked on our data, we continually fleshed out our code definitions. This made it easy to transform them into summaries that explained our organization's work with First Nations.

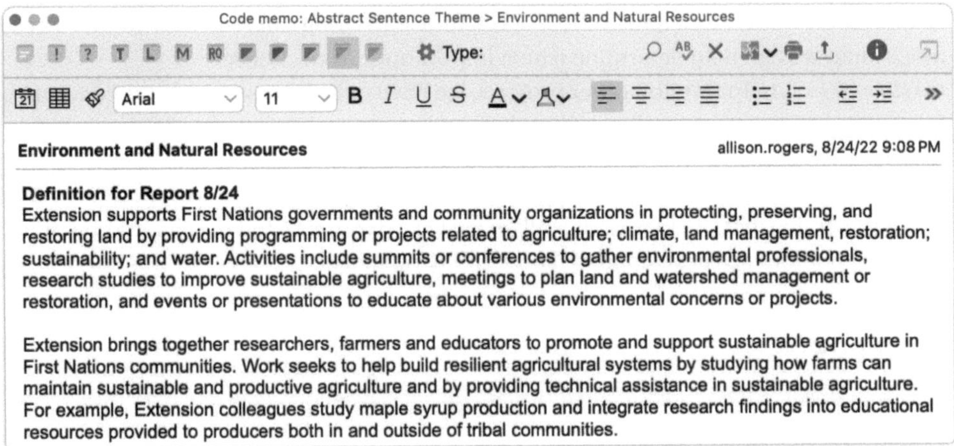

Fig. 16: Excerpt from an advanced code definition that we used in our final report

To create the report for our organization's strategic planning committee, we expanded on our code definitions to reflect the overall theme to briefly discuss all sub-themes and to discuss how each of the emerged themes related to the broader organizational strategic plan. In addition, we provided subcode statistics for each theme and overviews of the prevalence of each theme based on our organizational structure. Finally, we provided our stakeholders with lists of data that were sorted by theme and sub-theme. With this, we had equipped them with both a synthesis of our organization's work with First Nations and a structured inventory that they could use for subsequent analysis.

6 Lessons learned

We learned two important lessons in our project:

- *Reflecting on whether to code empty cells or not upon import.* When importing data from Excel files, MAXQDA also imports cells that do not have content (that is, when a report was not filled out completely or respondents skipped a question). MAXQDA provides the option to code this empty content, or to not code it. Coding empty cells upon import has the advantage that each document has the same visual structure in MAXQDA. Not coding empty cells has the advantage that the frequency of responses to each field can be more quickly assessed in the Code System. We found that it is helpful to determine early on which representation of the data will be more supportive of future analysis steps. We additionally found that running "mock analyses" based on imported data can be helpful to determine which functions in MAXQDA to use to bring analysis flow to life. These mock analyses can help determine which import options to choose.
- *Go slow to go fast.* In this and other projects, we have found it essential to "go slow to go fast," that is, to code a small batch of data and to review and discuss in depth before moving on to coding more information. This lowers the opportunity cost of overhauling the coding scheme early on, and it prevents the need to re-code massive amounts of data mid-project. Further, it ensures that all analysts develop a shared understanding of the concepts and themes developed and used in the process.

Bibliography

Boyatzis, R. E. (1998). *Transforming qualitative information: Thematic analysis and code development.* Sage.

Braun, V., & Clarke, V. (2006). Using thematic analysis in psychology. *Qualitative Research in Psychology, 3*(2), 77–101. https://doi.org/10.1191/1478088706qp063oa

Braun, V., & Clarke, V. (2022): *Thematic analysis. A practical guide.* Sage.

Kuckartz, U., & Rädiker, S. (2023). *Qualitative content analysis: Methods, practice and software* (2nd ed.). Sage.

Mayring, P. (2021). *Qualitative content analysis: A step-by-step guide.* Sage.

Lawrence-Lightfoot, S., & Hoffman Davis, J. (1997). *The art and science of portraiture.* Jossey-Bass.

Sanders, C. B., & Cuneo, C. J. (2010). Social reliability in qualitative team research. *Sociology,* 44(2), 325-343. https://doi.org/10.1177/0038038509357194

About the authors

Christian Schmieder serves as Assistant Director for Data Governance at the University of Wisconsin – Madison, Division of Extension. He has used MAXQDA since 2005 in research, evaluation, and institutional analysis contexts. Christian is a MAXQDA trainer and research consultant since 2009 and specializes in the use of QDAS in teamwork; research/evaluation/assessment project management; and institutional adaptation of QDAS. His research and publications focus on qualitative methods pedagogy and the use of QDAS in qualitative analysis.

ORCID: https://orcid.org/0000-0003-1324-6141

Allison Rogers is the Data Services Specialist at the University of Wisconsin – Madison, Division of Extension. She provides MAXQDA and qualitative data analysis support for strategic planning and program evaluation at the Division of Extension. Her past research has centered on how spatial, quantitative, and qualitative data can guide conservation decision-making.

Using MAXQDA for Combining Visual and Textual Analysis: An Example From a Participatory Photovoice Research Project

Elena Samonova

Abstract

In recent years the repertoire of qualitative research has been enriched by various visual methods. One of such methods is photovoice, which enables participants to express their views through the means of photographs. This chapter is based on a photovoice participatory research project conducted in 2020 in rural Sierra Leone (West Africa). It focuses on the analytical procedures used in this project and illustrates the ways in which MAXQDA software can be used to conduct a combined analysis of visual and textual data. It describes various MAXQDA tools such as Creative Coding, MAXMaps, and Compare Cases & Groups that were used at different stages of the analysis. This chapter is not only useful for those researchers who would like to analyze a photovoice project, but for everyone who works with both visual and textual data.

Key MAXQDA features covered

- ✓ Coding
- ✓ Creative Coding
- ✓ Internal Links
- ✓ Document memos
- ✓ Compare Cases & Groups
- ✓ MAXMaps: Single-Case Model (Code Hierarchy)
- ✓ MAXMaps: Single-Case Model (Coded Segments)
- ✓ MAXMaps: Layers

1 Introduction

Qualitative research uses a variety of methods to gain a deeper understanding of the lived experiences of people, their everyday realities, values, and norms (Gibbs et al., 2002; Schell et al., 2009; Wang, 1999). In recent years the repertoire of qualitative research has been enriched by various visual methods, which add value to traditional methods such as interviews and observations by capturing rich multidimensional data and providing insights into participants' perspectives on the world around them (Mah, 2015). One of such methods is photovoice, which enables participants to express their views through the means of photographs. This method that was first introduced in the 1990s by Wang and Burris (1994), is widely used in research of lived experiences of various groups of people, including those

Samonova, Elena (2024). Using MAXQDA for combining visual and textual analysis: An example from a participatory photovoice research project. In: S. Rädiker & Michael C. Gizzi (Eds.), The practice of qualitative data analysis. Research examples using MAXQDA, volume 2 (pp. 149–164). Berlin: MAXQDA Press.
https://doi.org/10.36192/978-3-948768188_8

who are most vulnerable and powerless (Devine & McGillicuddy, 2019; Luttrell, 2010; Luttrell, 2020). It stresses the importance of agency and voice of research participants, and promotes dialogue between participants, researchers, and stakeholders (Luttrell, 2013).

This chapter is based on a photovoice participatory research project conducted in 2020 in rural Sierra Leone (West Africa). The project was part of a larger longitudinal mixed methods Safe Learning Study that examined gender dynamics in children's lives, literacy, and well-being (Devine et al. 2021). The study consisted of an annual survey of children and teachers in 100 schools over the period of three years, accompanied with an in-depth qualitative study in case study communities that involved interviews, group discussions, and several participatory projects, including photovoice. The photovoice component of this large project aimed to deepen our understanding of children's everyday experiences in school and, in particular, to explore how children frame their school environment (Samonova et al., 2022).

2 Data collection and methodological approach

My photovoice project was conducted in February and March 2020 in three case study communities in northern Sierra Leone. In each community, 8 children (4 boys and 4 girls) enrolled in class 2 took part in the photovoice project. The majority of participants were 7 or 8 years old, however some were as old as 12. Additionally, in one community older children enrolled in class 6 were invited to participate in this activity. The research project followed all required ethical procedures, including obtaining informed consent from parents or guardians of children and assent of child participants. Pseudonyms are used throughout this text.

After the initial training, the children were provided with digital photo cameras and asked to take 5 photos of things they like and 5 photos of things they don't like in school. After the activity was completed, I conducted individual semi-structured interviews with the children, enabling them to explain their photos and share their daily experiences, aiming to gain a deeper understanding of children's everyday experiences in school. The task was intentionally formulated as open as possible to allow students to share their own perspectives and experiences without adults' guidelines. In total, the students took more than 200 photos which revealed a wide range of interests, from narratives related to school infrastructure, to the pride of being a good student.

To analyze data gathered during the photovoice activity, I applied a combination of semiotic analysis of the images and thematic analysis of both images and transcripts. Thematic analysis is widely used in social sciences to identify patterns within and across data and to examine lived experience and people's worldviews (Boyatzis, 1998). Semiotic analysis, in turn, regards images as signs made up of signifiers or objects shown on the image itself and signified or concepts that these objects represent (Barthes, 1967). The analysis of both levels of images helped me to gain a better understanding of what children wanted to show in their photos, as well as to gain insights into the local systems of meanings and social relations. This combination of textual and visual analysis allowed to include both verbal and nonverbal data in the analysis (Catalani & Minkler, 2009; Wang, 1999) and thus to overcome some limitations of using just one type of data. Moreover, closer semiotic analysis of photos provided additional insights into the everyday school practices, school infrastructure, and social norms related to education and gender.

3 Setting up the MAXQDA project

MAXQDA allows users to import various file formats including texts, PDFs, Excel files, images, and videos. In this research project two main file formats were used: Word documents and PDF files. In order to store and analyze images efficiently, all photos taken by each case study child were grouped together and saved as one PDF file named after a child's pseudonym. These PDF files together with Word documents with interview transcripts were imported into a new MAXQDA project, using ***Import* > *Texts, PDFs, Tables*** from the main menu. The document names reflected the place of the school and the interviewed child.

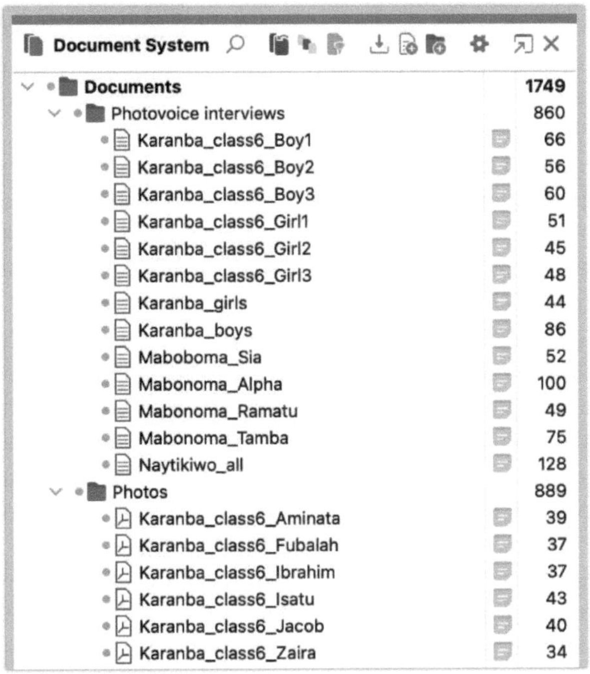

Fig. 1: Document System with two document groups, one for each data type

I used document groups to organize my data in the Document System. As Fig. 1 shows, I had two groups: "Photovoice interviews" and "Photos." The first group contained interview transcriptions, while in the second group the PDFs with photos were stored. The organization of project data into groups made it easy to find a certain document and also enabled efficient analysis of data using various MAXQDA tools, including Compare Cases & Groups tool, and such visual tools as Code Matrix Browser.

The initial analysis of data gathered during the photovoice project included three major steps: (1) coding of textual data, (2) coding of visual data, and (3) establishing links between two types of data in order to enrich the analysis, whereas the two latter steps were often taken simultaneously. Later a further analysis of coded segments was conducted in order to identify differences and similarities across the cases and develop a framework for understanding of children's perceptions of safety and danger.

4 Coding and linking the data

4.1 Coding the interview transcripts

The first stage of the analysis involved coding the interview transcripts, applying thematic analysis as the main analytical approach. Thematic analysis is a method of identifying and interpreting themes or key patterns in qualitative data (Clarke & Braun, 2017). It is recognized as a good tool to identify patterns within and across data and is often used for the analysis of lived experience and people's worldviews (Boyatzis, 1998).

This research project used a hybrid approach to thematic analysis which combined both deductive coding using a pre-developed codebook (Crabtree & Miller, 1999) and inductive data driven coding (Boyatzis, 1998). The first step was deductive coding: I used a codebook that was developed for the entire Safe Learning Study based on 5 main research areas of the project, namely teaching and learning, gender dynamics, well-being, socio-cultural dynamics, and impacts of NGO interventions. Codes from this codebook were used to analyze both textual and visual data. However, as this photovoice project provided participants with an opportunity to express their views and perspectives freely, new topics emerged, which were not covered by the pre-developed codebook. That is why the deductive coding process was supplemented by inductive coding, which involved the creation of new codes that emerged from the data. These two coding processes happened simultaneously and supplemented each other.

At this stage, most of the basic features of MAXQDA were used: segments of text were coded by dragging and dropping highlighted segments to codes. The option to use different colors for different coded segments was very useful at this stage: I marked different thematic areas with different colors, which made it easy to find segments related to certain themes while screening the document (Fig. 2).

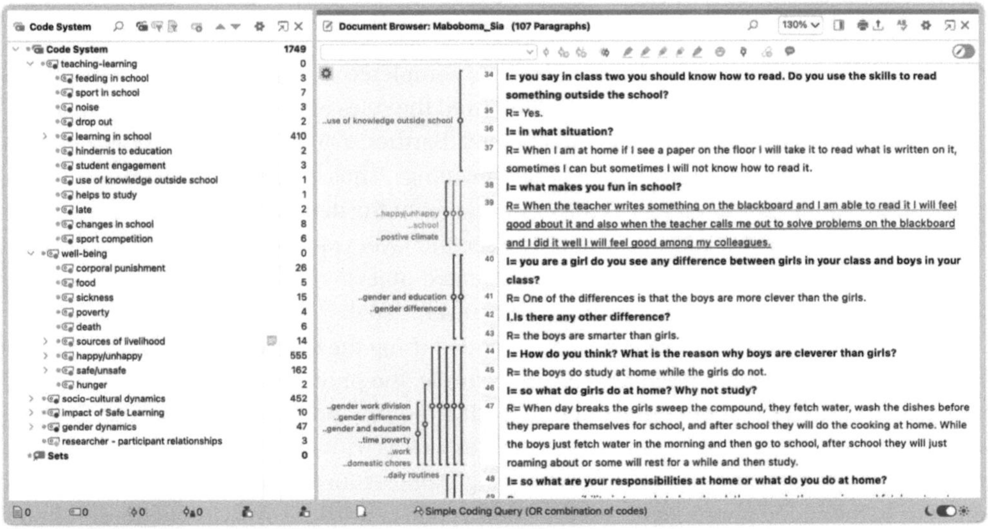

Fig. 2: Interview text in the Document Browser coded with codes having different colors

After the coding, I deleted all deductive codes that were not used in this research from the code system. As a result, I had over 100 codes in total arranged into 5 thematic areas: teaching and learning, well-being, socio-cultural dynamics, impacts of NGO interventions, and gender dynamics (Fig. 3).

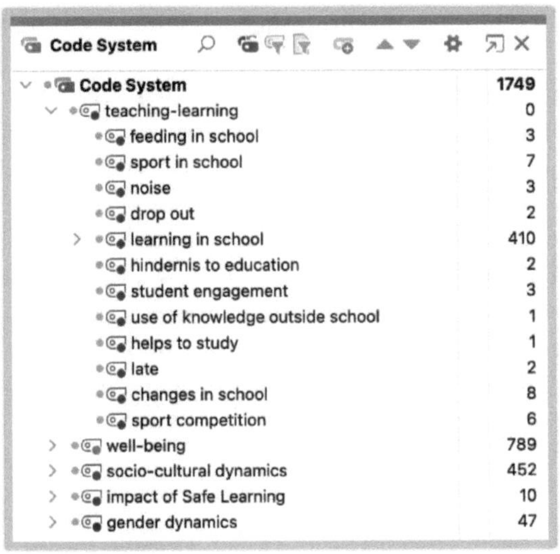

Fig. 3: Extract from the Code System after deleting empty codes

4.2 Coding and linking the photos

Once the initial coding of the textual data was completed, I started the coding of photos taken by the children. During this stage, I followed the rules of semiotic analysis which distinguishes between the signifier and the signified (Barthes, 1967), or in other words, between the objects portrayed on the image and their meanings. Thus, there were two layers of analysis of visual data: the first one was the examination of the denotation level of the photo or finding out what or who is shown there. The second layer was the analysis of the connotation level, which revealed what meaning presented objects or people had and what story was hidden behind the image (see also van Leeuwen, 2005).

On the denotation layer the images were coded using the hybrid approach of deductive and inductive coding described above. For example, the photo of a blackboard was coded using such codes as "school infrastructure," "classroom," and "teaching materials," which were included in the pre-developed codebook, as well as with new codes such as "brilliance in class." For this stage I used the same coding frame as for the interview texts. The later analysis of the coded photo segments provided a good contextual overview of the children's living conditions that were often taken for granted and not addressed in the interviews.

The connotation layer, in turn, involved a more complex coding process. It was important to include children's views that they expressed in interviews in the analysis to ensure the correct understanding of the meaning of photos. Thus, it required the use of more sophisticated MAXQDA functions, such as the creation of internal links. This allows users to establish connections between two different documents, videos, or images within one MAXQDA project. In this research example, I utilized internal links to connect children's photos with the description of images which children provided during their interviews. Such links allowed me to read children's explanations without going back to the interview transcript while looking at the photo (Fig. 4). This enhanced the accuracy and authenticity of the connotation analysis of the photos. As MAXQDA links are bi-directional, I could also see the linked part of the photo children talked about while reading the interview transcript (Fig. 5).

The other useful MAXQDA feature at this stage of the data analysis was the ability to write various kinds of memos. It is possible to create document and code memos as well as free memos that are suitable for documenting general thoughts and making notes on the whole project. In my research project most memos were document memos, which refer to the images taken by children and often include such background information as where the photo was taken, what is on the photo and any kinds of other insights that were gathered during the fieldwork. Fig. 6 shows an example of such a memo.

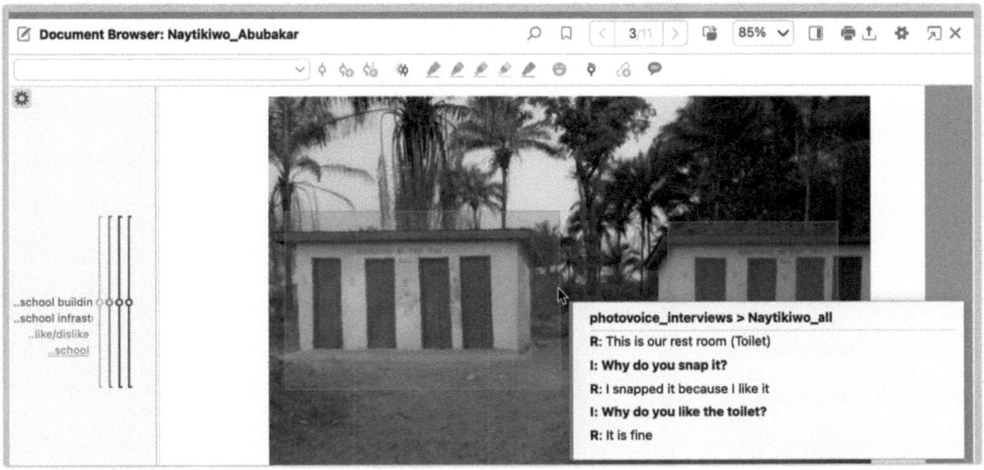

Fig. 4: Internal Link between a photo and an interview. The linked interview text is shown when hovering over the blue box indicating the linked image segment in Document Browser.

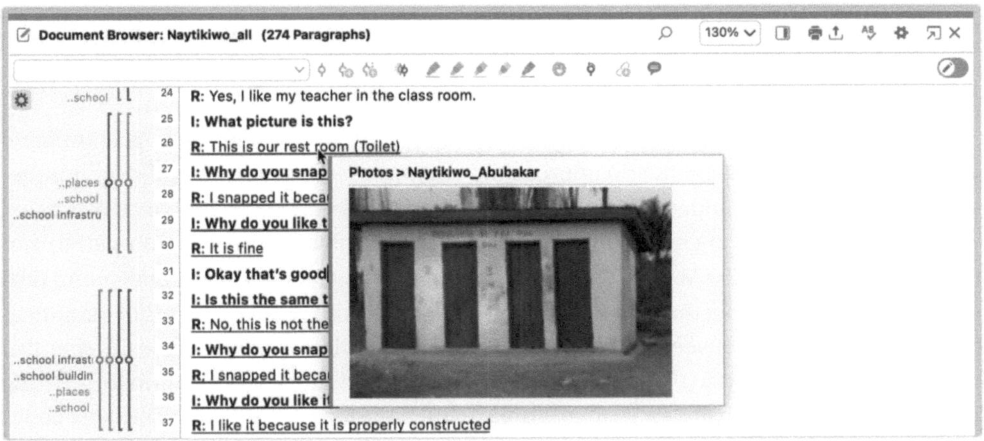

Fig. 5: Internal Link between interview text and photo. The photo segment is shown when hovering over the blue underlined text segment in Document Browser.

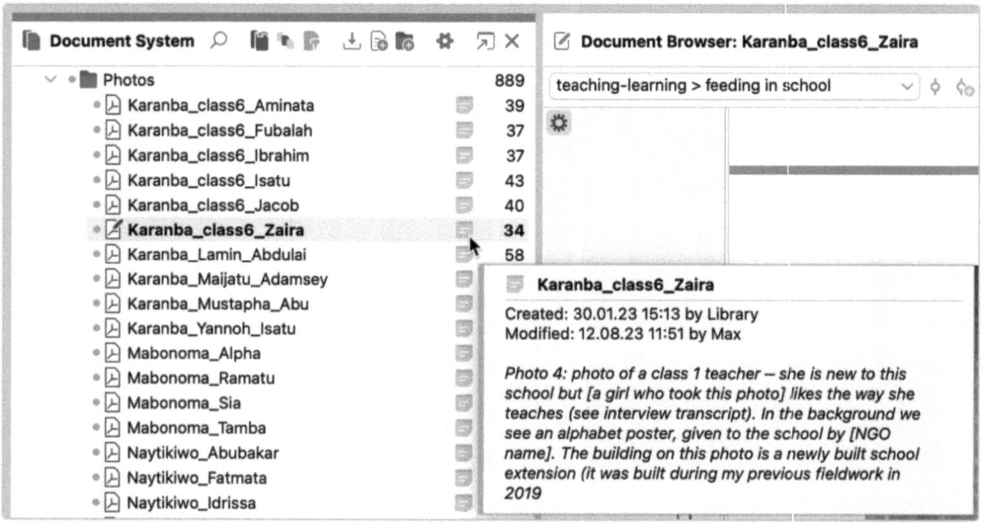

Fig. 6: Document memo containing descriptions of the photos

Such memos allowed me to share my insights from the fieldwork with my colleagues who were not in the field and make sure that in all future analytical procedures and research publications these photos will be interpreted accurately.

Once coding of images was finished, the coding system was reorganized. As mentioned above, this project used the hybrid approach to coding, which means a significant number of new codes were developed during the analysis and these new codes had to be organized within a coding frame to enable faster analysis and identification of common patterns of meanings in the data. The MAXQDA Creative Coding tool (available in the ***Codes*** menu tab) allowed me re-organizing the codes effectively. It bolsters the creative process of identification of relationships between codes and developing theories and hypotheses. Using this tool, I was able to get a visual overview of the codes, incorporate new codes into the existing thematic areas, and create new thematic areas. The first step here was to insert new codes to the Creative Coding workspace and separate them into broad groups. Then the groups of codes were examined and if they suited into one of the existing categories, connections between the groups and existing codes were established. Fig. 7 shows the reorganized groups of codes that fall into the thematic category "well-being". Later the relationships between all thematic categories were re-examined and several categories were merged into bigger ones.

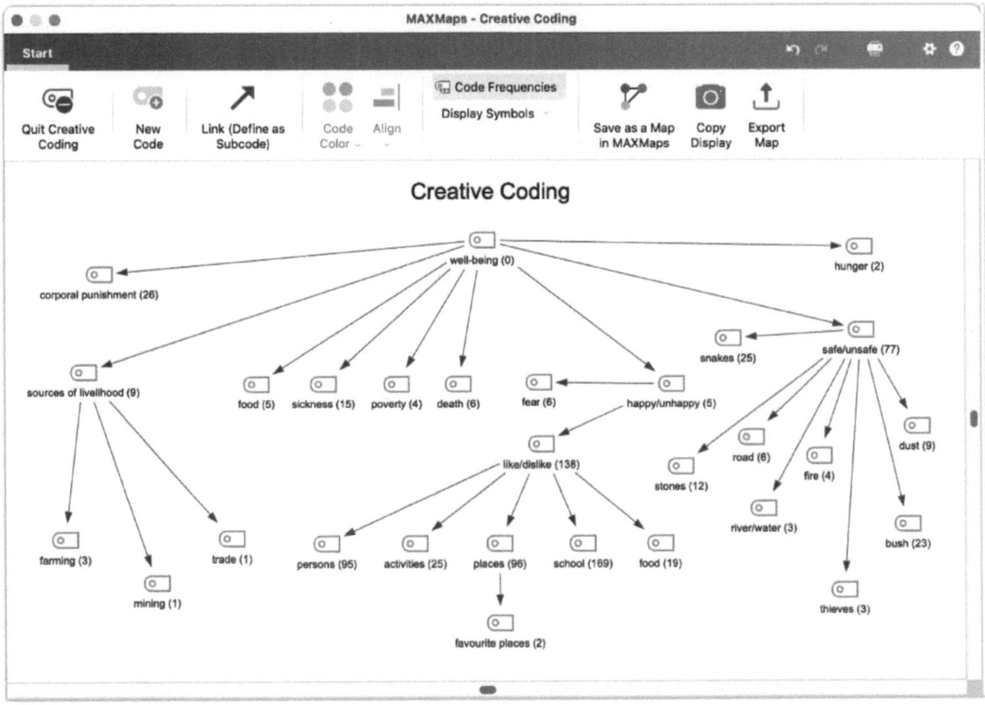

Fig. 7: Creative Coding: Final reorganization of codes that fall into "well-being" category

5 Analyzing the coded and linked transcripts and photos

Once these initial coding procedures were completed, the next stage of the analysis began: the integrated analysis of the data. This section discusses the use of two MAXQDA tools for data analysis, MAXMaps and Compare Cases & Groups tool, which allow users to examine individual cases and identify differences and similarities across cases.

5.1 Utilizing MAXMaps

MAXMaps allows users to visualize codes and coded segments as well as connections and relations between different codes and documents in a concept map. For this research project, this tool was particularly useful because it can provide an overview of both textual and visual fragments, which allows the integrated analysis of both types of data.

I first created document-based maps using several of the built-in templates. After opening ***Visual Tools > MAXMaps***, I selected ***New Document Model > Single-Case Model (Code Hierarchy)***. The resulting concept map provided an overview of what codes were applied to a specific document. This was useful for the analysis of individual cases: it provided an overview of the themes that a particular child addressed during the photovoice exercise. Fig. 8 shows a single-case map for all codes that were assigned to the interview transcript of one of the case study children. From this map, it was easy for me to identify the themes that emerged from the photovoice exercise: for example, we see that during the photovoice activity this child focused on well-being and safety, experiences of learning, and cultural practices.

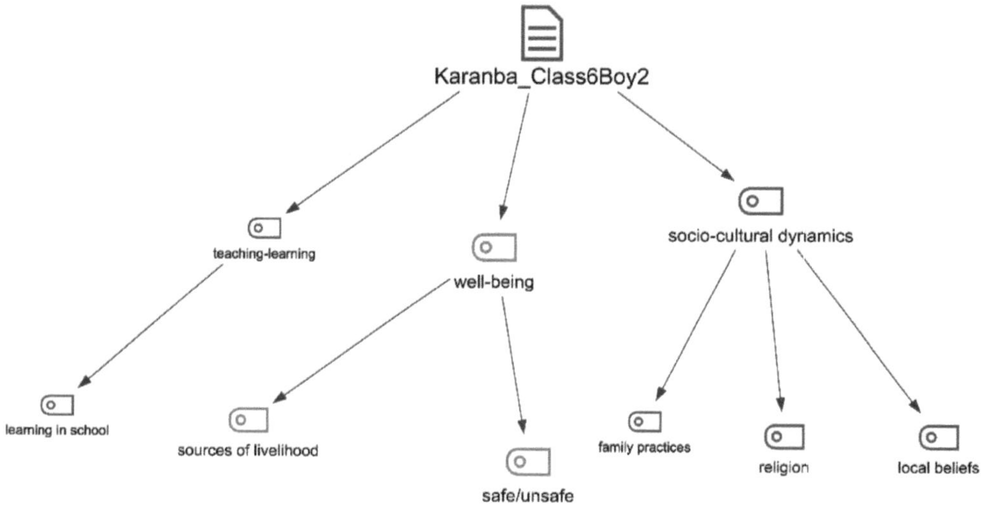

Fig. 8: Single-Case Model (Code Hierarchy), showing a case-based map for one child

MAXMaps allowed me not only to create a map showing the codes assigned to this document, but also to create a map showing the coded segments of a document. This allowed me to see all coded segments in one map, without having to read the entire interview transcript again. A similar map could be created for visual images as well: Fig. 9 shows a visualization of all codes and coded segments from photos taken by one of the boys.

I created the visualization by selecting ***Single-Case Model (Coded Segments)*** from the ***New Document Model*** dropdown in the MAXMaps window. After requesting this model, a list of all documents appeared, and I dragged the needed document onto the interactive map field. Once the document was selected, a new menu appeared on the left side, which allowed me to identify elements to be included in the map, such as memos, codes, and coded segments. Under the section "codes," I could decide how many of the most frequent codes to include in the map. The section "coded segments" allows users to choose what types of coded segments will appear: for example, one can click on ***Change label to: coded text*** and see all textual fragments associated with codes presented on the map. For creating Fig. 9, I selected the option ***Change symbol to: coded image*** to see all image segments.

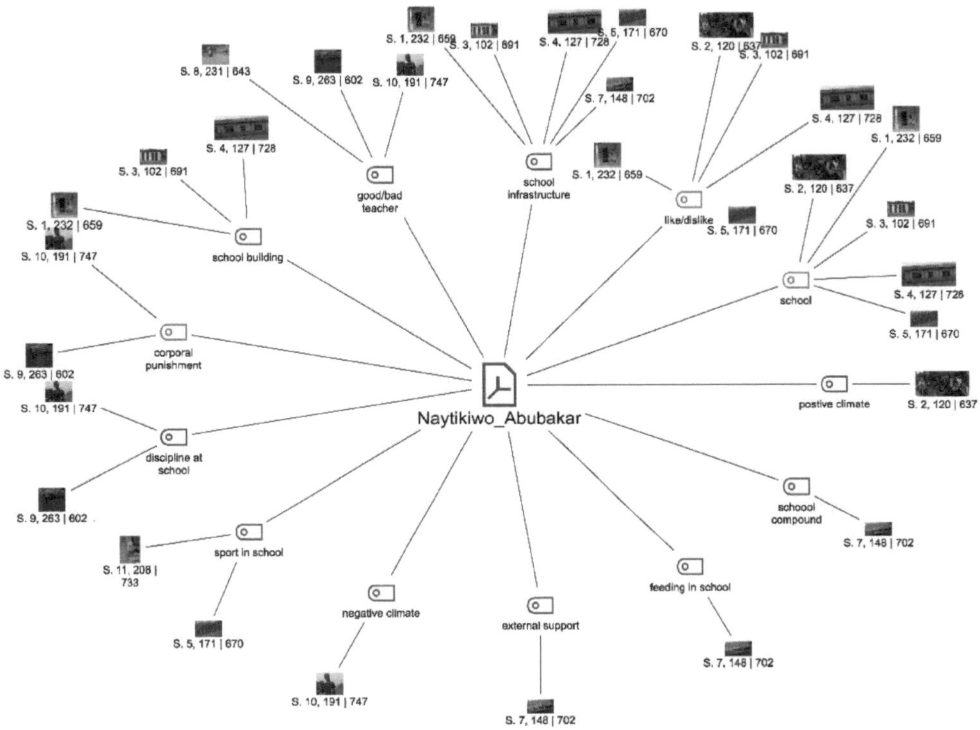

Fig. 9: Single-Case Model (Coded Segments) showing the coded image parts for one child in a case-based map

Using MAXMaps, it is also possible to automatically create a map that compares the codes applied to different documents (Fig. 10). In order to do so, I chose the ***Two-Cases Model*** option in the ***New Document Model*** drop down in MAXMaps and then dragged a textual document with the interview transcript of a child and a document containing photos taken by this child. Please note that the resulting map presented in Fig. 10 did not compare two cases in the literal meaning but compared two documents of the identical case. Such a map shows codes associated with each document only at the sides, and those which are common to both in the middle.

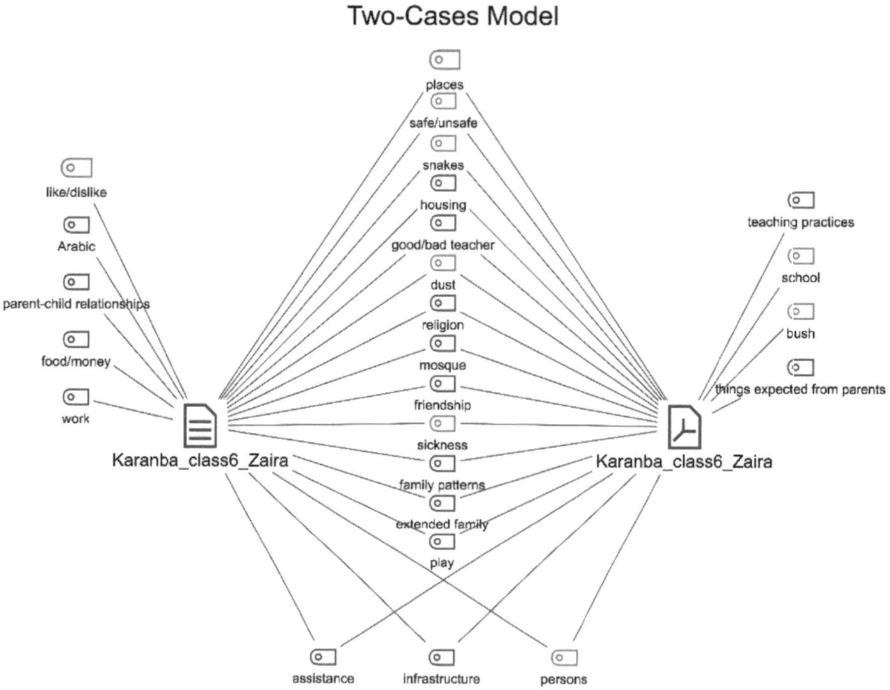

Fig. 10: Two-Cases Model, comparing the codes used for textual and image coding

I wanted to avoid having too many codes on one map, so I defined which layers of the map should be visible. I usually left only codes and coded segments visible while hiding the connections between codes. This made the map less messy and easier to understand. To make it happen, I went to the ***Start*** tab in MAXMaps and clicked on the ***Layers*** icon. A new menu appeared on the left side where I could select which of the automatically created layers I wanted to see (Fig. 11). I even created my own layers to make the map more focused. In some cases, I left visible only segments assigned to certain codes, while other codes were not displayed. This procedure helped me to analyze children's views on a particular topic.

The second type of map used in the analysis of the data is the code-based map called Single-Code Model, which gives an overview of all subcodes, and coded segments associated with certain codes. This type of map is useful for the analysis of particular thematic areas. For example, in Fig. 12, we can see a map for the code "corporal punishment"—it provides a good overview of children's experiences with corporal punishment in school and children's views on this practice. As with the previously described models, during the creation process, I could decide what I wanted to see on the map (for example, coded image parts instead of a generic coded segments symbol) and what elements not to include. After the map was created automatically, I refined the arrangement of the elements.

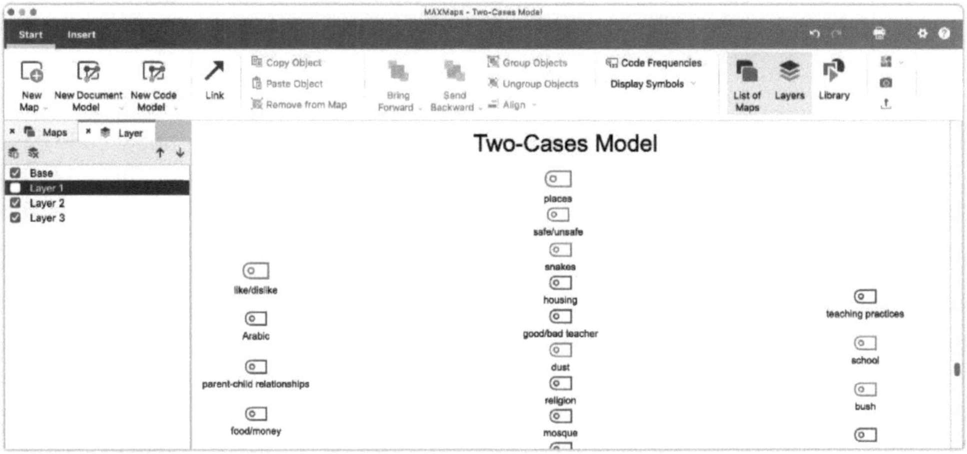

Fig. 11: Using layers in MAXMaps to focus on specific parts of the visualization

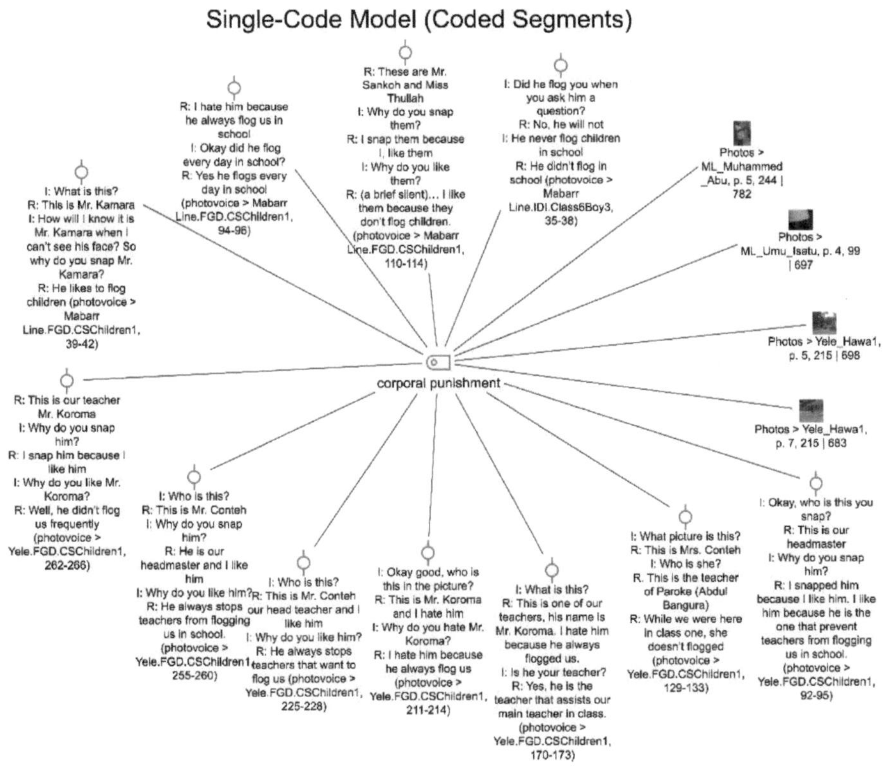

Fig. 12: Single-Code Model (Coded Segments), a code-based map showing the coded segments from interviews and photos for one selected code

5.2 Utilizing Compare Cases & Groups feature

While MAXMaps provides a good opportunity to examine individual cases and codes, ***Compare Cases & Groups*** can help with the analysis of differences and similarities across cases. This tool can be found in the ***Analysis*** menu tab and allows the user to compare code data (qualitative comparison) and code frequencies (quantitative analysis). For this research project, I applied qualitative comparison of coded segments. I used this tool a lot during the analysis as such a comparative analysis of cases is one of the most important techniques in qualitative analysis. Having a clear overview of experiences of different case study children helped me to identify patterns and dynamics within the sample and to make some conclusions about perspectives and experiences of different groups of participants.

The feature to compare cases and groups enables users to decide whether they want to compare individual documents or whole documents groups and documents sets. In my project, I compared individual documents such as interview transcripts of different children with each other. While creating the comparison table, users can choose what codes and documents they want to analyze and get a table with all coded segments associated with selected codes. Such a presentation of the data makes it easy to identify any discrepancies in participants' answers. In Fig. 13, we see a table with all coded segments associated with a major code "safe/unsafe" and its subcodes. The table allowed me to read all coded segments from different interview transcripts and compare them with each other.

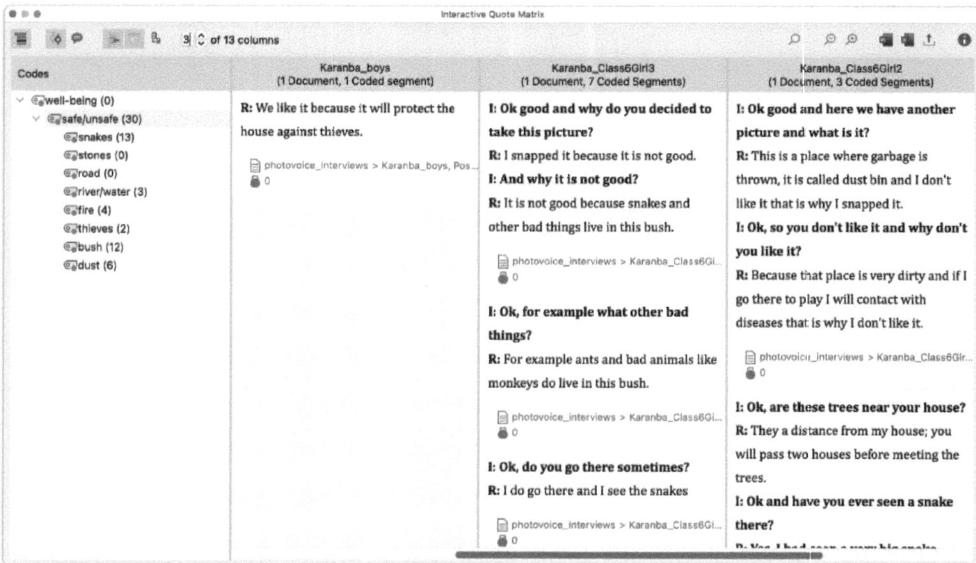

Fig. 13: Compare Cases & Groups tool showing the coded segments for one selected code in the left pane for three children

This analysis was very useful for developing a better understanding of differences between children's experiences in different case study villages. For example, from the table shown in Fig. 13, it became clear that in one of the villages children's perceptions of safety and dangers were significantly influenced by traditional practices of initiation, while in other villages children did not mention these practices, while doing photovoice. These findings inspired a further analysis of the role of traditional practices in children's lives across different communities.

6 Lessons learned

This project demonstrates the ways in which MAXQDA may help to conduct a combined analysis of visual and textual data. In my research project, I particularly learned the following:

- MAXQDA tools can be useful at different stages of the analysis starting from the initial coding to more sophisticated analysis of individual cases and identification of common patterns of meanings and differences across case studies.
- Creative Coding can be effectively used during the hybrid deductive/inductive thematic analysis of data to reorganize the coding frame, while memos can provide background information during the semiotic analysis of images.
- Internal links between visual images and interview transcripts can help to develop a better understanding of visual data and help with the semiotic analysis of images.
- Such tools as MAXMaps and the Compare Cases & Groups feature can be used during the further stages of combined textual and visual data analysis. MAXMaps were found useful in the analysis of individual cases and codes, while the Compare Cases & Groups tool provides good opportunities for a comparative analysis across case study communities.

Bibliography

Barthes, R. (1967). *Elements of semiology.* Macmillan.

Boyatzis, R. E. (1998). *Transforming qualitative information: Thematic analysis and code development.* Sage.

Catalani, C., & Minkler, M. (2010). Photovoice: A review of the literature in health and public health. *Health Education & Behavior, 37*(3), 424–451. https://doi.org/10.1177/1090198109342084

Clarke, V., & Braun, V. (2017). Thematic analysis. *The Journal of Positive Psychology, 12*(3), 297–298. https://doi.org/10.1080/17439760.2016.1262613

Crabtree, B. F., & Miller, W. F. (1992). A template approach to text analysis: Developing and using codebooks. Sage.

Devine, D., Bolotta, G., Samonova, E., Sugrue, C., Sloan, S., Symonds, J., & Capistrano, D. (2021). Becoming *'brilliant'*: Generationing education and development in rural Sierra Leone. *Childhood, 28*(2), 262–278. https://doi.org/10.1177/0907568220981159

Devine, D., & McGillicuddy, D. (2019). Explorations of care and care injustice in the everyday lives of Irish Traveller children. *Gender and Education, 31*(5), 618–630. https://doi.org/10.1080/09540253.2019.1609653

Gibbs, G. R., Friese, S., & Mangabeira, W. C. (2002). The use of new technology in qualitative research: Introduction to issue 3 (2) of FQS. *Forum Qualitative Sozialforschung/Forum: Qualitative Social Research, 3*(2).

Luttrell, W. (2010). "A camera is a big responsibility": A lens for analysing children's visual voices. *Visual Studies, 25*(3), 224–237. https://doi.org/10.1080/1472586X.2010.523274

Luttrell, W. (2013). Children's counter-narratives of care: towards educational justice. *Children & Society, 27*(4), 295–308. https://doi.org/10.1111/chso.12033

Luttrell, W. (2020). Children framing childhoods: Working-class kids' visions of care. Policy Press.

Mah, A. (2015). Visual methods: DTC qualitative research methods. *PowerPoint presentation. Department of Sociology University of Warwick, England.* https://www2.warwick.ac.uk/Fac/Soc/Sociology

Samonova, E., Devine, D., & Luttrell, W. (2022). Under the mango tree: Photovoice with primary school children in rural Sierra Leone. *International Journal of Qualitative Methods, 21*, 160940692110531. https://doi.org/10.1177/16094069211053106

Schell, K., Ferguson, A., Hamoline, R., Shea, J., & Thomas-Maclean, R. (2009). Photovoice as a teaching tool: Learning by doing with visual methods. *International Journal of Teaching and Learning in Higher Education, 21*(3), 340–352.

van Leeuwen, T. (2005). *Introducing social semiotics.* Routledge.

Wang, C., & Burris, M. A. (1994). Empowerment through photo novella: Portraits of participation. *Health Education Quarterly, 21*(2), 171–186. https://doi.org/10.1177/109019819402100204

Wang, C. C. (1999). Photovoice: A participatory action research strategy applied to women's health. *Journal of Women's Health, 8*(2), 185–192. https://doi.org/10.1089/jwh.1999.8.185

About the author

Elena Samonova is a postdoctoral researcher at the University of Bremen, Germany. She has a PhD in social sciences from the University of Helsinki. She has used MAXQDA since 2019 in various research projects and teaches MAXQDA in workshops.

ORCID-ID: https://orcid.org/0000-0001-6078-7739

Using MAXQDA for Interpretative Analysis: Analyzing Four Interviews (Almost) Without Coding

Andreas Müller

Abstract

MAXQDA has been used to implement an interpretative approach to analyze interviews following Saša Bosančić's Interpretative Subjectivation Analysis. This research approach integrates techniques from grounded theory and sequential analysis in a strongly theory-guided analysis. This chapter demonstrates a way to implement such an interpretative methodology with MAXQDA. Here, the focus lies on how sequential analysis, both as an individual researcher and in a group setting, can be implemented in MAXQDA. For this, the usage of in-documents memos and color coding was crucial. Linking codes to in-document memos helped to identify overarching patterns of interpretation and to arrive at a dense and theory-rich interpretation. Overall, the chapter shows that MAXQDA can be useful for very detailed and interpretative analysis just as well as for category-oriented approaches. Codes do not need to stand in the focus of working with MAXQDA, instead the software can be a great platform to integrate various steps of the research process.

Key MAXQDA features covered

- ✓ Color coding (highlight coding)
- ✓ In-document memos
- ✓ Document memos
- ✓ Link codes to in-document memos
- ✓ MAXMaps: Free map

1 Introduction

With the onset of the 21st century, life, jobs, and identities became increasingly individualized. Patchwork biographies have become popular and societal blueprints of jobs, careers, and lifestyles have lost much of their normative power (Sennet, 2010). At the heart of this analysis lies the concept of the entrepreneurial self (Bröckling, 2007). According to this theory, policies are increasingly envisioning citizens as entrepreneurs of their own life using their skills, time, and other assets in a methodic or entrepreneurial way. A primary example of this concept are sole proprietors who work as one-person companies and usually sell their skills openly on the market.

Müller, Andreas (2024). Using MAXQDA for interpretative analysis: Analyzing four interviews (almost) without coding. In: S. Rädiker & Michael C. Gizzi (Eds.), The practice of qualitative data analysis. Research examples using MAXQDA, volume 2 (pp. 165–179). Berlin: MAXQDA Press. https://doi.org/10.36192/978-3-948768188_9

My research focused on how established female entrepreneurs make meaning of their own situation and frame their identity in the dimensions of power, flexibility, gender, health, and qualification. Therefore, the following research questions guided the theory-driven analysis:

> "What modes of subjectivation do female sole proprietors use in the contemporary working environment? How do they make meaning of their subjective position and what subject-positions do they use to identify or distinguish themselves?"

This project is used as an example for how a strongly theory-guided and interpretative methodology can be implemented with MAXQDA.

2 Data collection and methodological approach

To examine the research questions, four problem-centered interviews (Witzel, 2000) have been conducted with female sole proprietors from various branches of the economy. Saša Bosančić's (2014, 2019) Interpretative Subjectivation Analysis (ISA) served as the primary methodological approach. This approach is rooted in the sociology of knowledge approach to discourse (SKAD) based on Keller (2011) and tries to breach the gap between a structuralist and an individualist perspective on discourse analysis and subjectification. For analyzing interviews, Bosančić suggests a combination of sequential analysis (Oevermann, 1979) and grounded theory (Glaser & Strauss, 1967). Sequential analysis is characterized by an extensive line-by-line interpretation of text where many different readings are created to uncover the internal logic of the case. Bosančić integrates this with a more coarse-grained analysis used in selective coding from grounded theory and arrives at three key stages, illustrated by Fig. 1.

While following this analysis layout, several key questions appeared regarding the specific implementation in MAXQDA:

1. How to identify relevant segments for sequential analysis?
2. How to implement sequential analysis both as a single researcher and as a group of analysists who meet face to face?
3. How to reconstruct the internal logic of each case?
4. How to create patterns of interpretation for the analysis based on this previous work?
5. How to present the results?

For each of these five questions, a solution was implemented using functions of MAXQDA that will be explored in the following sections 3.1 to 3.5.

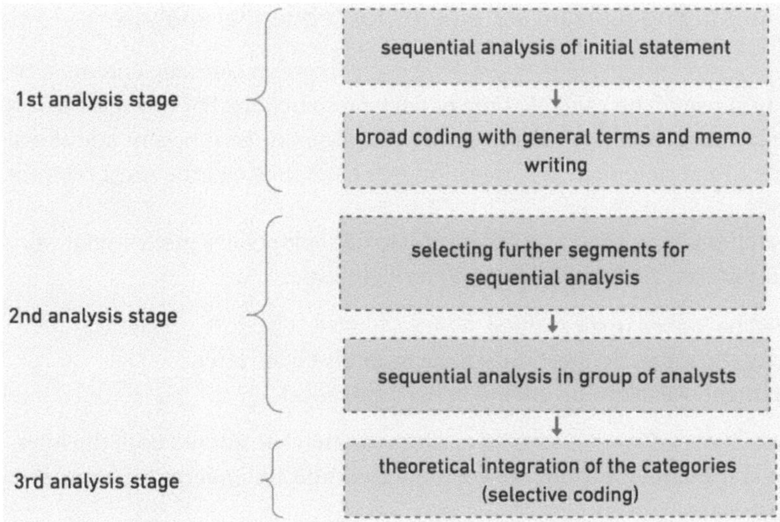

Fig. 1: Three stages of interpretative subjectivation analysis which iterate between sequential analysis and coding, drawn from Bosančić (2014)

3 Implementing subjectivation analysis in MAXQDA

The four interviews were automatically transcribed using the transcription feature of Office 365 and manually corrected by the researcher. When importing the transcripts into MAXQDA, the transcripts were connected to the original audio files via timestamps so that the original audio statements could always be considered when interpreting a key statement. For sequential analysis, it is crucial to have the ability to reference brief text segments, including specific words, phrases, metaphors, etc., employed by the interviewees. Therefore, the numbering in Document Browser was altered from counting paragraphs to counting lines by right-clicking on the transcript text and selecting the option ***Convert to Line Numbered Text*** (Fig. 1).

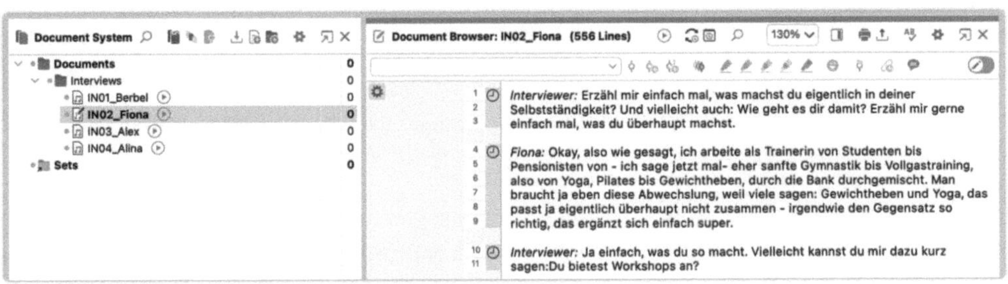

Fig. 2: The data after the import with activated line numbering

3.1 Color coding: Identifying relevant statements for sequential analysis

Sequential analysis is a time-intensive method. Especially in group settings, one must be careful to make the best use of the valuable time of fellow researchers. For this reason, it is important to carefully consider which data to spend this time on. To pinpoint additional segments beyond the initial statement, the question emerged: how can the most relevant sections be identified?

In previous research projects, I found it very useful to use color codes in the initial work with text (Kuckartz & Rädiker, 2023), following a street-light logic:

- ❖ Red: unclear, must be looked up or verified.
- ❖ Yellow: relevant for the research question, will be properly coded later.
- ❖ Green: a key statement, will likely be quoted in the final report.

In this project, a more nuanced system seemed appropriate that considered both the internal logic of the case and the relationship between the case and the theoretical approach. The following color codes were used:

- ❖ Case-internal inconsistency (yellow): The segments seem to contradict what was said earlier or what is known about the interviewee.
- ❖ Personal perplexity (blue): The segment surprises the analyst on a personal or emotional level.
- ❖ Theoretical affirmation (green): The segment confirms or fits well with existing theories.
- ❖ Theoretical dissonance (red): The segment seems to contradict existing theories.
- ❖ Self-narrative (magenta): The person tells a story or anecdote that illustrates who they are.

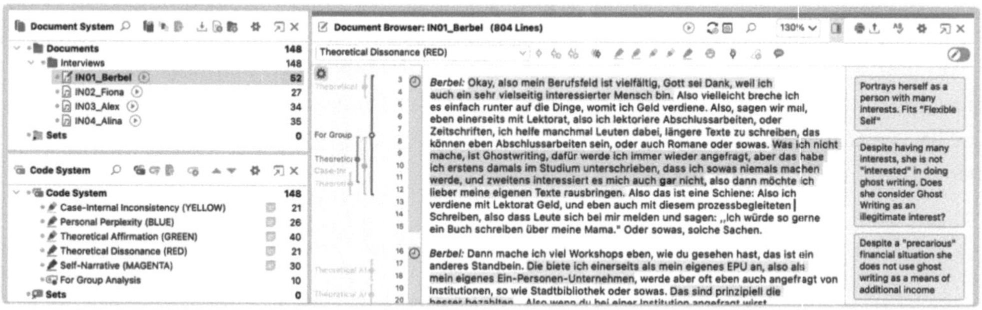

Fig. 3: An interview coded with color codes. Starting with "Despite," the coding comments in the right sidebar focus on the perceived contradiction right away.

As illustrated in Fig. 3, I wrote a comment for each segment coded with a color code (visualized in blue boxes right to the text). The segments captured with color codes were then reviewed based on these written comments. The codes "Theoretical Dissonance" and "Case-internal Inconsistency" proved especially productive. After reviewing all color-coded segments, I selected a hand full of them and copied them into a code labeled with "For Group Analysis" (also illustrated in Fig. 3 at the bottom of the Code System). This continuous process of gathering important statements for group analysis accompanied my work of conducting sequential analysis alone as illustrated in the following section.

3.2 In-document memos: Sequential analysis of identified statements (alone and with an analysis group)

In-depth sequential interpretation of text lies at the heart of sequential analysis. To implement this, two components are key: first, conducting an in-depth interpretation of short segments of the text as a single researcher, and second, interpreting segments of the text

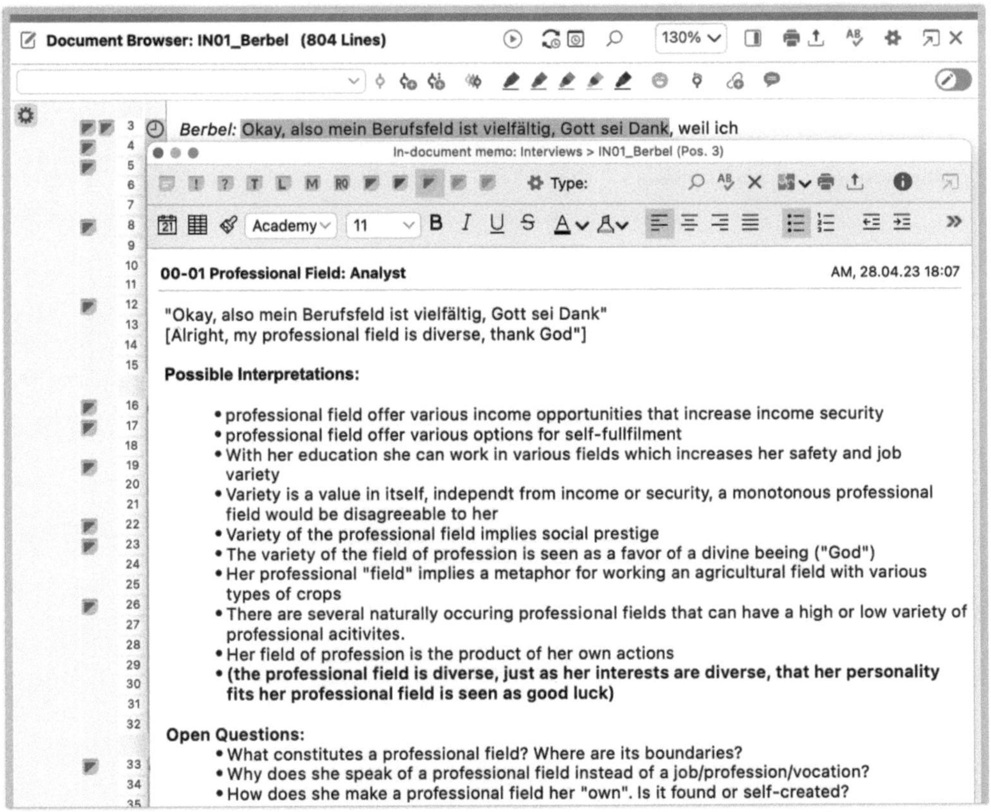

Fig. 4: In-document memo for the initial statement. The blue memo icon indicates that the memo was written by me alone. The memo window can be used to visually block the further text of the document to enable a strictly sequential interpretation process.

collaboratively with a group of analysists in a face-to-face meeting. To document and retain in-depth interpretations, I used in-document memos as visualized in Fig. 4, which shows the interpretation of the initial statement "Alright, my professional field is diverse, thank God" in one interview. The in-document memo contains the original statement, various interpretations of it and any remaining questions. The text in bold and brackets was added later to indicate what became the dominant interpretation of this segment.

After I interpreted several segments alone and identified them by using color codes (see section 3.1), I asked a group of researchers to meet face-to-face and analyze the same sequence of segments. For this, the analysts began with one of the identified text segments from which they continued their analysis in a sequential order. Once the analysis of this sequence was completed, the other analysts moved on to the next segment that I had identified. In these group sessions, I took the role of taking notes and abstained from the discussion. All analysts received a paper copy of the interview that they used for discussion, while I recorded notes in MAXQDA using a new in-document memo (Fig. 5). These memos were given a red memo icon to distinguish them from those previously written alone, which I indicated using a blue memo icon.

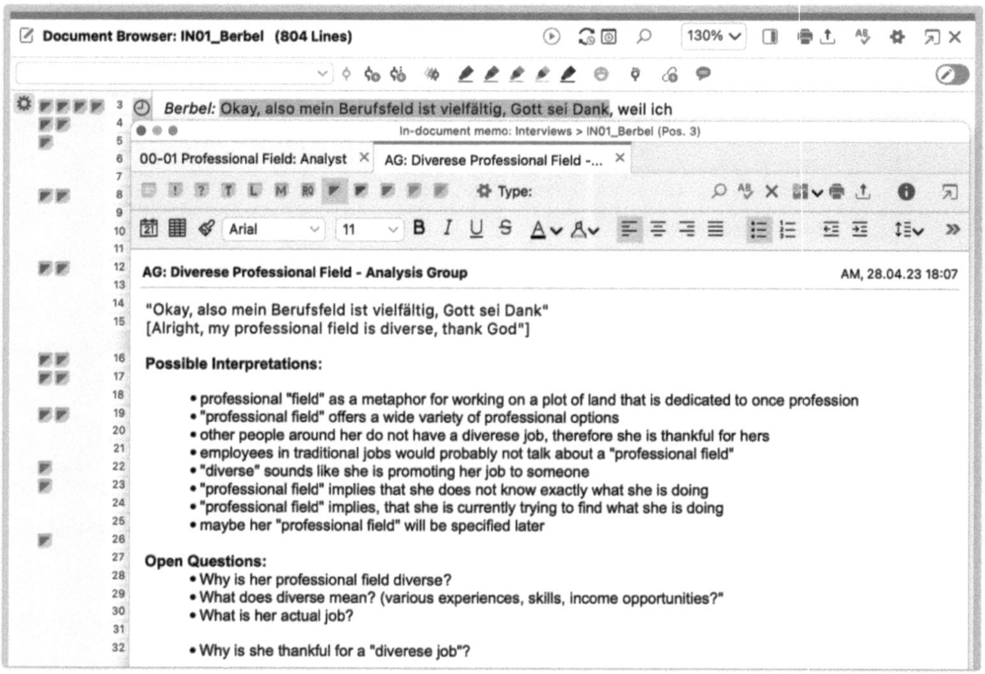

Fig. 5: A second in-document memo for the initial statement. The red memo icon indicates that the memo is based on the interpretation of the analysis group. This way, two parallel in-document memos are connected to the same interview segment to keep track of the two independent interpretations.

After the analysis group finished discussing one segment, the in-document memo was reviewed together to make sure that it reflected the outcome of the discussion well. In my project, only two different readings (one by me, and one by the group) of the same sequence of segment were created. However, the same approach could be used to create readings with further analysis groups. For this step, MAXQDA served as an important note taking tool, that allowed enabling the convergence of various interpretations and the text.

3.3 Document memo: Writing detailed case portraits

In sequential analysis, it is important to reconstruct the internal structure of a case. Furthermore, it was key in this theory-guided approach to reflect on the case from a specific theoretical perspective. Therefore, writing extensive document memos that contained a detailed case portrait was a crucial step. The example shown in Fig. 6 is an abridged version of the memo for one case, which is in its full length 2,000 words long.

For writing these memos, a consistent structure was followed:

- *Personal Motto.* A short quote from the interview that summarizes the central attitude of the interviewee.
- *Biography.* An extensive note on the biography and living conditions of the interviewed person.
- *Thematic Chronology.* A thematic summary of the main contents following the order that occurs within the interview.
- *Self-Image.* A description of how the interviewed person talks about herself.
- Narrative framework: A description of the overarching story that the person tells through the interview.
- *Subjective Theories.* A bullet point list of the convictions or opinion that this person holds about other people or how the world operates.
- *Case Structure Hypotheses.* Any hypotheses that may explain the internal logic of the case.
- *Open Questions.* Any open or even unanswerable questions for this case.
- *Topic Summaries.* Short summaries focusing on each of the five guiding topics of the interview guidelines that were constructed based on theoretical assumptions.
- *Theoretical interpretation.* An interpretation reflecting the case based on the leading theories used in this approach.

These extensive memos allowed to create an in-depth interpretation of each case and to think clearly about the relationship of the case to the theory. This also ensured that the internal logic of the case and the story of the woman interviewed was not lost when focusing on single segments or interpretative patterns. The five topic summaries were later used to create a case comparison table with summaries.

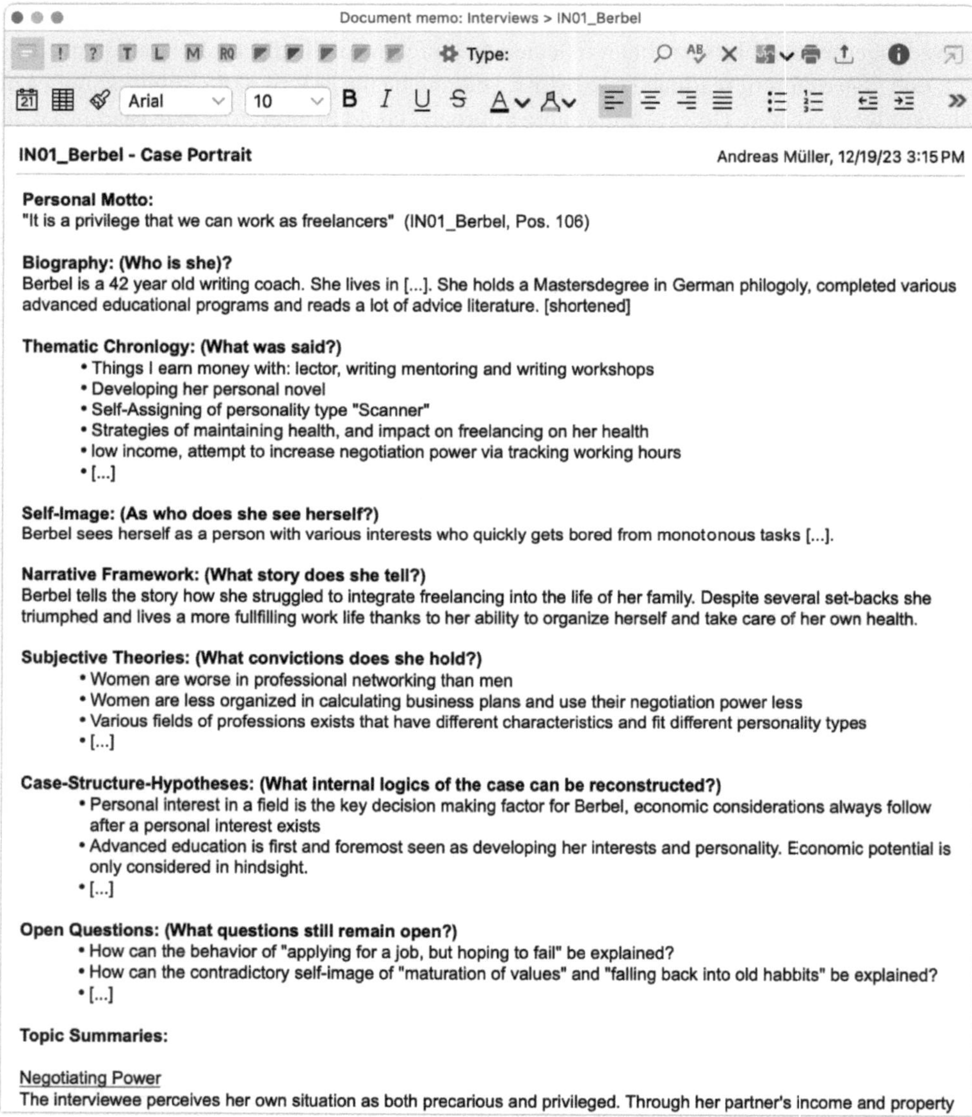

Document memo: Interviews > IN01_Berbel

Type:

Arial 10

IN01_Berbel - Case Portrait Andreas Müller, 12/19/23 3:15 PM

Personal Motto:
"It is a privilege that we can work as freelancers" (IN01_Berbel, Pos. 106)

Biography: (Who is she)?
Berbel is a 42 year old writing coach. She lives in [...]. She holds a Mastersdegree in German philogoly, completed various advanced educational programs and reads a lot of advice literature. [shortened]

Thematic Chronlogy: (What was said?)

- Things I earn money with: lector, writing mentoring and writing workshops
- Developing her personal novel
- Self-Assigning of personality type "Scanner"
- Strategies of maintaining health, and impact on freelancing on her health
- low income, attempt to increase negotiation power via tracking working hours
- [...]

Self-Image: (As who does she see herself?)
Berbel sees herself as a person with various interests who quickly gets bored from monotonous tasks [...].

Narrative Framework: (What story does she tell?)
Berbel tells the story how she struggled to integrate freelancing into the life of her family. Despite several set-backs she triumphed and lives a more fullfilling work life thanks to her ability to organize herself and take care of her own health.

Subjective Theories: (What convictions does she hold?)

- Women are worse in professional networking than men
- Women are less organized in calculating business plans and use their negotiation power less
- Various fields of professions exists that have different characteristics and fit different personality types
- [...]

Case-Structure-Hypotheses: (What internal logics of the case can be reconstructed?)

- Personal interest in a field is the key decision making factor for Berbel, economic considerations always follow after a personal interest exists
- Advanced education is first and foremost seen as developing her interests and personality. Economic potential is only considered in hindsight.
- [...]

Open Questions: (What questions still remain open?)

- How can the behavior of "applying for a job, but hoping to fail" be explained?
- How can the contradictory self-image of "maturation of values" and "falling back into old habbits" be explained?
- [...]

Topic Summaries:

Negotiating Power
The interviewee perceives her own situation as both precarious and privileged. Through her partner's income and property

Fig. 6: Document memo of one of the interviews. "[...]" indicates omission from the original memo text which was much longer.

3.4 Linking memos with codes: Creating interpretative patterns

Until this step, hardly any coding had been conducted, except for color coding. Most of the work was accomplished using in-document memos and document memos. After these steps, the key question that emerged was how to develop interpretative patterns. In accordance with Bosančić (2014, p. 272), an interpretative pattern can be seen not only as a pattern that structures a public discourse, but also as one that structures the self-identity and subject positions of individuals and that becomes visible in their actions and opinions.

For the task of identifying these patterns, the feature of linking codes to memos played a pivotal role. First, the extensive document memos (see section 3.3) were revisited and ideas for a code system were gathered in a free memo. Once this was done, preliminary codes were created to reflect the interpretative patterns and were defined via a code memo (Fig. 7). These codes were refined throughout the following process.

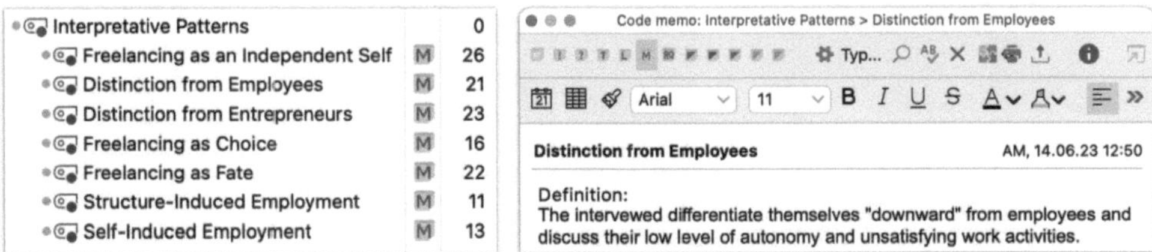

Fig. 7: The resulting patterns of interpretation in the code system of MAXQDA (left) and an example for a definition (right).

With these codes in mind all previously written in-document and document memos were revisited. Whenever a relevant pattern appeared in one of the memos, this memo was linked to the appropriate code by dragging the code from the Code System window and dropping it into the memo window (Fig. 8).

For example, a memo in which freelancing was described as the necessary mode of work because of once own personality traits was linked to the code "Freelancing as Fate" (Fig. 8). All memos that are linked to a corresponding code could easily be accessed via right-clicking on a code in the code system and selecting ***Linked Memos***. After refining the code system, these codes were used to code all previously color-coded segments. For this, the Smart Coding Tool (available in the ***Codes*** menu tab) was used to easily assign the codes based on the segment comments written earlier (see section 3.1).

This extensive iterative process enabled me to reconstruct the patterns of interpretation in the form of a code system (Fig. 7), using the theory-rich memos and color codes. This elevated the data to a high level of abstraction and preserved the interpretations of the group of analysts and myself.

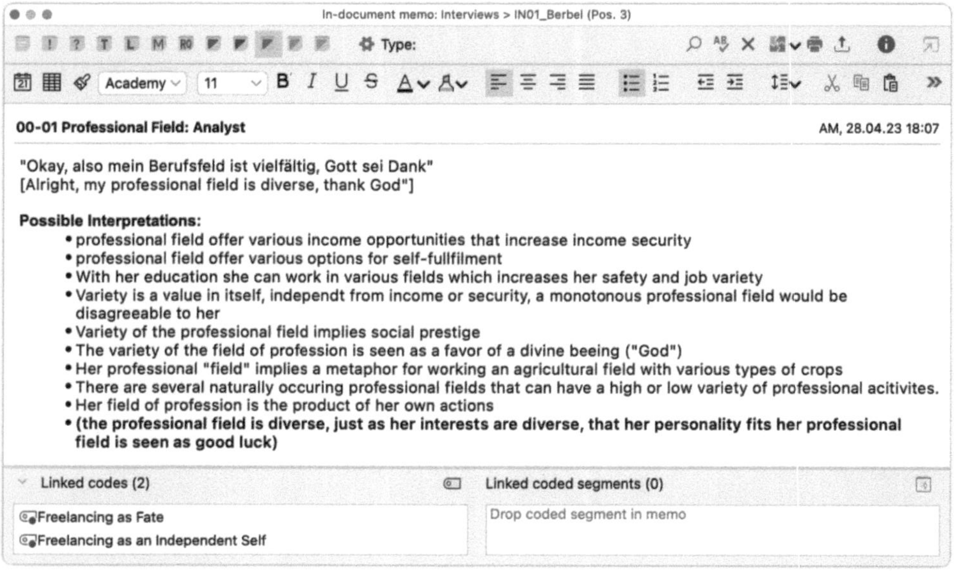

Fig. 8: Linking memos to codes for the interpretative patterns. This memo is linked to "Freelancing as Fate" and "Freelancing as an Independent Self".

3.5 Table of summaries and MAXMaps: Presenting the results and creating the basis for a typology

Interpretative methods do not lend themselves easily to visualizing or even quantifying results. Therefore, I saw myself faced with the challenge of presenting and communicating my results well. To achieve this objective, I faced two key challenges: The first was to summarize the findings of the five topics that were already outlined in the interview guideline and to contrast these with the individual cases. The second challenge involved visualizing the patterns of interpretation that emerged throughout the analysis and connecting them to each respective interviewee.

Creating a case-comparison table with summaries

To address the first challenge, I condensed the results by creating a table with summaries for the five guiding topics of the interview guideline (Fig. 9). In the case portrait (see section 3.3), a summary of each of the five guiding topics had been written. These were transferred over into a table in Microsoft Word. Each summary was highly condensed to allow for a case-by-case comparison. The final table (Fig. 10) allowed me to compare the four cases based on the five central themes of the interview guideline. It became clear that there is no universal "type" in this data but that each woman positions herself on a spectrum of opinions.

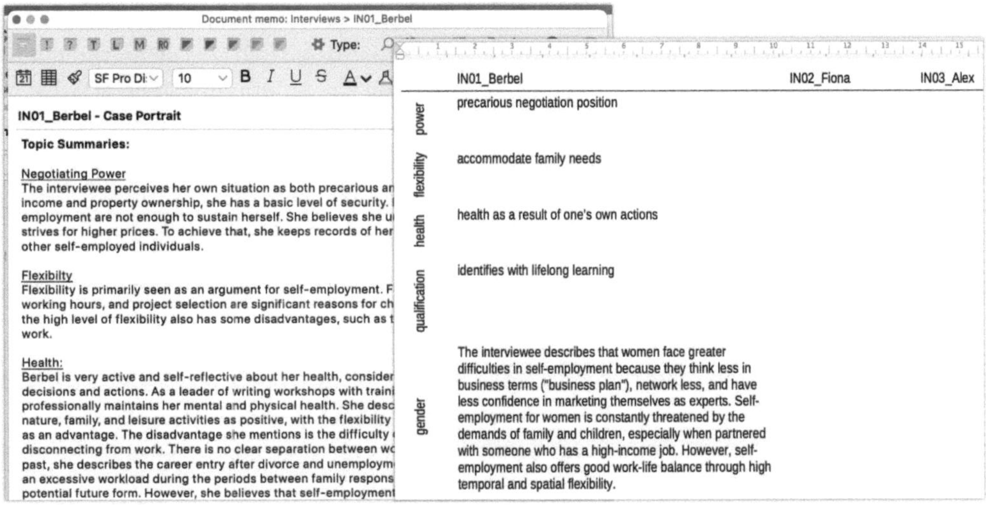

Fig. 9: The process of creating a manual table of summaries based on a document memo. The memos were copied over into a table in Microsoft Word and then reduced to a short statement.

	IN01_Berbel	IN02_Fiona	IN03_Alex	IN04_Alina
power	precarious negotiation position	financial ease	strong cooperative relationship	low dependence on individual customers
flexibility	accommodate family needs	adjust to the time windows of clients	adapt to own and familial needs	adapts to market and client requirements
health	health as a result of one's own actions	profession demands and promotes personal health	allows to work despite health restrictions	rewarded with good health conditions after a burdensome transitional phase
qualification	identifies with lifelong learning	low interest in further education due to high qualification	achieved through cooperation with partners	through volunteering due to a completed education
gender	self-employment is threatened by family needs	little importance of gender differences	self-employment as a chance for good income and high flexibility	self-employment as a privilege that women must always fight for

Fig. 10: Manually created table of summaries based on document memos. Grey shading indicates that the person is taking a contrasting opinion compared to their peers in this topic.

Visualizing the patterns of interpretation in MAXMaps

To achieve the second goal of visualizing the seven reconstructed patterns of interpretation I used MAXMaps. The seven interpretative patterns (see Fig. 6) form one general pattern, which is "Freelancing as an Independent Self," indicating that the interviewees described freelancing as a form of self-fulfillment and part of their personal goals in life. The other six interpretative patterns were grouped into three pairs:

- "Distinction from Employees and Entrepreneurs": They usually distinguished themselves both from dependent employees and from entrepreneurs who follow primarily economic interests.
- "Freelancing as Choice or Fate": All interviewees described themselves both as making intentional choices towards freelancing and freelancing being their fate because of their inherent nature.
- "Self-induced and Structure Induced Employment Situation": Regarding freelancing as an option for women they describe non-independent employment situations both as self-induced (lack of confidence, risk-aversion, lack of motivation) and as induced by the structure of society (gender expectations, parental duties, institutional barriers).

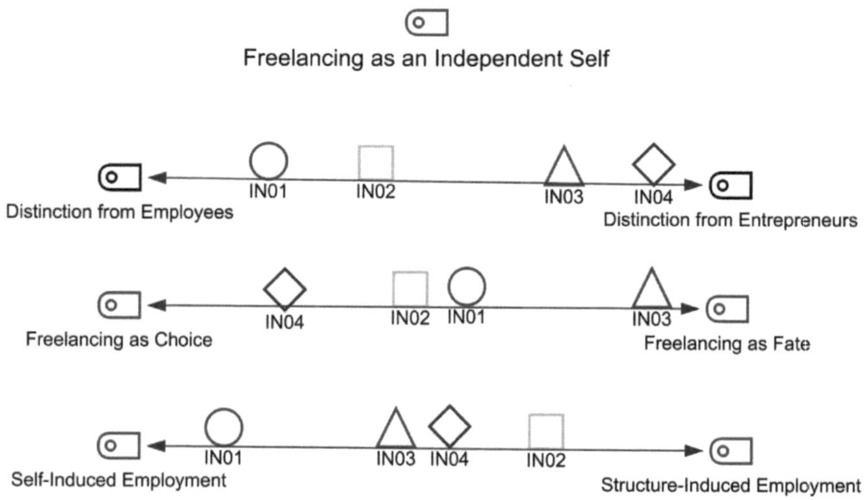

Fig. 11: Concept map created via MAXMaps. Codes and documents were placed manually. Because one document cannot occur twice on the same map, symbols (circle, diamond, square and triangle) were used to represent the four interviews.

To visualize these results and relationships in a concept map (Fig. 11), I started ***Visual Tools* > *MAXMaps*** and inserted all seven codes into an empty map. I placed the pairs as poles of a spectrum that I connected with arrows, using ***Start* > *Link*** from the MAXMaps menu tab.

Next, I utilized four shapes (circle, rectangle, triangle, diamond) to represent the four cases on this spectrum. Based on my document memos and by examining the codes with the interpretative patterns applied to each interview, I positioned each case on this spectrum.

For example, IN01 (blue circle) strongly identifies via her distinction from employees. Although she also mentions it, distinguishing herself from entrepreneurs is not crucial to her. Furthermore, she takes a medium position between freelancing as choice and fate. She describes freelancing both as her destiny and as a goal that she is constantly working for, which puts her in the middle of the spectrum. Finally, she sees the reason why many women are in regular employment situations as their own fault for not being determined enough. Although she also mentions structural barriers to self-employment for women, they play a minor role in her argument. This way, MAXMaps was of great help to answer the research question on how these female sole proprietors make meaning of their subjective position and how they distinguish themselves from others. This visualization was key to communicate my findings.

4 Overview of the analysis process

Fig. 12 illustrates and summarizes how the challenges for conducting subjectivation analysis were addressed by creating a workflow using several MAXQDA functions.

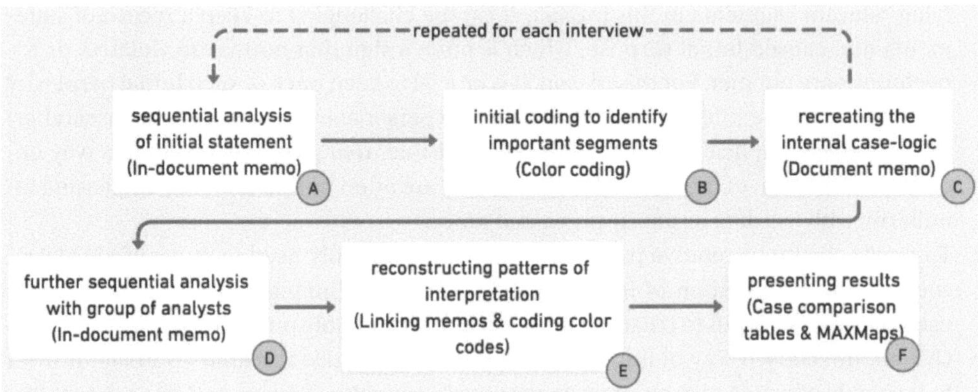

Fig. 12: The steps taken, and tools used to implement the research approach. The first three steps were conducted for every interview, the remaining only for specific sections of the data.

To conduct the sequential analysis, in-document memos were utilized to create a detailed interpretation of the initial section of an interview. In close connection with this step, color codes were employed to identify further relevant segments for subsequent in-depth analysis. Once the in-document memos and color codes were created for one document, a case portrait was written for every interview. This step was followed by another sequential analysis, this time in a group of researchers and implemented using in-document memos again. Once the group sessions were completed, the reconstruction of the patterns of interpretation was conducted by linking codes with memos and coding the initially identified and color-coded segments. Then, selective coding was implemented to rework and apply the patterns of interpretation to the entire material. Finally, the results were summarized and juxtaposed by topic for each case in a table and presented using MAXMaps.

5 Lessons learned

This chapter demonstrated how MAXQDA can be used to implement an interpretative, sequential, and theory-guided approach. Applying this approach using MAXQDA resulted in several lessons learned:

- One benefit of using MAXQDA as a tool for recording analytical notes is that it keeps these notes very close to the data. MAXQDA allowed me to keep an overview of interpretations of various analysis groups. Personally, I can highly recommend taking notes during a live, face-to-face analysis session within MAXQDA. This way, no insights were lost and writing extensive protocols from memory became unnecessary. Likewise, I was able to continue working right away with the interpretations provided by the other analysts.
- A systematic approach to use the color coding feature proved very beneficial for identifying relevant segments in this project. It can be challenging to keep a record of statements that caused initial surprise, which is often a sign that norms are violated, or expectations are not met. For this reason, it is crucial to keep track of such initial perplexity (based on the case internal logic, the theory, or personal experiences of the researcher) to make these implicit structures and norms visible. Using color codes in this way ensures preservation of these initial surprises that are often buried under an increasing familiarity with the data or poorly organized notes.
- To create the interpretative patterns, some less commonly used features of MAXQDA, such as the combination of in-document memos and linking codes to memos, were used. It proved fruitful to create a code system based mainly on memos.
- Overall, the chosen way of implementing the interpretative research approach proved to be highly effective in preserving continuously emerging insights and was straight forward enough to ensure purposeful use of time and resources.

Bibliography

Bröckling, U. (2007). Das unternehmerische Selbst: Soziologie einer Subjektivierungsform. Suhrkamp.

Bosančić, S. (2014). *Arbeiter ohne Eigenschaften.* Wiesbaden.

Bosančić, S. (2019). *Die Forschungsperspektive der Interpretativen Subjektivierungsanalyse.* In: Geimer, A., Amling, S., Bosančić, S. (Eds.) *Subjekt und Subjektivierung (pp. 43–64).* Springer, Wiesbaden. https://doi.org/10.1007/978-3-658-22313-7_3

Glaser, B. G., & A. L. Strauss. (1967). *The discovery of grounded theory. Strategies for qualitative research.* Aldine.

Kuckartz, U., & Rädiker, S. (2023). *Qualitative content analysis: Methods, practice and software* (2nd ed.). Sage.

Oevermann, U., Tilman A., & J. Krambeck. (1979). Die Methodologie einer „objektiven Hermeneutik" und ihre allgemeine forschungslogische Bedeutung in den Sozialwissenschaften. In H. G. Soeffner (Ed.), *Interpretative Verfahren in den Sozial- und Textwissenschaften* (pp. 352–434). Metzler.

Keller, R. (2011). The sociology of knowledge approach to discourse (SKAD). *Human Studies 34*(1), 43–65. https://doi.org/10.1007/s10746-011-9175-z

Sennett, R. (2010). *Der flexible Mensch. Die Kultur des neuen Kapitalismus.* Berliner Taschenbuch Verlag.

Witzel, A. (2000). The problem-centered interview. *Forum: Qualitative Social Research, 1*(1) Art. 22. https://doi.org/10.17169/fqs-1.1.1132

About the author

Andreas Müller has been a professional MAXQDA trainer for over 5 years, and is a research and methods coach and contractual researcher. He is experienced in a wide array of qualitative methods and works with clients from diverse academic disciplines, including healthcare, educational sciences, and economics. Andreas specializes in the analysis of qualitative text and video data, as well as mixed methods data.